THROUGH THE PAST DARKLY

THROUGH THE PAST DARKLY

History and Memory in François Mauriac's *Bloc-notes*

NATHAN BRACHER

The Catholic University of America Press
Washington, D.C.

The paper used in this publication meets the minimum requirements of American National Standards for Information Science—Permanence of Paper for Printed Library materials, ANSI Z39.48-1984.
∞

LIBRARY OF CONGRESS CATALOGING-IN-PUBLICATION DATA
Bracher, Nathan, 1953–
Through the past darkly : history and memory in François Mauriac's Bloc-notes / by Nathan Bracher.
p. cm.
Includes bibliographical references and index.
ISBN 0-8132-1380-0 (cloth : alk. paper)
1. Mauriac, François, 1885–1970. Bloc-notes. I. Title.
PQ2625.A93B6328 2004
844'.912—dc22
2003022644

Sine nomine

CONTENTS

ACKNOWLEDGMENTS

I am grateful to Texas A & M University for the Faculty Development leave that allowed me to complete my research and draft the initial manuscript of this book, and for the generous grant awarded by the Program to Enhance Scholarly and Creative Activities through the Office of the Vice President for Research of Texas A & M University that allowed me to complete the writing of this book and prepare it for publication.

Chapter 3, "An Uncertain Idea of France," is an adaptation of an article first published as "Mauriac and Decolonization: Civilization, History, and National Identity," in *Contemporary French Civilization* 18, no. 2 (Summer–Fall 1994): 167–87. I have incorporated another article, "The Dreyfus Affair in François Mauriac's *Bloc-notes*," also published by *Contemporary French Civilization* 26, no. 1 (Winter–Spring 2002): 12–29, into Chapter 2, "The Story of History," and Chapter 5, "In Search of Times Past." I wish to thank *Contemporary French Civilization* and its editor Lawrence R. Schehr for granting permission to republish this material.

The definitive version of this book has greatly benefited from the careful reading and helpful suggestions provided by Professors Jean-Pierre Cauvin and George E. Gingras, and by the close oversight of Susan Needham, the managing editor of The Catholic University of America Press.

Most importantly, I thank my wife, Françoise; my three boys, Christoph, Benjamin, and Andrew; my mother, Gladys Bracher; and my dear friend Robert Leslie: without their unfailing support and inspiration, this project would have never come to fruition.

THROUGH THE PAST DARKLY

1 THE PRESENCE OF THE PAST

Mais en quoi les prises de position d'un simple écrivain, à des époques révolues, dans des questions dépassées et oubliées du grand public, auraient-elles quelque chance de retenir ceux qui m'écouteront? (François Mauriac, "Jeudi 29 février 1968," BN V, 38)[1]

[*Just how could the stances once taken by a mere writer on outdated issues forgotten by the general public have any chance of interesting those who will be listening to me?*]

Coming from a Nobel Prize–winning novelist whose literary chronicles and political editorials had for more than twenty years left no one indifferent amid France's raucous debate, such modest words sound disingenuous in a French context. Contrary to what is the case in the United States, where change, the abandonment of Old World ties, and the conquest of new frontiers are inscribed into the national mythology, the past matters, and matters greatly, in contemporary France. From the picturesque rural landscapes sculpted by countless generations of human habitation to the venerable walls of chateaux and cathedrals woven into the urban habitat, the past is a palpable part of everyday French life. Even today, as a postindustrial economy and a media-saturated culture

1. All references to François Mauriac's *Bloc-notes* are taken from the five volumes edited and annotated by Jean Touzot (Paris: Éditions du Seuil [Points-Essais], 1993), henceforth designated by "BN" with the appropriate volume and page numbers.

threaten to relegate agrarian traditions to oblivion, an ever-increasing number of festivals and "sites classés" (officially recognized and protected landmarks, buildings, and places) celebrate the rhythms and customs of a "vieille France" that now "is history" in every sense of the word. Commemorations of historical events have indeed become so prevalent that they sometimes seem to leave little room for current developments.

But France's passion for the past goes far beyond antiquarian hobbies and nostalgia: its history often spills out of the confines of textbooks and museums to vie for front-page headlines. Witness the series of scandals involving high-level French collaboration with Nazi Germany and the complicity of the French state in the deportation of Jews to death camps: rocked in 1992 by the arrest of Paul Touvier; in 1993 by the bizarre assassination of the former head of the Vichy police, René Bousquet (more than incidentally a close friend of then-president François Mitterrand); in 1994 both by Touvier's conviction for crimes against humanity and by Mitterrand's acknowledgment of his own work as a Vichy bureaucrat; in 1997 and 1998 by unprecedented public acts of repentance by Catholic bishops and French police, and by an equally unprecedented six-month-long trial and conviction of another former Vichy bureaucrat, Maurice Papon, who had furthermore enjoyed a stellar postwar career at the highest levels of public administration and government, public debate of the 1990s in France was often dominated—if not obsessed[2]—by the unfinished business of the German Occupation that had ended some fifty years earlier.[3]

And just when the "Vichy syndrome" finally seemed to have abated, new controversies over the use of torture—now unapologetically

2. See "The Future of an Obsession," in *Vichy: An Ever-Present Past*, ed. Éric Conan and Henry Rousso, translated and annotated by Nathan Bracher, with a foreword by Robert O. Paxton (Hanover, N.H., and London: University Press of New England, 1998), 197–211.

3. See, among many others, my articles on the resurgence of political conflicts occasioned by the Papon trial: "Memory Null and Void?: The Broken Record of Vichy Polemics in the Papon Case," *Contemporary French Civilization* 23, no. 1 (Winter–Spring 1999): 65–80; "La Mémoire vive et convulsive: The Papon Trial and France's Passion for History," *French Review* 73, no. 2 (December 1999): 314–24; and "The Trial of Papon and the Tribulations of Gaullism," in *The Papon Affair: Memory and Justice on Trial*, ed. Richard J. Golsan (New York: Routledge, 2000), 115–30. See also Richard J. Golsan, *Vichy's Afterlife: History and Counterhistory in Postwar France* (Lincoln: University of Nebraska Press, 2000).

avowed by a French general claiming to have been acting under government orders—and the treatment of the Harkis (Algerians having sided with France) in the Algerian war have flared up and once again brought the discussion of the past to fever pitch.[4] In the face of the particularly cruel civil war in Algeria and continuing ethnic tensions on French soil, France's treatment of the Algerian rebels—which, as we shall see, prompted Mauriac to articulate not only his most stinging indictments of his compatriots but also some of his most compelling reflections on history—is an issue that matters intensely to former protagonists of the war on both sides, to youth of North African descent, and even to the French public in general, for obvious reasons. But what about the brief (four-year) venture of the poet Victor Hugo, arguably the greatest French literary figure of the nineteenth century, into the political arena? Among the plethora of events and publications marking the bicentennial of Hugo's birth, the publication of Jean-François Kahn's 950-page *Victor Hugo: Un Révolutionnaire* by Fayard in December 2001 in an edition intended for the general reader speaks volumes: one hundred and fifty years after the fact, commentary offered by a literary figure on public events clearly receives considerable attention.

The French take not only their nation's history, but also the commentary of writers and intellectuals on that history, very seriously for several reasons. In the first place, the past matters in France precisely because its very presence is ubiquitous and unavoidable. Whereas Americans might trace the historical beginnings of their nation back some six hundred years, to the time when the first Spanish explorers set foot on the New World, a "discovery" duly commemorated by Columbus Day, France's national memory reaches back for more than two millennia to the Gallic tribes' feisty resistance to Julius Caesar's attempt to bring them under Roman dominion, a scenario richly—if whimsically[5]—mythologized to the immense delight of French readers of every age

4. The scandal surrounding the use of torture by French forces in Algeria resurfaced in May 2001, when retired general Paul Aussaresses published *Services spéciaux, Algérie 1955–1957* (Paris: Perrin). See Appendix, Section A.

5. Christian Goudineau points out that Rome's presence was largely established by the time of the revolt led by Vercingetorix, who had moreover once fought alongside the Romans. See "Nos ancêtres les Romains," *L'Express*, 9 September 1999, pp. 10–13. See also Christian Goudineau, *César et la Gaule* (Paris: Errance, 1990).

and persuasion who have enthusiastically followed the escapades of Astérix and Obélix for over four decades. That a comic book series so explicitly rooted in the past—a past over two thousand years distant from the present—should now be celebrated as part of France's distinctive cultural patrimony is emblematic of historical roots running infinitely thicker and deeper than in the United States.[6] In France, the past matters because countless historical figures and events have left an indelible mark on the nation's landscapes and memory.

The loom of French history has indeed woven a rich tapestry whose legacy, for all its depth and fascination, at times appears so omnipresent as to stifle innovations and creativity.[7] Paradoxically, however, the numerous and often radically opposed regimes, constitutions, and social orders that have occupied the public scene throughout the many domestic upheavals and international ordeals that France has endured from the 1789 Revolution to the 1958 instauration of the Fifth Republic (itself threatened at its inception by failed military takeovers and attempted assassinations) have, due precisely to the fragile and sometimes ephemeral nature of these various regimes, led the French to situate their collective identity in a putatively common past. First institutionalized by French schools in the nineteenth century and then consecrated as one of the cultural bastions of the Third Republic, the academic discipline of history provided an essential element of cohesion in a nation deeply divided along social and ideological lines. And it achieved this result by thematizing the nation's fundamental bone of contention: the French Revolution.

With an inherent focus on the changes leading from one regime to the next, the study of history carried a certain progressive tendency: political orders and revolutions were no longer seen as divinely sanctioned but rather as formed by historical events that could be analyzed and understood.[8] The academic discipline of history has thus exerted a significant progressive influence. Modern France, observes Pierre Nora, liber-

6. See Olivier Delcroix, "Astérix, le dernier mythe français," and Jean-Marie Rouart, "Héros de la France franchouillarde," *France-Amérique*, 5–11 February 2000, p. 32. See also Alain Duhamel, *Le complexe d'Astérix* (Paris: Gallimard, 1985), 10, 15–16.

7. Cf. Olivier Duhamel, "Eux et nous," *L'Express*, 21 August 1997, p. 21.

8. Antoine Prost, *Douze leçons sur l'histoire* (Paris: Seuil, 1996), 22–27.

ated itself from the rural, Catholic, artisanal society governed by memory precisely by thinking its traditions, rituals, and customs in terms of a history that identified their finite origins and traced their evolution through the vicissitudes of time.[9] And from Marx and Lenin to Sartre, Derrida, and Foucault, points out Alain Finkielkraut, the most subversive strains of historicism have been characterized by their emphasis on the radical contingency of human institutions: if the present order has been constructed on artifice and arbitrary convention, then human beings can take control of their own destiny and invent a more desirable order by destroying or "deconstructing" the ancien régime on all levels.[10]

But it would be a serious error to overlook the stabilizing, even conservative, strain also present in the academic discipline of history and implicit in the French passion for the past. For even the decidedly antiroyalist history manuals of the early Third Republic taught schoolchildren to revere not only their supposed ancestors, "nos ancêtres les Gaulois" (our ancestors the Gauls), but even the noble lineage of kings, "ces rois qui firent la France" (these kings that made France), who had molded France into a preeminent European power. Pupils were thus encouraged to celebrate the rich heritage of "French civilization" so painstakingly acquired not only through the successive endeavors of such cultural icons as Charlemagne, Henry IV, and Descartes, but also thanks to the anonymous efforts of a venerable "chain of generations," the innumerable common folk with whose blood, sweat, and tears the cathedrals were erected and the territory defended.[11] While it is true that Maurice Barrès's cult of homeland and ancestry—"la terre et les morts" (the land and the dead)—provided the basis for a stridently conservative, highly xenophobic nationalism that revealed its sinister tendencies throughout the Dreyfus affair, one would be gravely mistaken to portray the attachment to the past as a preserve of the right wing. For the positive valorization of the past in France is also manifested in the wide-

9. Pierre Nora, "Entre mémoire et histoire: La problématique des lieux," in *Les lieux de mémoire, Vol. 1: La République* (Paris: Gallimard, 1984), xvii–xviii.

10. Alain Finkielkraut, *L'humanité perdue* (Paris: Seuil, 1996), 57–64.

11. Cf. Laurence Wylie and Jean-François Brière, "Points de vue français sur le temps," *Les Français*, 3rd ed. (Upper Saddle River, N.J.: Prentice-Hall, 2001), 32–49.

spread search for "roots," as individuals and groups—many of whom conspicuously place themselves on the left—from all political and geographical sectors seek to affirm a cultural, ethnic, linguistic, or religious identity grounded in particular traditions, ancestors, and historical experiences.[12]

The reference to durability and permanence as a gauge of quality and character for everyone and everything from political figures to architecture to wine is clearly no longer an indication of allegiance to the Right but rather constitutes a cultural trait observable even in the most conspicuous representatives of the Left. Reflecting on his visit to the United States in 1945, Sartre—who could hardly be suspected of harboring conservative leanings—expressed rather disdainful bemusement toward the American view of the past as a vulgar "résidu" (leftover) to be disregarded or bulldozed in laying out the brave new world's cities.[13] Equally telling were the inaugural gestures made by François Mitterrand, whose victory in the 1981 presidential election was widely hailed among the various constituencies of the Left in France as a long-awaited triumph over the Gaullist conservatism that had so long dominated the Fifth Republic. The inauguration ceremonies were highlighted by the homage paid to illustrious socialist predecessors, as Mitterrand solemnly marched up the steps of the Pantheon to lay a rose on the tombs of Victor Schoelcher (who led the fight for the abolition of slavery), Jean Jaurès (doubtless the greatest voice for peace and social justice in the early twentieth century, assassinated on the eve of World War I), and Jean Moulin (the leader of the mainland Resistance tortured to death by Klaus Barbie).

Simply stated, the question of the past—and therefore the question of history—carries with it the question of identity, as disputed and problematic as both may be. Here again, anyone doubting this connection could observe the statement by François Mitterrand during a 1982 ministerial meeting: "Un peuple qui n'enseigne pas son histoire est un peuple qui perd son identité" (A people that does not teach its history is a peo-

12. Cf. François Furet, *L'atelier de l'histoire* (Paris: Flammarion, 1982), 24, and Tzvetan Todorov "Les usages de la mémoire," in *Mémoire du mal, Tentation du bien* (Paris: Robert Laffont, 2000), 175–91.

13. Jean-Paul Sartre, "Villes d'Amérique," in *Situations III* (Paris: Gallimard, 1947), 108.

ple that is losing its identity).[14] As Prost points out, the very fact that no one from any quarter in France bothered to take exception to Mitterrand's pronouncement (whose patent fallacy Prost readily demonstrates with the counterexamples of Great Britain and the United States, countries that maintain their national identity without emphasizing history) constitutes virtually indisputable evidence that the French define their identity through history.

Returning to the question raised in the epigraph, we are now poised to articulate the current interest in the stances articulated by François Mauriac—admittedly no "mere writer" by any account—in response to seemingly distant events and over issues virtually forgotten by the general public. There are in fact several salient reasons why we should devote great attention to Mauriac's journalism of the 1950s and 1960s. To begin with, his passion for history is emblematic both of contemporary French culture and of postwar politics. The *Bloc-notes* contains many reflections on turn-of-the-century French politics and culture, and vivid recollections of an agrarian, Catholic society slipping into oblivion in the midst of a thoroughly urbanized and secularized consumerism; such pages are symptomatic of France's increasing attachment to the past in the wake of the rapid changes of the postwar years now referred to as "les Trente Glorieuses," the "Thirty Glorious Years," of economic growth and prosperity named after "les Trois Glorieuses," the "Three Glorious Days," of the 1830 uprising against Charles X.

On another level, however, Mauriac's incisive commentaries on contemporary events as seen in the light of history are emblematic of preoccupations shared by an entire generation of postwar intellectuals in France. For most, France's traumatic World War II experiences had shattered what might have remained of an ethereal pursuit of truth and beauty in a literary domain uncompromised by the contingencies of politics. In a nation that had been invaded and occupied by Nazi Germany; abandoned and betrayed by the Vichy regime's political, military, and administrative leaders; torn by civil strife between a largely communist Resistance and a pro-fascist militia; and liberated by foreign intervention (but only after having suffered great human and material

14. Mitterand's remark is cited by Antoine Prost, in *Douze leçons sur l'histoire*, 16.

devastation), any hope of retreating to a realm of pure ideas and aesthetics was totally illusory, particularly during the period when the communist-controlled Comité National des Ecrivains maintained a stranglehold on literary life. The cataclysmic struggle between the Axis and the Allies had threatened the future of the planet and of humankind, and had played itself out with particular violence on French soil. It was in this context that Sartre so dramatically stated that writers and intellectuals experienced "freedom" as never before precisely when France was under the thumb of the Nazis: "Jamais nous n'avons été plus libres que sous l'occupation allemande" (Never were we so free as under the German Occupation).[15] Since each gesture and every word unavoidably constituted an act that took on political meaning in the crucial struggle for hearts and minds, writing for underground newspapers required men and women of letters to put their lives on the line, as both Sartre and Mauriac themselves indeed did.

This urgent moral necessity for political commitment in a time of war was to become the postwar historical imperative of an *engagement* on all fronts, as the Parisian intelligentsia spearheaded by Sartre and *Les Temps modernes* enjoined their contemporaries to follow the march of history. A particular confluence of ideology and circumstance thus led the dominant figures of the intellectual scene in postwar France to elaborate both political allegiances and literary creations in reference to a history understood as the universal drive of the proletariat for economic and social liberation, of which the Soviet Union provided the prime example and leadership. These French intellectuals had perceived the military debacle, political implosion, and moral collapse of the Third Republic as the judgment of history not only on an inept leadership but also on democratic institutions that, even before the war, had been considered by many on both the right and the left as unadapted to modern reality.[16] Vichy's ambitions of rolling back the institutional breakthroughs of 1789 and abolishing the reforms of the Popular Front by means of a "National Revolution" on the domestic scene and collabora-

15. Jean-Paul Sartre, "La République du silence," in *Situations III*, 11.

16. Cf. Tony Judt, *Past Imperfect: French Intellectuals, 1944–1956* (Berkeley, Los Angeles, and Oxford: University of California Press, 1992), 15–25.

tion with Hitler in the international arena had totally discredited right-wing Maurrassian alternatives to parliamentary democracy. Conversely, the massive participation of French communists in the Resistance was seen as a parallel to the Soviet Union's defeat of Hitler's *Wehrmacht*, which had first been driven back by the Red Army's heroic defense of Stalingrad in the winter of 1942–1943 before being finally crushed between the pincers of Allied forces in the spring of 1945. Nazi Germany's defeat was subsequently used to accredit communist claims of embodying the forces of history that would lead to the emancipation of humanity.[17]

It is now widely acknowledged that the postwar intellectual scene was for some thirty years dominated by the Left, that leftist intellectuals viewed artistic creation and politics as subordinate to the imperatives of history, and that this history was conceived in Marxist-Hegelian terms. What is not recognized, however, is that Mauriac's courageous condemnations of torture in Algeria as well as his rich commentaries on culture and society of the 1950s and 1960s—both of which have justly won an enduring place for the *Bloc-notes*—are framed in reference to history, albeit in a decidedly non-Marxist mode. Penned in response to the dramatic events unfolding from one day to the next, Mauriac's editorials extend far beyond the anecdotal or topical by incorporating contemporary developments into the ongoing story of humanity past and present.

In a sense, the *Bloc-notes* is like France: history and memory compose the very texture and matrix of Mauriac's editorials. He lives and thinks historically, constantly viewing people, events, and regimes in relation to the legacy of the past as well as to the ongoing drama of society. He also sees his journalism as participating in the larger narratives by which this legacy and ongoing drama of both French society and humanity in general are constituted, communicated, and preserved. Writing neither as a professional historian nor as a philosopher, he elaborates no theory, paradigm, or master narrative to be invoked in interpreting the affairs of the day.

Yet there is method in his meaning, and Chapter 2 of the present

17. Cf. Michel Winock, *Le siècle des intellectuels* (Paris: Seuil, 1997), 414–20.

book accordingly analyzes the various components of the "history" operative throughout the *Bloc-notes.* The value of Mauriac's historical reflections resides to no small degree in the fact that he engages the present through the filter of the rich, if tragic, legacy of the past without pouring events into some preestablished ideological mold. Like other intellectuals speaking out against torture and oppression in North Africa, Mauriac thus deplores the shadow that the Dreyfus affair continued to cast over all of French society in the twentieth century, and in particular over the French army's role in Algeria. Rejecting metaphysical notions of history as driven by some immanent force or directed to some ultimate end, Mauriac adamantly refuses to see either the hand of God or the dialectics of liberation in the course of human affairs. And yet, like Zola, whose valiant defense of Dreyfus exemplified the unfettered conscience of the intellectual engaged in the fight for justice and human rights throughout the twentieth century, and not unlike Sartre, whose impassioned—if decidedly belated—engagement in the early 1940s made him the "maître à penser" (master thinker) for the postwar generation,[18] Mauriac felt the urgency of clearly situating himself within the historical drama of his time.

Sartre and *Les Temps modernes* certainly held no monopoly over the ethics of *engagement* that were to become the touchstone for an entire generation. Mauriac's tendency to present the immediate political drama as unfolding in the light of history is thus emblematic both of a national culture so inclined to recall its rich historical patrimony and of postwar French intellectuals' focus on humanity's historical destiny. And yet Mauriac's approach to history and his invocation of the past are not consonant with any ready-made ideology. His many returns to the Dreyfus affair are a case in point. Referring to both the Dreyfus affair and the Algerian war, he unequivocally condemns the racial and religious bigotry pushing French nationalists to violate fundamental human rights pursuing ruthless military and social agendas. So doing, he clearly places these editorials in the Left's tradition of protests against an oppressive order. It was moreover precisely the repression so visible in

18. See Jean-François Sirinelli, *Deux intellectuels dans le siècle: Sartre et Aron* (Paris: Fayard, 1995).

the events of the 1950s in Morocco and Algeria that led Mauriac to reflect on the unjust order dominating the French political scene from the medieval epoch of feudal lords to the twentieth-century reign of industrial magnates. He moreover questions the Catholic Church's traditional alliance with such powers. In essence, contends Mauriac, the same anti-Semitic authoritarians first demanded Dreyfus's head despite his total innocence, then later, under Vichy, collaborated with the Germans and delivered Jews to the Nazis, and finally, in Algeria, resorted to torture, arbitrary detention, and "disappearances" to repress an uprising against the French colonial regime.

To emphasize continuity while struggling for justice and human rights, that is, for change, for a singular departure from the established way of doing things, is singularly paradoxical, particularly in France. For contrary to what is usually the case (even when invoked by the founders of the Third Republic or François Mitterrand, as we have already seen), Mauriac establishes a strong continuity between the Dreyfus affair, the Vichy government, and the war in Algeria with no intention of claiming legitimacy or prestige for some political leader or regime. Instead, he undertakes a more general assessment of the fascist elements in French politics, questions the conventional narratives of France's past, and even explores the larger problems of human identity posed by major cataclysms of the twentieth century, as we see in Chapter 4.

The two ostensibly opposite leanings implicit in the study of history, namely, the emphasis on change and contingency favoring the progressive aims of the Left versus the focus on continuity and patrimony bolstering the conservative views of the Right, are thus both present in the *Bloc-notes.* Hardly to the same extent, however: the stress on continuity and the affection for the rich legacy of the past far outweigh observations on the arbitrary and artificial. Mauriac does indeed qualify common or "official" versions of France's past as "a compilation of lies" recorded to protect vested interests, but he invariably articulates his appeals for justice and humanity in reference to history's seemingly endless chain of crimes that the reader of the *Bloc-notes* finds again and again designated as a "brouillamini d'erreurs et de violences" (imbroglio of errors and violence) and the unending saga of Cain and Abel.

Mauriac's approach to history sets him apart from other leading figures on the postwar French intellectual scene in another important way. While he rejects in no uncertain terms the "master narrative" proposed by communism, he does not fail to point out the economic and social contingencies responsible for glaring omissions in the epic depicting France as the torchbearer of civilization. Yet he does not elaborate any master narrative of his own. Unlike the many fellow travelers among the Parisian intelligentsia who were sure that history was on their side and that the future of human society lay in the hands of the Communist Party and the Soviet Union, Mauriac eschews all such historical messianism and refuses to champion one narrative or ideology of history over another. Even during his unswerving and arguably overzealous loyalty to Charles de Gaulle during the late 1960s, Mauriac repeatedly called attention to the idealistic, constructed nature of the general's epic narrative of France's past. If Mauriac enthusiastically embraced it as a political project (which indeed raises a number of thorny questions), he never mistook it for an authentic account of French history.

The very form of the *Bloc-notes* is antithetical to the construction of any such master narrative: fragmented into commentaries on readings and political developments associated with specific, successive days, Mauriac's editorials follow changing moods and circumstances, though with recurring themes, first and foremost of which is history. Specific events and personalities are compared and contrasted with myriad other situations and figures of the past, all within the overarching framework of the story of humanity. His intent in the 1950s, however, is not to claim that any particular individual, doctrine, or group embodies some immanent force or ultimate end of human history. On the other hand, Mauriac's virtually unconditional allegiance to a Charles de Gaulle presented as the embodiment of the French nation is another story, one that requires the more nuanced assessment provided in Chapter 5.

In his most strident attacks on the unjust order responsible for torture, oppression, and dire poverty both in North Africa and in mainland France, Mauriac nevertheless stresses the continuities linking the current state of affairs to notable precedents, and in particular the Dreyfus affair. Instead of viewing the particular political problems at hand as epiphenomena of some underlying, impersonal force of history, and thus instrumentalizing specific occurrences to illustrate a preexistent ideology, he explores the various issues raised by France's colonial conflicts in reference to a larger, ongoing drama. History in the *Bloc-notes* is the universal context that allows Mauriac to relate incidents of widely divergent epochs and national contexts both to each other and to the larger question of human identity. In sharp contrast with those postwar French intellectuals who saw human identity as a derivative of historically contingent social and economic structures, and who accordingly subordinated ethics to political imperatives, Mauriac approaches history as an eminently human, even personal, story.

We find ethics and human identity inextricably tied to history in the *Bloc-notes* precisely because these editorials contain historical narratives engaging the responsibility of writer and reader alike. Mauriac's narration of history in the *Bloc-notes* thus forms the major axis of inquiry for the four central chapters of the present book. Mauriac does not concern himself with narrative theory in and of itself, and neither shall we. As posed by the recent writings of Tzvetan Todorov, however, the narration of history raises crucial issues of memory, that is, of how the past is appropriated and used in the present to commemorate events, define identities, and inform political stances. Just as Mauriac clearly situates himself with respect to both current events and textbook accounts of France's past, and thus assumes responsibility as a narrator of French history past and present, so shall we situate his approach to history with respect to the pivotal figures and developments that defined the contours of the 1950s and 1960s in France, including the Marxist doctrine of history espoused by the Parisian intelligentsia, the moral and political crises of decolonization, the return to power of Charles de Gaulle, and the cult of *lieux de mémoire* (places of memory) in the wake of the urbanization and consumerism that were eclipsing the ancestral traditions of a largely rural, Catholic culture.

We can indeed measure the mettle of Mauriac's approach to history by considering it in the context of the major political dramas and social transformations in postwar France. While the *Bloc-notes* constantly filters the present through the past, portraying personages and events as emerging from a heavy sediment of history, it is also true that this keen scrutiny of current developments prompts Mauriac to consider France's past in a new light. Thus in Chapter 2, "The Story of History," we see that if, on the one hand, Mauriac's many returns to the Dreyfus affair illustrate his fundamentally historical perception of the contemporary world, it was, on the other hand, the colonial abuses in North Africa that led him to identify the Dreyfus affair as a touchstone for French politics of the first half of the twentieth century. Chapter 3, "An Uncertain Idea of France," shows that in lashing out against torture in Algeria (thus depicted as the legacy of the Dreyfus affair), Mauriac came to rethink the heroic saga of France as a beacon of enlightenment and refinement that he himself had previously invoked in defense of France's presence in both North Africa and Indochina, and even questioned the very notion of "civilization" upon which such claims of a "civilizing mission" had been based.

Mauriac's new—or at least heightened—awareness of injustice in both the narrative record and political practice compels him to reassess France's history. Beyond his specific stands on the pressing issues of torture and oppression in France's colonies, however, he engages the larger issues of history as posed not only by the dramatic upheavals of colonial wars and a rapidly changing society, but also by the major cataclysms of the twentieth century that shook the very notion of humanity. It is in this context that Chapter 4, "The Lessons of History," examines Mauriac's use of the past in denouncing crimes perpetrated by French forces of order during the Algerian war from November 1954 through July 1962. Though seldom recognized as such, Mauriac's vociferous condemnation of torture, arbitrary detentions, and disappearances in Algeria were as precocious as they were courageous.[19] These protests began with an editorial penned at the very outset of the war, and drew a flood of hate mail and even death threats from the OAS.[20] that were hardly idle talk. Coextensive with these forays into the contemporary political are-

19. See Jean-François Sirinelli, "Mauriac, un intellectuel engagé," in *François Mauriac entre la gauche et la droite*, ed. André Séailles (Paris: Klincksieck, 1995), 153–54.

20. The OAS (Organisation de l'Armée Secrète [Secret Army Organization]) was a group intent on maintaining French control of Algeria and preventing any form of independence. With bombings and assassinations, it carried out a particularly vicious campaign of terror both in Algeria and in mainland France during the last phase of the war from 1960 to 1962.

na, however, are an underlying series of Montaigne-like *essais* that pose the question of humanity (and barbarity) in terms of history.

Mauriac engages in an uncompromising assessment of history and of the unprecedented violence of the twentieth century in order to explore human identity. He therefore takes up many of the issues examined by Tzvetan Todorov in his *Mémoire du mal, Tentation du bien* (Memory of evil, temptation of the good). Todorov argues that while it is indeed essential for human beings to seek their identity through the narration of the past, we must reconcile the scholarly demand for objectively verifiable truth with the seemingly contradictory imperative of providing a moral assessment of the historical record. The key, contends Todorov, is to avoid the conventional paradigms of historical narration in which one's own group appears either as triumphant heroes or innocent victims (and rarely, if ever, as perpetrators of crimes); events should instead be narrated from the multiplicity of perspectives of those involved, and assessed not just in terms of their benefits or damage to the interests of one specific group. Ultimately, the various episodes of the past—and in particular, those most heavily charged with ethical implications, such as enslavement, genocide, and mass deportation—must be related to the notion of a universal human identity that human groups and societies of all times and places nevertheless share in spite of their ethnic and cultural particularities.

Using Todorov's paradigms of historical memory and narration, we observe that in drawing lessons from events as disparate as the conquest of the Americas, the French Revolution, the Dreyfus affair, and World War II, Mauriac avoids the instrumentalization of history. He evaluates events past and present not according to prearranged social, national, or ideological categories, but rather according to the humanity or inhumanity of their protagonists.

Chapter 5, "In Search of Times Past," invokes Pierre Nora's notion of the *lieu de mémoire* to explain how Mauriac's editorials constitute a conscious crystallization of the past, as he attempts to rescue the pathos of public and private experience from oblivion. The *Bloc-notes* thus provides an eloquent, firsthand account of France's profound evolution in the 1950s and 1960s as experienced by a Frenchman who had come of age within the institutions and mores of the nineteenth century. In this context, Mauriac pens editorials not so much to teach the lessons of history, but rather to revive it, to immortalize the seemingly ephemeral experiences of times past, to reveal the rich sediment of humanity inscribed on the countrysides, landscapes, and constructions that testify to both the triumphs and the crimes of previous generations. He seeks in particular to capture the unique identity constituted on personal, social, and national levels precisely by the accumulation of experience over the years. Mauriac's many returns to the past thus serve not only as a filter through which contemporary events and issues are to be interpreted, but ultimately form one of the *lieux de mémoire* that have come to constitute the fabric of France's collective memory and its very identity.

Mauriac's attachment to French identity as constituted over the course of the nation's rich, if often highly conflictual, past best explains why he so enthusiastically espouses de Gaulle's "certaine idée de la France."[21] He idolizes the general to the point of retreating from the uncompromising denunciations of unjust, oppressive order so characteristic of the *Bloc-notes* of the 1950s, and sides politically with de Gaulle even when conceding that the general is morally and factually errant.

Chapter 6, "The *Bloc-notes* in History," contrasts Mauriac's approach to history with that of the two dominant figures of the 1950s and 1960s in France, Sartre and de Gaulle. In the final analysis, we will see that he eschews what Finkielkraut aptly terms the "enchantment" of history by ideology. Mauriac's approach to history is not without its own tensions and contradictions. Given the empirical, flexible humanism with which

21. The phrase comes from the opening lines of Charles de Gaulle's *Mémoires de Guerre, Vol. 1: L'appel* (Paris: Plon, 1954), 1:

> Toute ma vie, je me suis fait une certaine idée de la France. Le sentiment me l'inspire aussi bien que la raison. Ce qu'il y a en moi d'affectif imagine naturellement la France, telle la princesse des contes ou la madone aux fresques des murs, comme vouée à une destinée imminente et exceptionnelle.
>
> [Throughout my life I have maintained a certain idea of France. It has been inspired by both reason and sentiment. The affective part of me naturally imagines France like the fairy-tale princess or the madonna of wall frescoes, destined for an imminent, exceptional destiny.]

This "certain idea of France" thus became the hallmark of the general's discourse and politics of grandeur.

he engages day-to-day events, the opposite would in fact be surprising.
But even in his unswerving fidelity to de Gaulle, which exasperated so many of his friends on the left, Mauriac was not blinded by the dogma of any one social or political group: while impressed by a politics of "grandeur" that so closely corresponded to his own vision of history and politics, he nevertheless—even at the very outset of de Gaulle's tenure in the summer of 1958—called explicit attention to the artificial, contingent nature of the general's highly idealistic narrative. While he admired the general's historical discourse and political vision, Mauriac never took it to be an accurate record of the past, but on the contrary remained sensitive to the violence and injustice of history from which France—even under de Gaulle—was hardly exempt.

Mauriac subscribed to de Gaulle's "certaine idée de la France" as a dynamic reaffirmation of a culture, society, and national identity painfully acquired through the many vicissitudes of French history. Nothing could be farther from Mauriac's mind than the idea of creating a tabula rasa in history by liquidating that past and its decidedly onerous heritage. Here again, the contrast with his contemporaries among a Parisian intelligentsia largely won over to a Marxist perspective on history and politics is dramatically apparent, for Sartre and other fellow travelers readily endorsed revolutionary violence as the necessary means of ridding humankind of the shackles impeding progress toward a utopian future. If so many French intellectuals pursued for so long the fantasy of revolution, it was in no small part because, as Finkielkraut points out, they viewed existing values and institutions as mere "constructions" of history to be destroyed and swept away in order to clear the way for a newly constructed humanity and society.[22]

Such moral and intellectual hubris is foreign to Mauriac. He makes no attempt to identify one underlying cause of historical evil precisely because he never reduces the figures and events of history past and present to a single discursive or ideological concept. History in the *Bloc-notes* remains indeterminate, richly opaque and polyvalent, irreducible to ideological paradigms.[23]

22. Alain Finkielkraut, *L'humanité perdue*, 56–57.
23. Cf. Michel Winock, *Le siècle des intellectuels*, 440.

I have made a conscious effort to respect this indeterminacy in my own analyses and commentary. As indicated in the synopsis offered above, each of the following chapters explores a constellation of issues surrounding a different component of Mauriac's approach to history in the *Bloc-notes.* I have not hesitated to cite these editorials extensively for several reasons. First, I wanted to foreground the empirical richness and rhetorical verve so characteristic of Mauriac's treatment of specific events as well as of the larger questions of history, ethics, and identity. I also wanted to let his editorials echo the profound repercussions thus perceived in such unspectacular phenomena as the publication of a new novel by Françoise Sagan, the creation of a new television program, or the construction of an airport. More importantly, however, I sought to avoid the truncated citations that can so easily lead to erroneous interpretations. Throughout the book I have stressed Mauriac's original manner of thinking history concretely, in terms of the specific historical images, figures, and events that constitute the very substance of the *Bloc-notes:* close textual commentary is indispensable if we wish to analyze his thinking in a precise, rigorous manner. Implicit in each of these avenues of investigation is the overarching thesis that, contrary to what is most often presumed, Mauriac did indeed have his own autonomous thought on history and politics. Before delivering any global assessment of Mauriac's perspective on history in the context of the 1950s and 1960s and considering the enduring viability of Mauriac's approach to the past, let us first follow the rich contours of that thought as embodied in the *Bloc-notes.*

2 THE STORY OF HISTORY

> Quel roman plus poignant que celui-là? Quelle histoire inventée l'emporterait en intérêt sur celle que je raconte ici et qui ne s'invente pas? . . . Alors nous professons que la lecture des romans nous ennuie et qu'aux plus belles histoires imaginées, il faut préférer l'inimaginable Histoire. ("Préface," BN II, 10)
>
> [*What novel could be more poignant than that one? What concocted story could evoke greater interest than the one that I tell here, which cannot be made up? . . . And so we profess that we are bored with reading novels and that the unimaginable story of history is to be preferred over the most beautiful stories imagined.*]

One only has to read a few of Mauriac's editorials to observe that history permeates his writing, informs his position on virtually all subjects, and constantly provides the essential frame of reference. The past is everywhere present in the *Bloc-notes*, as Mauriac filters his perception of current events through a vast repertoire of figures and episodes from French history. In the preface to the first volume, he specifically identifies history as the nexus of his writing. Changing moods may have directed his attention in a number of directions, just as pressing political concerns may have compelled him to engage in polemics. And yet the basic formula remains constant:

> . . . quelqu'un est là, avec ses idées, ses goûts, ses humeurs, les conditions d'une vie ordinaire, et chaque semaine, *il réagit à l'histoire telle qu'elle se fait sous son regard.* Cet affrontement de l'individuel et de l'universel, c'est tout le *Bloc-notes.* (BN I, 37; emphasis mine)

> [. . . someone is there amid the circumstances of an ordinary life with his ideas, his tastes, his moods, and each week, *he reacts to history being made under his very eyes.* This confrontation of the individual with the universal is what the *Bloc-notes* is all about.]

In all their apparent diversity, the editorials of the *Bloc-notes* nevertheless transcend the topical because they participate in *history.*

Recent critical commentary has to a certain extent acknowledged the importance of history in the *Bloc-notes.* Bernard Cocula speaks of "cette longue méditation sur l'Histoire que constitue aussi le *Bloc-notes*" (this long meditation on history that the *Bloc-notes* also forms).[1] He further characterizes Mauriac's editorials as a "product" of historical events,[2] and even claims that Mauriac "becomes one" with history in some instances.[3] And although Malcolm Scott points out that, like de Gaulle, Mauriac valued the continuity and permanence of French identity as constituted by its rich literary and cultural patrimony and that he considered French history as indissociable with France's unique geography,[4] neither Scott, nor Cocula, nor anyone else has analyzed the rich spectrum of signification that Mauriac creates through his countless invocations of history.

This chapter is devoted precisely to that task: we shall first delineate the various senses of "history" operative in the *Bloc-notes* and then explain how Mauriac situates himself, his texts, and his readers with respect to both past and present events. It will be less a matter of *what* Mauriac thinks about such and such a topic than of *how* he conceives, perceives, and represents "history" in his journalism. We shall see that history functions not merely as a décor, nor even as a rhetorical artifice, but rather as the crucial medium through which Mauriac engages his readers and confronts the most pressing issues of his time.

From the beginnings of the *Bloc-notes* in 1952 until its final phase in 1969 and 1970, the historical drama most frequently invoked by Mauriac

1. Bernard Cocula, *Mauriac, le Bloc-notes* (Bordeaux: L'Esprit du Temps, 1995), 63.
2. Cocula, *Mauriac, le Bloc-notes,* 53.
3. Cocula, *Mauriac, le Bloc-notes,* 81.
4. Malcolm Scott, *Mauriac et de Gaulle* (Bordeaux: L'Esprit du Temps, 1999), 24–26.

is the Dreyfus affair.[5] A careful examination will allow us to see how Mauriac uses such events as a basic point of reference and how these many returns to the affair are emblematic of his overall understanding of history. At the turn of the century, the Dreyfus affair ultimately marked the triumph of anticlerical progressives and put to shame the nationalists claiming to be staunch defenders of the Church and French cultural tradition. It might at first glance seem paradoxical, if not incongruous, for such a profoundly Catholic, culturally conservative,[6] and fervently patriotic admirer of de Gaulle's "certaine idée de la France" (of which we will have much more to say in Chapters 3 and 5) to hark back to the momentous scandal of fifty years earlier as an emblem of both political turpitude and intellectual courage. Beyond the fact that his political, social, and even metaphysical stances often escape the a priori's of religion and class in France, however, these many reflections on the Dreyfus affair are in a sense only natural for a French writer who thinks in a fundamentally historical mode. Prefacing his *Mémoires politiques* in 1967, Mauriac presents himself as

> ... un écrivain ... qui a émergé à la vie de l'esprit, et donc à la vie politique, dans les premières années du siècle et qui depuis bientôt trente ans ne s'est pas privé de la commenter.
>
> Il y a émergé à un certain moment de l'Histoire, dans une ville de province, et dans une famille très singulière (comme toutes les familles) et à un certain échelon social.[7]
>
> [... a writer ... who first became involved in intellectual and therefore political affairs during the early years of the century and who for almost thirty years has not refrained from commenting on it.
>
> He began his career at a certain moment of history, in a provincial

5. Cocula points to no less than seventy-one references to the affair in the *Bloc-notes* (54).

6. Mauriac took a dim view of many cultural developments of the "Trente Glorieuses." He frowned on an increasingly media-saturated culture as well as on the increasing eroticism of contemporary literature, cinema, and popular music. He also took a dim view of the *nouveau roman* (new novel), deploring its willing fragmentation of the human subject, and the New Wave in cinema, criticizing its preoccupation with the present as arrogant.

7. François Mauriac, *Mémoires politiques* (Paris: Grasset, 1967), 7.

town, and in a very singular family (as are all families) and on a certain social level.]

Mauriac goes on in the same passage to indicate that the numerous incursions into French history that characterize both the *Bloc-notes* and the *Mémoires intérieurs* are indispensable for understanding his present positions.

Throughout the *Bloc-notes* Mauriac depicts himself as deeply rooted in the past: just as his affective sensibility remains indelibly marked by the rural landscapes and provincial rhythms of daily life at Malagar (the place of his birth and childhood in the Bordeaux region which he often describes in his editorials), so his historical outlook and political views remain linked to the specific social and political contexts surrounding his youth. Mauriac's thinking is thus historical not only because he explicitly grounds it in a particular set of events but also because he presents it as developing in constant relation to that point of departure.

Since his birth on 11 October 1885 made him a childhood witness to the stormy controversy over Alfred Dreyfus, Mauriac identifies the affair as the foundation of his long experience of France's twentieth-century vicissitudes. This knowledge, he contends, has given him a greater perspicacity than younger political adversaries: "J'en juge mieux que vous à cause du plus grand espace d'une vie d'homme que je tiens sous mon regard, puisque la mienne s'étend de Dreyfus à de Gaulle" (BN V, 48; I am a better judge of these matters than you because I can observe a longer span of human life, since my own extends from Dreyfus to de Gaulle). Here and elsewhere he speaks of the affair as framing his childhood and adolescence:

> L'histoire que j'aurai vécue à partir de mon enfance (je me souviens de l'Affaire Dreyfus) était déjà une histoire criminelle. (BN IV, 396)

> . . . l'affaire Dreyfus: elle coïncida avec mon enfance. J'ai songé souvent que le jour radieux de ma première communion, le 12 mai 1896, Alfred Dreyfus était dans sa case de l'île du Diable et souffrait. (BN V, 23)

> [The history that I have experienced from my childhood on (I remember the Dreyfus affair) was already a history of crime.

. . . the Dreyfus affair: it coincided with my childhood. It has often occurred to me that on the glorious day of my first communion, 12 May 1896, Alfred Dreyfus was suffering in his hut on Devil's Island.]

Perhaps even more important than this connection with his moral and political roots is Mauriac's perception of the Dreyfus affair as a political watershed bringing to the surface the major forces that would play themselves out in subsequent moments of crisis in France. Looking back over the first seven decades of the twentieth century, Mauriac concludes: "L'affaire Dreyfus fut au départ un bain révélateur, comme plus tard l'Occupation, qui départagea les Français. . . ." (BN V, 279; As was later the case with the Occupation, the Dreyfus affair at first acted in the manner of a developing bath that separated out opposing factions of the French people. . .). The Dreyfus affair is seen as a revelation of things to come, and in particular of the conflicts in Morocco and Algeria.

Numerous passages throughout the *Bloc-notes* trace the seeds of many other later tribulations back to the Dreyfus affair. Not surprisingly, first and foremost is the deeply rooted anti-Semitism that was to develop particularly virulent and destructive strains during the World War II era. Reflecting on the deep-seated hostility toward Jews in France, Mauriac sees the Dreyfus affair as symptomatic of a long tradition of Catholic anti-Semitism from which he himself was not exempt as a child:

> Ce qui est vrai, c'est que même avant qu'éclate l'affaire, le juif existait pour nous comme un être à part. . . .
>
> Le pauvre Dreyfus trouva donc en nous un terrain longuement préparé où son horrible histoire allait prendre racine, devenir un grand arbre—un grand arbre indéracinable.[8] (BN V, 23–24)
>
> [The truth is that even before the outbreak of the Dreyfus affair, the Jew existed for us as a being apart from others. . . .

8. Like virtually all literary enthusiasts in France during the 1890s (according to Michel Winock), Mauriac was steeped in the novels of Maurice Barrès. Given the importance of the image of the plane tree in *Le Roman de l'énergie nationale*, the sentence ironically alludes to Barrès the author of *Les Déracinés*, and of course the champion of anti-Dreyfusard nationalism rooted in "la terre et les morts" (the land and the dead). See Winock, *Le siècle des intellectuels*, 9–13.

Poor Dreyfus thus found in us ground that had for a long time been made ready for the horrible story that would take root in it and grow into a huge tree—a huge tree that could not be uprooted.]

The very same anti-Semitism prominent in the Dreyfus affair would resurface in the Occupation years, when the "divine surprise"[9] of the Third Republic's downfall satisfied the right-wing rancor that had long been seething. Certain sectors of the French populace were thus delighted to see the Third Republic discredited in the humiliating defeat of May and June 1940 and the Jews persecuted under Vichy:

> Je songe à cette espèce d'êtres à qui la débâcle causa (nous en sommes tous témoins) une sorte d'enivrement, qui ont adoré cette force triomphante, cet écrasement du Front populaire exécré sous les tanks et sous les bombes des nazis et à qui la persécution et la destruction de la race juive parurent délicieuses. L'affaire Dreyfus allait connaître enfin un dénouement selon leur coeur. ("Samedi 20 février 1965," BN IV, 32)
>
> [I am thinking of the sort of people (and we all witnessed it) who became rather giddy in observing France's debacle, who adored this triumphant force, this crushing of the hated Popular Front under the Nazis' tanks and bombs; people who took delight in the persecution and destruction of the Jewish race. The Dreyfus affair was finally culminating in a way that pleased them.]

To confirm the validity of Mauriac's analysis of the Vichy era as a sequel to the Dreyfus affair, one only has to recall the words of one of the most notorious anti-Dreyfusards of all, the same Charles Maurras who had greeted the demise of the Third Republic and the instauration of Vichy as a "divine surprise": upon his postwar conviction for treason, he blurted out "C'est la revanche de Dreyfus!" (This is Dreyfus's revenge!)[10]

Mauriac brings the ramifications of the Dreyfus affair even closer to

9. Charles Maurras, who had throughout the early twentieth century spearheaded right-wing, anti-Semitic attacks on the Third Republic with his newspaper *L'Action française* as well as with his political organization of the same name, heralded the arrival of Pétain and the Vichy regime as a "divine suprise." See Julian Jackson, *France: The Dark Years, 1940–1944* (New York: Oxford University Press, 2001), 140–41. Maurras was moreover one of the main ideological sources of the Vichy regime's "National Revolution."

10. Pierre Birnbaum, *L'affaire Dreyfus: La République en péril* (Paris: Gallimard Découvertes-Histoire, 1994), 95.

the present by pointing out that the same ones who sought revenge for the Dreyfus affair during the Vichy years later hoped for a military putsch during the Algerian turmoil. It was they, insists Mauriac,

> . . . qui triomphèrent et qui frémirent de joie avec Hitler et par Hitler: l'affaire Dreyfus allait connaître son véritable épilogue et le Juif paierait, cette fois! Ceux qui s'en pourléchaient les babines sont encore au milieu de nous et il n'y a pas si longtemps qu'ils se crurent au moment de prendre une dernière revanche—mais, cette fois, de Gaulle était là. ("Malagar samedi 15 avril 1967," BN IV, 432)
>
> [. . . who triumphed and shuddered for joy with Hitler and by Hitler: the Dreyfus affair was finally reaching its true epilogue and the Jew was going to pay this time! Those who were licking their chops are still among us and it was not so long ago that they thought they were about to get their last revenge—but this time de Gaulle was there.]

From Mauriac's perspective, the Dreyfus affair contained the germ not only of Vichy's authoritarianism and anti-Jewish policies, but even of nazism itself. Already in 1952, while responding to an article on Maurras, Mauriac explained why he adamantly refused to pay tribute to the founder and leader of the Action Française:

> Mais rien ne me fera m'incliner devant ce destin qui s'inscrit entre la glorification du faux Henry et les attaques antisémites de 1943. . . . Tout le nazisme est préfiguré dans la glorification du faux Henry—le plus immonde qui ait jamais été commis puisqu'il s'agissait de perdre un innocent, et dans cette fureur de 1943 que la vue de l'étoile jaune n'apaisa pas. (BN I, 45–46)
>
> [But nothing will bring me to pay tribute to this career that extends from his glorification of Henry's forgery to the anti-Semitic attacks of 1943. . . . All of nazism was foreshadowed by the glorification of Henry's forgery—the most disgusting forgery every perpetrated, since it was intended to have an innocent man condemned—and in the anti-Semitic furor of 1943 that was not appeased by the sight of the yellow star.][11]

11. Colonel Henry was one of the key witnesses for the prosecution, accusing Dreyfus of treason and espionage during the first trial. In the trial of Emile Zola, who had adamantly denounced the lies leading to Dreyfus's conviction, Henry produced a forged

On at least two occasions Mauriac even goes so far as to portray the Holocaust as a sequel to the Dreyfus affair. Paying homage to the writer and historian Jules Isaac, Mauriac comments: "La jeunesse est demeurée intacte chez cet octogénaire en dépit d'une expérience atroce et ininterrompue, de l'affaire Dreyfus aux crématoires dévorateurs de ses frères" (BN II, 250; This octogenarian's youth remains intact, even though he lived through an unbroken string of horrors extending from the Dreyfus affair to the crematories that consumed his fellow Jews).

On the part of such an ardent Gaullist writing at the height of the general's prestige, this willingness to link the Dreyfus affair to the very worst elements of nazism (as in the February 1965 and the April 1967 articles cited above) is particularly remarkable. Thanks to the epic strains of Malraux's stirring eulogy, the transferal of Jean Moulin's ashes to the Pantheon in December 1964 had marked the virtual apotheosis of Gaullism through the celebration of a supposedly united France's heroic resistance to the Nazi oppressor. There was no place in this heroic narrative for remembering indigenous anti-Semitism complicit with the Germans' execution of their "Final Solution" in occupied France. That, on the contrary, Mauriac should on several occasions point out the deep roots and subsequent ramifications of the anti-Semitism so visible in the Dreyfus affair confirms our initial observation: Mauriac's unswerving support of de Gaulle was not based on acceptance of the general's "certaine idée de la France" as an authentic statement of the historical record. Any misgivings as to Mauriac's supposed ideological dependence on de Gaulle should therefore be dispelled.

In Chapter 4, we will have more to say about Mauriac's repeated invocations of the Dreyfus affair in denouncing torture and oppression during the Algerian war. Before analyzing these lessons of "history," however, we must remember that the term takes on different meanings

---

letter seemingly corroborating Dreyfus's guilt. When the forgery was later exposed, Henry committed suicide; he was subsequently hailed as a "martyr" by leading figures of the anti-Dreyfusard press, including Maurras, who praised the willful falsification as patriotic. See Birnbaum, *L'affaire Dreyfus: La République en péril*, 39, 43–44, 60, 74. In May 1942, the Germans required all Jews in the Occupied Zone to wear a yellow star. Massive roundups of Jews conducted by French police and the resulting deportation of tens of thousands of Jews to Auschwitz were to follow in July and August 1942.

in different contexts, particularly in French, since the term "histoire" covers not only the various senses of the English word "history" but also includes the meaning of "story." In stating that he "réagit à l'histoire telle qu'elle se fait sous son regard" (reacts to history being made under his very eyes), Mauriac expresses a fundamental notion found throughout the *Bloc-notes:* looking at current events, he sees them as an ongoing drama. Just as he presents the defeatism, collaborationism, and anti-Semitism that emerged during World War II and the German Occupation as sequels to the Dreyfus affair, so the particular and the individual participate in a larger scheme of things that can be likened to a chess tournament: "Mais chaque partie ici engage l'histoire de la nation et celle du monde" (BN I, 202; But here each game impacts the history of our nation and of the world).

Instead of writing about isolated incidents or presenting random anecdotes, Mauriac is observing a series of actions unfolding over time, originating in the past and leading to the future. Events are interrelated: each new occurrence is like a new photo to be placed in a family album and understood in relation to other sets and series of pictures, or like another episode in a long saga. Hence the frequent use of one form or another of writing as a metaphor for history, as evident in the following examples:

> . . . l'histoire ne se corrige pas comme une copie. Le zéro que le destin donnera à l'équipe Laniel n'empêche pas *cette dissertation* de se poursuivre et d'être sans fin. (BN I, 138)

> . . . cette histoire à la fois criminelle et inepte, *cette histoire de dix ans écrite à l'encre rouge*, l'a été par des chrétiens, par ceux dont l'arrivée au pouvoir, le lendemain de la Libération, m'avait comblé de joie et de fierté. (BN I, 148–49)

> . . . c'est le petit professeur [Georges Bidault] que le destin a chargé d'ajouter *un chapitre* à notre histoire. (BN I, 171)

> Oui, il est temps encore. *Notre copie* n'est pas remise après tout: l'histoire de France continue et nous détenons encore le pouvoir d'en changer le cours. (BN I, 227)

> [. . . history cannot be corrected like a paper. The zero that Laniel's [governing] team is destined to receive will not prevent *this composition* from going on and being endless.
>
> . . . this story of history full of crime and ineptitude, *this ten-year story of history written in red ink*, was made by Christians who had filled me with joy and pride when they came into power just after the Liberation.
>
> This is the little professor [Georges Bidault] who was destined to take on the task of adding *a chapter* to our history.
>
> Yes, there is still time. After all, *our paper* has not been handed in: France's history goes on and we still have the power to change its course.]

Similar figurations of history as one form or another of a written text occur throughout the *Bloc-notes* and attest to the basic conception.

The recurring metaphor contains several key components. In the first place, historical events take place in chronological order: there is change, evolution, movement, and progression (not to be confused with progress). The ongoing drama of humanity brings something new and confronts societies with change and evolution. Second, the story of history is for Mauriac primarily—but as we shall see, not exclusively—that of the political life of nations, as peoples struggle for power, prosperity, and autonomy. As such, history is the cumulative result of myriad human actions. Third, history necessarily entails a written narrative: in each case, there is a human being (or a group) seeking to give an account of what happens, in order to record events, decipher their meaning, and transmit both their memory and meaning to others. Finally, Mauriac's "prose of the world" composes a text whose chapters are interconnected: past and present are not only linked by the chain of causes and effects, they are interrelated within the overarching story of history, since the narrative weaves them into one coherent whole. The past continues to weigh on the present, just as the present takes its meaning in relation to what has come before.

Hence Mauriac's frequent portrayal of things present against the backdrop of time: people and places are related back to the long process of sedimentation constitutive of their identity. Witness Mauriac's commentary on the annual pilgrimage to Chartres in May 1954, just when

France's stinging defeat at Dien Bien Phu and the continuing unrest in North Africa were bringing the issues of colonial violence and repression to a head:

> Ces douze mille garçons et filles de France réunis sous les voûtes les plus illustres de la chrétienté, dans la cathédrale de Péguy, au lendemain de Dien Bien Phu, quel silence les accueille! J'ai cru un moment que les pierres crieraient! Non que le cardinal ne leur ait adressé des paroles excellentes, celles mêmes qu'il devait leur adresser. Mais une autre voix, une voix non officielle aurait dû s'élever. . . . Quelle voix? Hélas! des générations chrétiennes se pressaient autour de la chaire du père Lacordaire,[12] comme il y eut des générations socialistes que la grande voix de Jaurès réveillait et remettait debout quand elles perdaient coeur. Quel silence, partout, dans cette France désemparée de 1954! Sur la dalle du soldat inconnu, nous devrions verser des larmes de sang; car cet inconnu, c'est l'homme qui se tait aujourd'hui. ("Lundi 10 mai 1954," BN I, 151)
>
> [What silence greets these twelve thousand young French men and women gathered here just after Dien Bien Phu, in Péguy's cathedral, under the most illustrious vaults of Christendom. I thought for a moment that the stones would cry out! The cardinal did not fail to deliver an excellent address in the very words he should have spoken. But a different, nonofficial voice should have spoken out. . . . What voice? Alas, there were generations of Christians crowding around Father Lacordaire's pulpit, just as, whenever they were disheartened, generations of Socialists were stirred back to their feet by the great voice of Jaurès. What silence there is everywhere in our bewildered France in 1954! We should shed tears of blood over the tomb of the unknown soldier, for today it is he who is remaining silent.]

Mauriac defines the pathos of the moment in reference to the history that continues to resound through the silence of the cathedral. Not only is the past present in the architecture and the memories connected with Chartres, it reverberates through analogies with previous moments of both French and Western European history, since Mauriac alludes to "la

12. The Dominican monk and priest Henri Lacordaire (1802–1861) worked actively in politics and journalism for the instauration of democratic institutions. See *Petit Larousse Illustré 1994* (Paris: Larousse, 1993).

chrétienté" (Christendom) and to the New Testament account of Jesus' entry into Jerusalem ("J'ai cru un moment que les pierres crieraient!" [I thought for a moment that the stones would cry out!]).[13]

It is important to rectify the misinterpretations that have arisen from such biblical allusions: contrary to what has been advanced by Malcolm Scott (71), there is no "mystical" element in Mauriac's approach to history. As abundantly illustrated by many passages of the *Bloc-notes* cited throughout the present book, Mauriac responds to intense echos of the past emanating from virtually every site highlighted in his editorials, from the childhood memories and venerable rural traditions connected with his ancestral residence at Malagar to the murmurs of history in the Palais Bourbon,[14] to the legacy of the ancien régime still palpable in the provincial château of Valmante,[15] to the rich social life of yesteryear centered on the Place Stanislas in Nancy,[16] to cite just a few examples. The underlying concepts of the continuity of French history and of the permanence of French national identity stem from nineteenth-century secular views of France's heritage formulated by Michelet, Guizot, Lavisse, and others. These are deeply seated, cultural notions shared by generations of schoolchildren—among whom we must include not only François Mauriac, but a certain Charles de Gaulle—who acquired their basic concepts of history under the Third Republic.

In one of his accounts of the National Assembly, we thus see Mauriac constantly depicting the immediate situation in relation to an extensive past, as when he speaks of "l'atmosphère bitumeuse de mauvais tableau d'histoire" (the sooty atmosphere of a second-rate historical painting), and deplores the mediocrity of contemporary orators in comparison with their illustrious predecessors: "nous soupirons: 'Ah! Jaurès, Briand, c'était autre chose . . .'" [Jeudi 10 juin 1954, BN I, 170; We sigh: "Ah! Jaurès and Briand were of another category . . ."]. Mauriac goes on to explain that his perception of the Chambre des Députés has been indelibly marked by momentous occasions of the twentieth century:

13. Cf. Luke 19.39–40.
14. See below and BN I, 170.
15. See below and BN I, 484–85.
16. See "Mulhouse, jeudi 23 juin 1964," BN IV, 284–85.

Oserai-je tout dire? Cette tribune, pour moi, ne sera jamais plus celle où Clemenceau, épuisé de joie, monta le 11 novembre 1918. Elle reste celle d'où, un jour de juillet 1940, l'immonde Rosenberg fit la leçon à la France profanée. (BN I, 170)

[Shall I go ahead and say what I really think? For me, this podium will never again be the one where Clemenceau, overwhelmed with joy, stood up to speak on 11 November 1918. It shall remain the podium where the obscene person of Rosenberg dished out his lesson to a desecrated France.]

Throughout the *Bloc-notes*, Mauriac continually frames the current situation with such allusions to events and figures of history: the experience of the past does not simply vanish but accumulates over the years, becoming ingrained in the particular character of persons, places, and things.

The imagery used in relating a visit to the chateau of Valmante testifies dramatically to the presence of the past: Mauriac presents the now declining estate as the material embodiment of selfish bourgeois ambition, and then explains the Catholic Church's disavowal of the worker priests as a symptom of a defensive posture that parallels the architecture of the bourgeois castle:

Valmante, samedi 20 juillet 1957

Aux portes mêmes de Marseille, ce beau domaine, tout vivant qu'il est, je le sens frappé à mort. Ce que le château recelait de précieux a été dispersé. Les armoires ouvertes ne défendent plus leurs secrets qui, dans une noble demeure comme celle-ci, sont les mêmes que dans les logis modestes où j'ai vécu: albums, photos dédicacées. . . . Quel parti pris d'être heureux, dans cette puissante bourgeoisie d'autrefois! . . . .

Je songe, ce matin, au petit nombre d'êtres qui ont refusé de se mettre à part de la multitude, qui ont choisi de se livrer à elle, de se confondre avec elle. Les prêtres-ouvriers. . . .

C'est que, comme la grande bourgeoisie, mais pour d'autres raisons, l'Eglise elle aussi est barricadée, hérissée de défenses: tout ce que dix-neuf siècles ont accumulé de sédiment sur d'antiques structures, vénérables mais humaines, trop humaines. (BN I, 484–85)

[Valmante, Saturday 20 July 1957

I sense that this fine estate, as lively as it is, has been mortally stricken. The chateau's valuables have been scattered about. Its open armoires are no longer guarding the secrets that, in a noble dwelling such as this, are the same as the ones in the modest homes where I have lived: photo albums, autographed pictures. . . . What determination to be happy on the part of this powerful bourgeoisie of yesteryear! . . .

This morning I am thinking of the few human beings who have refused to set themselves apart and chosen instead to give themselves over and join with the multitude. The worker-priests. . . .

The fact is that, like the most affluent sectors of the bourgeoisie, but for other reasons, the Church has also barricaded itself in and put on spiked armor, in the form of all that the nineteen centuries of sediment has accumulated over its old and venerable, but human, all-too-human structures.]

Specifically designated in these last lines, the rich deposit of the past, figured palpably by the massive architecture and furniture of the chateau, weighs heavily on the present.

Mauriac's view of contemporary events, however, is in no way hostage to antiquarian nostalgia: in the passage just cited, the ancient constructions are "vénérables" but flawed ("humaines, trop humaines" [human, all-too-human]) and represent in fact a handicap to be overcome. We must moreover recall that this piece was written for *L'Express* amid the highly charged atmosphere of the "Battle of Algiers" that, in July 1957, had already been raging for months. Throughout these tense times marked by pitiless acts of terror on the part of the Front de Libération National (FLN), the dominant rebel movement fighting for an independent Algeria, and equally ferocious repression on the part of the French military and police, Mauriac not only condemns the use of torture but makes repeated appeals to bring down the colonial walls of social privilege and exclusive power that constituted the chief impediments to a peaceable and just solution to the tragedy in Algeria. The same is true throughout the *Bloc-notes:* while constantly recalling the various historical figures and developments instrumental in shaping the present, Mauriac's editorials convey his own particular perception of history by depicting the immediate situation as a part of a much larger drama.

The piece devoted to the celebration of France's national holiday in 1957, once again at the height of the Battle of Algiers, is particularly revealing: far from beholden to some "mysticism" or reactionary historicism, this editorial undercuts the declining Fourth Republic's attempt to exploit the heroic vision of the past that the official commemorations marking the anniversary of the storming of the Bastille were attempting to convey. For as noted by Jean Touzot (BN I, 481n), the 1957 rendition of the ritual 14 July parade down the Champs-Elysées featured General Massu and his paratroopers, who were using torture and summary executions to repress terrorism in Algiers. The 14 July display was thus an attempt to legitimate this brutal campaign by affirming a continuity with the revolutionaries who had toppled the ancien régime in 1789.

Mauriac not only refuses to take this reference to the past at face value, he proceeds to undermine the entire spectacle by underscoring its artificiality: he uses literary allusions for ironic commentary, juxtaposes the staged spectacle with the reality of current military and judicial practices in Algeria, and finally inserts the parade into the "atemporal" drama of human existence as defined by Saint Bonaventure. Paradoxically, it is by mocking the French government's would-be exercise of heroic memory that Mauriac conveys a powerfully historical perception.

Mauriac begins by calling attention to his own particular position as a spectator exterior to the official celebration:

> Dimanche 14 juillet 1957
>
> En ma qualité "d'exhibitionniste de l'intelligence et du coeur" je me suis gardé d'aller sur les Champs-Elysées. Il m'a suffi de voir défiler les paras sur l'écran de la télévision. Je me vante même de les avoir admirés plus à loisir que si M. le président de la République m'avait fait asseoir à sa droite. L'écran devenait, à certains moments, une tapisserie vivante de visages vus d'aussi près qu'il était possible, à moins de se cogner. Le téléspectateur, si le coeur lui en disait, pouvait se livrer à des comparaisons entre ces types humains. Que de différences d'un corps de troupe à l'autre, et à l'intérieur d'une même unité! Qu'il y en avait de nobles et qu'il y en avait de vils! J'ai fait là-dessus de ces réflexions qui ne valent que pour nous-même et que la sagesse conseille de ne partager avec personne! (BN I, 480–81)

> [Sunday 14 July 1957
>
> In my capacity as "an exhibitionist of the heart and mind," I refrained from going to the Champs-Elysées. I was content to watch the paratroopers parading on television. I can even boast of taking in the spectacle in a more leisurely manner than I would have if the president of the republic had seated me on his righthand side. At times, the television screen became a living tapestry of faces viewed from as close as possible without bumping into them. If they so desired, viewers could indulge in comparing different types of people. What differences there were between one corps and another, and within the same unit! There were indeed individuals of a noble and of a vile sort. On that score, I made a few of my own reflections that wisdom counsels not to share with anyone!]

As Jean Touzot points out (BN I, 480n), the first sentence recalls the words that Robert Lacoste, then governor of Algeria, had used in trying to blame recurrent outbreaks of terrorist bombings on the journalists and intellectuals such as Mauriac who were leading the campaign against torture. Mauriac thus cites the words of the highest ranking French official in Algeria to frame his ironic dismantlement of the French government's 14 July propaganda.

Mauriac's status as an official persona non grata at the supposedly triumphant parade becomes the basis of the critical distance separating him from the commemoration that he, along with thousands of other "téléspectateur[s]," views ironically as a sort of "tapisserie vivante" (living tapestry) on his "écran" (screen). From this vantage point outside the spectacle, he exposes its illusory character, first of all by characterizing it as a *mise en scène*, a staged event that fails to hold him under its sway:

> Le moteur a tué les revues militaires en supprimant ce qui caracolait, voilà le vrai. (BN I, 481)

> . . . ce n'est pas cette mirobolante revue qui rassurera là-dessus les Français capables de quelque réflexion. (BN I, 481–82)

> Ah! tourner le bouton! Le téléspectateur est un dieu maître d'interrompre à la seconde une revue à grand spectacle, comme était celle-là. (BN I, 482)

. . . Il jouait au soldat, ce matin, sur les Champs-Elysées, prisonnier d'un vieux mirage. . . . (BN I, 483–84)

The truth is that, by eliminating prancing [horses], motorized vehicles have killed military parades.

. . . it is not this dazzling parade that will reassure those French citizens capable of thought.

Ah! Let's switch it off! The TV viewer is a masterful god who can at any second interrupt a spectacular parade such as this one.

. . . Captive of an old illusion, he was playing at being a soldier on the Champs-Elysées this morning. . . .]

Mauriac further heightens the irony with allusions that filter our perception of Lacoste and the official 14 July celebration through the words of Goering, Descartes, Baudelaire, and La Fontaine:

> Laissons là l'intelligence et le coeur, pour ne pas offenser M. Robert Lacoste qui serait capable de tirer son revolver, comme Goering. Reste le bon sens, la chose du monde la mieux partagée [selon Descartes dans le *Discours de la méthode*], c'est bien connu, et dont les diplomates étrangers ne sont pas non plus dépourvus. J'en voyais un qui, de son oeil de poisson froid, suivait cette parade. Qu'en pensait-il? Je crois l'avoir deviné, bien qu'il n'en ait rien dit à personne, et surtout pas, j'imagine, à M. le président de la République et à M. le président du Conseil. Il pensait, cet homme raisonnable, qu'un instrument doit être adapté à l'usage auquel on le destine. J'ignore ce que ferait la guerre atomique du beau joujou, dont ce matin, les musiques "versaient l'héroïsme au coeur des citoyens."[17] Je sais fort bien, en revanche, ce qu'en fait, ou plutôt ce que n'en fait pas, une guerre de partisans.
>
> Soyons juste: le moucheron n'est pas encore venu à bout du lion, comme dans la fable [de la Fontaine]. Mais le lion continuera de se battre les flancs de sa queue sans que le moucheron s'en trouve beaucoup plus mal, voilà ce qu'il faut craindre, et ce n'est pas cette mirobolante revue qui rassurera là-dessus les Français capables de quelque réflexion. (BN I, 481–82)

17. Touzot (481n) notes that these words are taken from Baudelaire's poem "Les petites vieilles" ("The Little Old Women") in *Les Fleurs du Mal (The Flowers of Evil).*

[Let's leave aside the heart and the mind in order not to offend Monsieur Robert Lacoste, who would be capable of drawing his revolver like Goering. There remains common sense, which as we all know [[and as Descartes asserts in *Discourse on the Method*]] is the most commonly shared commodity in the world, even among foreign diplomats. I saw one such diplomat coolly [[literally, "with an eye of a cold fish"]] taking in this parade. What were his thoughts on the matter? Even though he said nothing to anybody, and especially not, I suppose, to Mr. President of the Republic or to the Premier, I believe I figured it out. This reasonable man was thinking that any instrument should be fitted to its intended purpose. I don't know what nuclear warfare would do to the pretty plaything whose band "was making heroism well up in the hearts of city dwellers." I know quite well, however, what guerilla warfare does, or rather does not do, to such a force.

To be fair, the gnat has not yet overcome the lion, as in the fable [[of La Fontaine]]. But the lion will continue to switch his sides with his tail without doing much harm to the gnat. That is what must be feared, and it is not this dazzling parade that will reassure those French citizens capable of thought.]

Likening the French governor of Algeria to one of nazism's most infamous spokesmen and then citing poetry to deflate the military bravado exhibited on the Champs-Elysées, Mauriac appears every bit as much of a "cold fish" as the foreign diplomat decidedly unimpressed by the display.

But Mauriac does not limit his refutation of both Lacoste's and the paratroopers' pretensions of martial virtue to literary wit: a cold analysis of the actual military and judicial situation then prevalent in Algeria thoroughly discredits all claims to supremacy and domination through military might:

Evidemment, on peut toujours continuer. On ne peut pas dire qu'il n'en coûte rien, mais si cher qu'il faille le payer en vies humaines et en milliards, le plus facile est de s'en tenir à la méthode qui consiste à ne pas réfléchir et à fermer les yeux. L'immortelle péroraison de M. Lacoste l'a définie pour des siècles, cette méthode: "Je suis là, bien là, encore là, et je ferai tout ce qui est en mon pouvoir pour rester là." C'est le style "parole historique." Mais en clair, cela signifie: "Je laisserai faire tout ce qu'on voudra pour qu'on me laisse là." Car qui a les mains plus durement liées que ce faux proconsul? On dit qu'un cri lui échappe, parfois. (482)

[Of course, we can always continue in the same manner. We cannot say that there is no price to pay: as high as the cost may be in terms of human life and billions of francs, the easiest thing is to stick with the method that consists of closing our eyes and refusing to think. The immortal words of Monsieur Lacoste's oration have laid out this method for centuries to come: "Here I am, firmly in place, still there, and I will do everything in my power to stay there." Which in fact means "I'll let them do whatever they want so that they will leave me in power." For whose hands are bound more tightly than those of this phony proconsul? They say that at times he lets out a yelp.]

Mauriac thus makes a mockery of Lacoste's attempt at grandiose pronouncements for posterity by juxtaposing his "parole historique" (immortal words; literally, "historic speech") with the human and financial cost that France must pay for the war in Algeria.

Apparently disgusted with the televised spectacle, Mauriac finally turns the set off and meditates on Saint Bonaventure, whose commemorative day falls on 14 July. The metaphysical drama he finds in Bonaventure's philosophy, however, ultimately leads right back to current events, as the tortures and arbitrary detention practiced by French authorities in Algeria reveal the full scale of the government's hypocrisy and illusion in attempting to claim a heroic revolutionary heritage with the military parade on the Champs-Elysées:

> 14 juillet. . . . Même le 14 juillet ouvre sur l'intemporel. La prise de la Bastille nous détourne chaque année de penser à l'admirable saint dont c'est la fête aujourd'hui: Bonaventure, le docteur séraphique, disciple de saint Augustin, fils spirituel de saint François et fort hostile à Aristote. Je décide dans mon coeur de lui consacrer cet après-midi de sa fête et me voilà à la recherche du gros bouquin de Gilson sur la [*sic*] "la philosophie de saint Bonaventure." J'en relirai le premier et le dernier chapitre.
>
> L'évasion dans l'intemporel. . . . Mais il y a cette lettre d'un avocat d'Alger qui m'a été communiquée voici bientôt quinze jours, et à laquelle je n'ai pas encore fait écho. Nous voudrions nous unir, sur l'Alverne,[18] à François d'Assise et à son fils Bonaventure, mais il y a cette lettre d'un avocat d'Alger. Ah! nous devons nier qu'il y ait contradic-

18. Where, as Touzot (482n) points out, St. Francis received his stigmata.

tion: "On rejoint toute chose à partir du Christ et on revient à lui à partir de toute chose . . . ," dit Gilson, commentant Bonaventure. Je reprends donc la lettre:

"Mon cher ami, c'est le 22 juillet que doit s'ouvrir le procès du prétendu complot ultra-chrétien d'Alger. J'ai vu bien des procès depuis deux ans—jamais comme celui-là. Parce qu'il n'y a pas eu l'ombre d'un complot et que tous ces gens qui, après avoir été torturés physiquement et moralement, attendent en prison depuis des mois d'être jugés, n'ont rien fait d'autre que de témoigner individuellement, spontanément, en dehors de toute idée politique, par des actes de charité fraternelle, qu'ils étaient des chrétiens: 'A cela on reconnaîtra que vous êtes mes disciples. . . .' . . . Personne n'a osé modifier l'inculpation première 'atteinte à la sûreté de l'Etat' alors qu'en réalité ils sont poursuivis pour 'recel de malfaiteurs.' Entendez par malfaiteur tout musulman traqué ou affolé par le débusquage des paras et qui cherchait à se terrer n'importe où, sachant que, s'il était pris, il serait torturé. Personne n'a osé non plus rendre la moindre ordonnance de non-lieu, même en faveur de ceux qui, à l'évidence, n'ont rien à se reprocher, au point qu'ils furent laissés en liberté provisoire. C'est toute la charrette qui est renvoyée au tribunal militaire. . . . Il faut que vous entriez dans l'arène non pas pour les trente-quatre accusés seulement, mais parce que derrière eux il y a toute une conception de la vie et des rapports humains qu'il faut faire triompher."

Je rêve sombrement là-dessus, et reviens au Bonaventure de Gilson: "Bonaventure est rempli d'angoisse en voyant que l'oeuvre créée par un Dieu, réparée par le sang d'un Dieu, se défait chaque jour comme si tout ce qui peut choisir entre le néant et l'être, choisissait, par un aveuglement insensé, le parti du néant."

Le parti du néant: c'est lui, le maître. Il jouait au soldat, ce matin, sur les Champs-Elysées, prisonnier d'un vieux mirage, aveugle et sourd devant ce monde qui va s'édifier sans nous et contre nous et dont nous étions appelés par vocation à devenir la pensée vivante. (BN I, 482–84)

[14 July. . . . But even the fourteenth of July is a window opening onto the timeless. Every year, the storming of the Bastille leads our thoughts away from the admirable saint we celebrate today: Bonaventure, the Seraphic Doctor, Saint Augustin's disciple, spiritual heir of Saint Francis, and strongly unfavorable to Aristotle. Following my heart, I decide to devote this afternoon to celebrating his memory, and so here I am looking for Gilson's thick volume on "Saint Bonaventure's philosophy." I shall read the first and last chapters.

To escape into the realm of the timeless. . . . But there is this letter from a lawyer in Algiers that was sent to me about two weeks ago and to which I have not responded. We would like to join Francis of Assisi and his spiritual heir Bonaventure on the heights of Mount Alverne, but there is this letter from a lawyer in Algiers. But we must deny that there is any contradiction here: "We reach all things through Christ and through all things we come back to him . . ." says Gilson in his commentary on Bonaventure. I therefore take up the letter again:

"My dear friend, the trial of the so-called conspiracy of radical Christians in Algiers has been slated for July 22. I have seen many a trial over the last two years, but never any like this one. For there was never a hint of any conspiracy. After being physically and psychologically tortured, these people have waited in prison for months to go on trial. The only thing they did was, through individual and spontaneous acts of brotherly love, to bear witness to the fact that they were Christians: 'by this they will recognize that you are my disciples. . . .' . . . No one dared modify the first indictment for 'attacking state security' although they are in fact being prosecuted for 'harboring criminals.' By 'criminal,' understand any Muslims on the run or panicked by the paratroopers' house-to-house searches and seeking to hole up anywhere they could, knowing that if they were caught, they would be tortured. No one dared dismiss any of the charges, even against those who have clearly done nothing wrong and who had for that very reason been released on their own cognizance. The whole cartload has been sent before a military tribunal. . . . You must enter into the public arena not only for the sake of the thirty-four accused, but also because beyond them there is an entire way of thinking about life and human relations that must triumph."

I ponder somberly over the matter, and return to Gilson's book on Bonaventure: "Bonaventure is filled with anguish when he sees that what has been created by a God and restored by a God's blood is undone every day, as if, out of foolish blindness, all that can choose between nothingness and being made the choice for nothingness."

The choice for nothingness: that is what is in command. Captive to an old illusion, he was playing soldier on the Champs-Elysées this morning, deaf and blind to the world that is going to be constructed without us and against us, although our calling had been to become its living thought.]

In the end, the policies that were concretely represented by Massu and his troops in the parade and that the French government was trying to legitimate by means of the 14 July commemoration appear as mirages totally disconnected from the history being played out in Algeria.

Mauriac unsparingly ridicules the simplistic image of the past given by the parade. He nevertheless communicates a thoroughly historical understanding of both the Parisian spectacle (in all its artificiality and pretension) and the concrete military and judicial realities in Algeria by relating them to specific events of the past (such as the sending of entire cartloads of prisoners to the guillotine) and by presenting them in relation to an ongoing, universal human drama, as we shall again see in Chapter 4. And although Mauriac connects the stark political battles to a larger metaphysical struggle, there is strictly nothing "mystical" about either his mockery of the heroic message proposed by the 14 July parade or his stinging indictment of human rights violations perpetrated by French authorities in Algeria.

The synthesis Mauriac provides in looking back over the first four years of his *Bloc-notes* illustrates the various components of "histoire" operative in his editorials. This important text also bears quoting at length, and we have underlined its salient objects of commentary.

> Malagar, lundi 16 septembre 1957
>
> Dans la maison encore mal réveillée de mon absence, je me soumets à cette épreuve: relire le Bloc-notes depuis le premier jour où je commençai à le rédiger. Car il faudra bien finir par publier *ces pages où la vie politique d'une nation et la vie intérieure d'un écrivain mêlent si étrangement leurs eaux.* Il n'est pas question de tout retenir. Mais *la continuité fait tout le prix d'un travail de cet ordre—la durée.* Si je tombe dans le genre "morceaux choisis," tout sera gâché.
>
> Amère lecture. Nos échecs personnels n'entrent pour rien dans cette amertume. Mais *à travers le Bloc-notes, je refais la route que nous avons parcourue depuis cinq ans; ou plutôt je la domine et tiens sous mon regard l'enchaînement des causes et des effets.* Que cette longue infortune soit l'oeuvre des hommes, je l'avais toujours cru. Aujourd'hui, je le vois. Quelques politiciens dont les noms sont connus en ont été et continuent d'en être les agents—mais non certes contre la volonté de la nation. . . .
>
> Ce dont peu de Français de ces milieux [bourgeois] se montrent ca-

pables, c'est de *prendre conscience du monde nouveau qui a surgi en 1945 et auquel les puissances colonisatrices étaient appelées à s'adapter.* Ce qu'il nous en a coûté de dire non en Indochine et au Maroc n'a ouvert les yeux qu'au petit nombre. L'imbécile méconnaissance du rapport réel des forces dans le monde d'aujourd'hui, dont témoigne l'équipée de Suez, a-t-elle frappé chez nous beaucoup de gens? Je n'en jurerais pas. . . .

Non, *aucune fatalité dans le déroulement de cette histoire que le Bloc-notes reflète.* Le sultan du Maroc aurait pu n'être ni déposé ni exilé. Un statut nouveau où les deux peuples auraient trouvé leur compte pouvait être négocié. Un autre ministre que M. Guy Mollet n'eût pas donné tête baissée dans le piège tendu à Alger le 6 février 1956. Un autre n'aurait pas capitulé devant des tomates.

A y regarder de près, le seul de tous nos malheurs qu'il n'appartenait à personne de conjurer, c'est l'Assemblée issue des dernières élections. Le pire est sorti des urnes, qui le nierait? Car le pire, dans une démocratie, consiste à faire accomplir par un gouvernement dit de gauche la politique la plus aveugle et la plus meurtrière de la droite.

Alors à quoi bon tant d'agitation, et que ne vous occupez-vous d'inventer et de raconter des histoires, vous dont c'était le métier? Voilà sans doute ce que pensent bien des gens et la question qu'il m'arrive de me poser à moi-même. *Mais aucun échec ne prévaut contre cette vocation d'un écrivain jeté dans "le brouillamini d'erreurs et de violences" qu'est selon Goethe la politique:* dire en termes clairs ce qu'il croit être vrai sans le souci de ménager aucun intérêt ni aucune personne. (BN I, 509–11)

[In the house not yet completely awakened from my absence, I subject myself to the test of rereading what I have written in the *Bloc-notes* ever since the first day I began to compose it. For *these pages in which a nation's political life and the inner life of a writer intertwine so strangely* must in the end be published. Including everything is out of the question. But *the duration or continuity of such writing is what makes it so valuable.* Falling back into the "selected passages" genre would spoil everything.

It makes for bitter reading, but not because of my personal failures. However, *through the "Bloc-notes," I retrace the route that we have followed for five years; or, rather, I look down on it from on high, from where my eyes perceive the unbroken chain of causes and effects.* I have always thought that this long string of misfortunes is the work of men. Today, I see it. A few well-known politicians have been and continue to be the agents of these woes, but they have certainly not acted against the will of the nation. . . .

There are few French people from these [[upper-class]] social milieus who display the capacity *to take stock of the new world that sprung up in 1945 and summoned the colonial powers to adapt accordingly.* The price we paid for saying no in Indochina and Morocco opened the eyes of only a very few. Have many people been struck by the incredible failure to recognize the real structure of power in today's world as illustrated by the Suez fiasco? I wouldn't bet on it. . . .

No, *there was nothing inevitable or predetermined in this story of history visible in the "Bloc-notes."* It would have been possible for the Sultan of Morocco not to have been deposed or exiled. It was possible to negotiate a new statute accommodating the interests of both nations. A premier other than Guy Mollet could have avoided tumbling head-first into the trap set in Algiers on 6 February 1956. Another would not have given in under the [[barrage of]] tomatoes.

When we look at things closely, the only one of our woes that no one could have prevented was the National Assembly that resulted from the last elections. Who could deny that they resulted in the worst possible scenario? For in a democracy, the worst consists of having a supposed government of the Left carry out the blindest and most deadly policies of the Right.

So what good is it to get so upset, and why don't you just worry about inventing and telling stories, since that's your job? That is probably what a good many people are thinking and at times I ask myself the same question. *But for a writer thrown into "the imbroglio of errors and violence" of politics, to borrow Goethe's phrase, no failure can prevail over this vocation:* to say clearly what I believe to be true with no desire to go easy on any particular interest or person.]

This passage confirms our preliminary assessment: Mauriac specifies once more that the substance of his *Bloc-notes* is history, and that "cette histoire que le Bloc-notes reflète" (this story of history visible in the *Bloc-notes*) consists of the various events that make up the "vie politique d'une nation" (a nation's political life). The events form a coherent story, a drama that is evolving, moving forward (though not necessarily to any desirable end). As a writer, Mauriac is intent on analyzing the "plot" (the evolution of historical events) and pointing out the direction of events: he thus exhorts his readers to "prendre conscience du monde nouveau qui a surgi en 1945" (take stock of the new world that sprung up in 1945) and realize the obsolescence of the old colonial order.

We should not overlook what at first glance might seem to be incidental, secondary details. As is the case throughout the *Bloc-notes*, the day and date situate Mauriac and his discourse temporally, thus linking the public events and personal experiences discussed in his editorial to a particular moment. And as always when Mauriac writes from his home in the Bordeaux region, the name of his estate, "Malagar," provides much more than a picturesque rural setting: the precise geographical location coincides with the distinct and paradoxical stance that Mauriac adopts with respect to history. The quiet isolation of his traditional family residence and the bucolic beauty of its surroundings offer a sort of retreat from the clamor of Paris and from the sound and fury of history. This "retreat" allows Mauriac to step back, or *prendre du recul*, as the French like to say when seeking to integrate specific temporal and geographical details into a larger scheme of things,[19] and contemplate what has transpired as if from above, taking stock of events from a global perspective: "je refais la route que nous avons parcourue depuis cinq ans; ou plutôt je la domine et tiens sous mon regard l'enchaînement des causes et des effets" (I go back over the course that we have followed for five years; or rather, I look down on it from on high, from where my eyes perceive the unbroken chain of causes and effects).

A prima facie reading of Mauriac's text here could lead one to think that he has adopted the perspective of the omniscient narrator naively presuming the transparency of his subject matter, and thus laying claim to an objective discourse written from a supposedly exterior vantage point. But a closer examination reveals his stance as a writer to be in fact much more problematical than that of either Sartre (who, before skewering his Catholic counterpart with his famous "Dieu n'est pas un artiste; M. Mauriac non plus" [God is not an artist; neither is Monsieur Mauriac],[20] had accused Mauriac of trying to play God in manipulating the characters of his novels like puppets), or Malcolm Scott, who sug-

19. See Wylie and Brière, *Les Français*, 11–12.

20. Jean-Paul Sartre, "M. François Mauriac et la liberté," in *Situations I* (Paris: Gallimard, 1947), 57.

gests that in the *Bloc-notes* Mauriac was equally heavy-handed in his depiction of political figures.[21]

The first part of the passage must be read in conjunction with the last paragraph. For there we find not the privileged perspective of the God-like narrator contemplating an impersonal process of "l'enchaînement des causes et des effets" (the unbroken chain of causes and effects) from the comfortable detachment of some supposed intellectual firmament, but "un écrivain jeté dans 'le brouillamini d'erreurs et de violences' qu'est selon Goethe la politique" (a writer thrown into "the imbroglio of errors and violence" of politics, to borrow Goethe's phrase). The writer no longer appears as an observer above the melee looking down from Olympian heights, but as someone thrown into the thick of the battle. History is seen not as an impersonal process unfolding according to some sort of rational law or immanent force, but as a human, all-too-human, imbroglio.

The tension among these various elements stems from the paradoxical approach to history articulated throughout the *Bloc-notes.* Mauriac repeatedly returns to Goethe's phrase, just as he often depicts the violence in France's colonial conflicts as an implacable cycle offering little chance for a reasonable instauration of peace and justice. The following lines illustrate this bleak view:

> Obsédé de ce que j'ai entendu hier soir: ce drame de l'Afrique du Nord, je l'aurai vécu heure par heure. *Cette chaîne sans fin des deux terreurs* qui s'enfantent l'une l'autre, qui fait naître la répression de l'attentat, l'attentat de la répression, ce malheur a un aspect quotidien et que le journal nous rapporte: film policier monotone, film à épisodes. ("Vendredi 14 mai 1954," BN I, 153)

> Mais c'est toujours de *la même chaîne sans fin de représailles* qu'il s'agit, chaîne qu'il faudra pourtant briser. . . . ("Dimanche 30 mai 1954," BN I, 167)

> Car de quoi s'agit-il, sinon de rompre *cette fatalité de représailles en chaîne?* ("Dimanche 13 juin 1954," BN I, 173)

21. Scott, *Mauriac et de Gaulle,* 236.

C'est moi qui rêve en croyant que *l'affreux enchaînement de meurtres et de représailles* crée un climat peu favorable à la négociation? ("Vendredi 1 juin 1956," BN I, 354–55)

[I remain haunted by what I heard yesterday evening, and I have been living through North Africa's ordeal hour by hour. *This is an unbroken chain of two forms of terrorism* that give rise to each other, with the terrorist bombing engendering the repression, and the repression leading to more bombings. As related by newspaper reports, this tragedy takes on a routine, everyday aspect: a monotonous detective film in several episodes. . . .

But it is still a matter of *the same unbroken chain of reprisals*, a chain that nevertheless must be broken. . . .

For what does it involve, if not to break *this inexorable chain of reprisals?*

Am I the one who is dreaming in believing that *the awful chain of murders and reprisals* creates an unfavorable climate for negotiation?]

The recurring image of the chain figures a seemingly endless spiral of violence: as a metaphor[22] of the human story of history, the "brouillamini d'erreurs et de violences" (imbroglio of errors and violence) would seem to offer little more hope than does the myth of the Atreids.

Yet Mauriac adamantly refuses determinism of any stripe, be it moral or material: "Non, aucune fatalité dans le déroulement de cette histoire que le Bloc-notes reflète" (BN I, 511; No, there was nothing inevitable or predetermined in this story of history visible in the *Bloc-notes*). Just as he insists that history is driven by individual and collective human action (designating both "quelques politiciens" [a few politicians] and "la volonté de la nation" [the will of the nation] as "agents"), he maintains that it is up to human beings to change the course of events: "Oui, il est temps encore . . ." ("Samedi 27 novembre 1954," BN I, 227; Yes, there is still time . . .). And while the unrelenting violence and confusion of human affairs (not to mention the persistent

22. Malcolm Scott points out that this theme of a cycle of violence, often referred to as a universal process of "entre-dévorement" (mutual devouring), occupies a prominent place in Mauriac's novels; see *Mauriac et de Gaulle*, 30.

blindness of the French electorate stigmatized in the above quotation of page 511) could make it very tempting for the bourgeois Catholic member of l'Académie Française to retreat behind the walls of his comfortable estate, confine his interests to an "otherworldly" or "inner" spirituality, or seek refuge in the proverbial ivory tower of arts and letters, the author of the *Bloc-notes* continually throws himself back into the fray of politics and history.

Even so, Mauriac's preoccupation with history has not been duly recognized. Most recently, Malcolm Scott has suggested that Mauriac simply used his editorials to transpose the moral and psychological dilemmas depicted in his novels onto the political scene.[23] As we indicated in our introductory chapter, however, the *Bloc-notes* provides a keen perception of events past and present, and its author displays great sensitivity to the ethical and ideological issues of history on all levels. It is certainly true that, unlike such contemporaries as Jean-Paul Sartre or Raymond Aron, Mauriac does not approach the developments of the 1950s and 1960s through philosophical or socioeconomic theory, but rather from the perspective of a highly learned French Christian humanist assessing events in light of his own experience of the Dreyfus affair, World War I, the Popular Front, the German Occupation, the Liberation, and the purge.[24] He is clearly unconcerned with elaborating any abstract ideological system of historical interpretation.

History nevertheless does represent an ethical and ultimately a metaphysical drama for Mauriac, since he most often places the present in relation to the past not so much to relativize or demythify events as to endow them with fuller meaning. While his invocation of France's past takes on more conservative accents in the archgaullist *Bloc-notes* of the late 1960s (which we shall study carefully in Chapter 5), the history that

23. Scott, *Mauriac et de Gaulle*, 232–34.

24. Mauriac states this experiential perspective explicitly on several occasions, including the following passage: "Je domine à mon âge un grand intervalle d'histoire, car la politique m'a intéressé et même passionné très tôt: à douze ans, l'affaire Dreyfus déjà me tourmentait. Je tiens donc sous mon regard le personnel politique de soixante-dix années" ("Dimanche 17 janvier 1965," BN IV, 14; At my age, I look down over a long span of history, for I was interested and even intrigued by politics at a very early age: when I was twelve, I was already torn apart by the Dreyfus affair. I thus hold in my field of vision all the political personalities of the last seventy years).

infuses his editorials of the 1950s—and in particular, the period of the Algerian war—informs decidedly progressive condemnations of torture and endemic oppression, moreover published by the distinctly left-leaning *L'Express* of Jean-Jacques Servan-Schreiber.[25] As intuitive, literary, and topical as his treatment of events may be, Mauriac in no way ignores the larger ideological issues of the postwar era.

Returning to Mauriac's repeated rejection of historical determinism, we see, as in the passage cited above, that he refuses to attribute historical events to fate or to any other impersonal force, including, not surprisingly, Marx's notion of a dialectical march of events toward a classless society.[26] But we must equally note that Mauriac refuses to attribute the course of events to divine will: "Je n'ai jamais su voir les signes d'une intervention divine dans les événements de l'histoire" ("Jeudi 18 juin 1953," BN I, 79; I have never been able to see signs of divine intervention in the events of history). Mauriac repeatedly emphasizes the primacy of the human element in history, particularly when commenting on violence and injustice.[27]

This focus on the human, however, does not lead him to a monumental idea of history as the sum of great deeds by great men. On the contrary, Mauriac was fully aware of the ethical and ideological challenges of history understood as an exterior, objective process, a structure of sociopolitical circumstances often wreaking havoc on private lives, placing the individual in excruciating moral dilemmas. Such indeed was the "history" that held great sway over a whole generation of intellectuals weaned on the genteel detached humanism of Alain:[28] World War II confronted them with the shock of invasion, the humilia-

25. Sirinelli, "Mauriac, un intellectuel engagé sous la IVe République," 147–48.

26. See "Vendredi 4 janvier 1957" (BN I, 423–26), in which Mauriac offers an extensive discussion of how the events in Potsdam and Budapest in 1956 illustrate the failure of Marxism both as a system of thought and as a principle of government.

27. See my article "Facing History: Mauriac and Lévinas on Nazism," *Journal of European Studies* 23 (1993): 160–61, 173; and Scott, *Mauriac et de Gaulle*, 43.

28. Emile Chartier (1868–1951), known as "Alain," was a prominent exponent of an enlightened skepticism toward society and one of the leading advocates of pacifism during the interwar period. As an author and a philosophy teacher at the Lycée Henry IV in Paris, he influenced such key figures as Merleau-Ponty and Raymond Aron. See Sirinelli, *Deux intellectuels dans le siècle*, 64–75, 110–14; and Winock, *Le siècle des intellectuels*, 249–53, 316–18.

tion of military defeat and political debacle, the specters of Occupation and state collaboration, and the pains of resistance and liberation. The ethereal realm of arts and letters, pure ideas and aesthetic beauty, embodied in the shimmering works of writers such as Valéry and Giraudoux, had been outstripped by the march of history. Many could echo the words of Raymond Aron: "Une fois pour toutes, j'ai cessé de croire que l'histoire obéisse d'elle-même aux impératifs de la raison et aux désirs des hommes de bonne volonté" (Once and for all, I ceased to believe that history is driven by the imperatives of reason and the desires of men of good will).[29]

One of the landmark war experiences for French intellectuals was that articulated by Jean-Paul Sartre, the *écrivain engagé* for an entire generation: snatched away from the nonchalant life of a brilliant young philosophy teacher and budding writer, Sartre endured the boredom of the phony war, the constraints of POW life, and the shock of returning to occupied Paris. These brutal disruptions of his personal existence brought Sartre to the realization that intellectuals could not simply delight in brilliant thought and writing: instead, they had to take heed of the social and political context and actively seek to further the ends to which historical events were irresistibly leading.[30]

While Mauriac sees history neither as the embodiment of some immanent principle nor as a teleologically determined march of events, his *Bloc-notes* was often the first to decipher the signs of the times and spell out the implications of the profound evolution of the 1950s and 1960s. For example, he repeatedly points to the end of the colonial era as an incontrovertible historical reality demanding a new world outlook and a different set of policies: what was necessary was to "prendre conscience du monde nouveau qui a surgi en 1945 et auquel les puissances colonisatrices étaient appelées à s'adapter" (BN I, 510, cited above; take stock of the new world that sprung up in 1945, summoning the colonial pow-

29. Raymond Aron, *Leçon inaugurale au Collège de France*, 1er décembre 1970, Collège de France, 1972, p. 14, cited by Jean-François Sirinelli, in *Deux intellectuels dans le siècle, Sartre et Aron* (Paris: Fayard, 1995), 153, 160.

30. Annie Cohen-Solal, *Sartre* (Paris: Gallimard, 1985), 245–417. See also Sirinelli, *Deux intellectuels dans le siècle*, 153–58.

ers to adapt accordingly). Similarly, he decries "l'aveugle refus de tenir compte du réel, de ce qui est, et par exemple du fait que l'ère coloniale est partout révolue, et non point seulement dans les mots" (Samedi 25 mai 1957, BN I, 461; the blind refusal to take stock of reality, of what really exists, beginning with the fact that the colonial era is everywhere and definitively a thing of the past, and not just verbally). The *Bloc-notes* moreover testifies to a remarkable acumen for the profound social, political, and cultural changes that were just beginning in the 1950s and 1960s, including the impact of the automobile, the advent of the consumer society, the obsolescence of parliamentary regimes in French politics, and the far-reaching influence of the media. While often stressing the continuity of historical events and analogies with the past, he was acutely aware of the radical difference separating the society of 1950s and 1960s from France's rural past. (Cf. Chapter 5 below and "Malagar, vendredi 16 octobre 1964," BN III, 532–35.)

Mauriac was not just a perspicacious observer of what were then subtle, yet major, transformations of French society. The *Bloc-notes* also shows him probing the historical contingencies of his own life and questioning the social structure and political order upon which his private domain was based. With respect to the young Moroccans whose future had been blocked by France's oppressive policies, Mauriac ruefully avows a sense of personal implication:

> Ces garçons se savent condamnés d'avance, ils ont renoncé à tout bonheur temporel, ils n'ont pas d'avenir, nous l'avons détruit. Sentiment intolérable d'appartenir à la race qui opprime. (BN I, 75)
>
> [These young men already know that they have been condemned [[to a life of misery]]. They have given up on finding any happiness in this world. They have no future, for we have destroyed it. I have the unbearable feeling of belonging to the race that oppresses.]

Similarly, Henry James's description of the sumptuous life of high society in Victorian England prompts Mauriac to reflect on his own privileged position in French society:

> Quel art de vivre! Quelle indifférence au prix que devaient payer les quatre cinquièmes des sujets de Sa Gracieuse Majesté pour les délices

de ce petit nombre! Toute civilisation exquise repose sur l'esclavage. Sinon elle ne serait pas exquise. Les immenses revenus nécessaires à la vie de l'aristocratie anglaise de ce temps-là, à ses châteaux, et à ses chasses, à l'entretien de sa domesticité, comme à celle de toutes les aristocraties à toutes les époques, exigent de bas salaires et le refus de toute législation sociale.

Dès que l'État secourt les individus, il utilise l'argent qui servait à édifier ce monde enchanté dont s'émerveillait le jeune Henry James. Qu'il l'a aimée, cette Angleterre des églises encapuchonnées de lierre, des châteaux élizabéthains à pignons de briques rouges et à fantômes, les tapis de gazon roulé, les cottages à treillis, les tavernes de village, les chasses au renard. . . . Je n'ai rien connu de tel; mais à un rang infiniment plus modeste, je fus en France un de ces privilégiés-là. Tenté, comme les contemporains de Henry James, d'accepter les conditions de cet ordre, de cet équilibre, de me dire: "C'est la nature qui est injuste au départ, et qu'y faire, sinon de l'accepter comme une loi?" (BN I, 139)

[What an art of living! What indifference to the price that four fifths of Her Gracious Majesty's subjects had to pay for the exquisite pleasures of these few! Every exquisite civilization reposes on slavery: otherwise it would not be exquisite. The tremendous incomes required for the life of the English aristocracy of the time, for its castles and its hunting expeditions, for maintaining its contingents of servants, as was the case for all aristocracies of every time, require low wages and the refusal of social aid legislation.

As soon as the state comes to the aid of individuals, it uses money that had served to construct the world of enchantment at which the young Henry James had marveled. How he loved that England of churches hooded in ivy, Elizabethan castles with their red brick gables and their ghosts, the rolling carpets of grass, the cottages with trellises, the village pubs, the fox hunts. . . . I have experienced nothing like that; but on an infinitely more modest level, I was one of those privileged people in France. Like Henry James's contemporaries, I was tempted to tell myself: "It's nature that is unjust at the outset, and what is to be done about it other than to accept it as a law?"]

Few could more powerfully unveil the socioeconomic framework of oppression that supported the refined elegance of James's Victorian England. (See also "Pâques 1955," BN I, 261–62, for similar observations on the privileged position of the writer.) The maxim "Toute civilisation exquise repose sur l'esclavage. Sinon elle ne serait pas exquise" (Every exquisite civilization reposes on slavery: otherwise it would not be exquisite) is not just a brilliant witticism, but a matter of personal reflection; in spite of his privileged position in society and letters, Mauriac was not oblivious to historical angst. In this passage, he clearly exposes aestheticism as an illusion (if not a lie), confronts the more general social and historical context of artistic and literary production, and acknowledges his own implication in events.

Facing history, reading the "prose of the world," and heeding the "moral of the story" of history prove taxing: time and time again in the *Bloc-notes*, Mauriac voices his weariness with the turmoil of events (notably in the 14 July 1957 piece analyzed above), as he yearns to dwell in the timeless beauty of his country home, lost in the reminiscences of his boyhood days or in his literary and spiritual meditations. And time and time again, he finds himself compelled to take part in the political struggle, as we vividly see in the following passages, written just before France's defeat at Dien Bien Phu:

> L'horreur, en Indochine, est à son comble! O sang injustement répandu! Nausée, tout à coup, tentation de fuite; échapper à ce "brouillamini d'erreurs et de violences," comme Goethe définit la politique. Droit à l'éternité qui à mon âge commence en deça de la mort. Comme au théâtre, quand nous sommes en avance, le rideau n'est pas encore levé, mais nous écoutons la rumeur de ce qui se passe derrière . . . du côté de l'intemporel. Nous sommes déjà dans la pièce non encore commencée. Permission donnée au vieillard de détourner son coeur et sa pensée de ce qui est le mal absolu. Dans l'ordre politique, la guerre d'Indochine est, spirituellement, le mal absolu. Ah! je comprends que Charles Du Bos ait tant aimé le vers de Keats: "L'âme est en elle-même un monde et a suffisamment à faire chez elle." Oui. Mais trop tard: je suis engagé, au sens matériel du terme, comme un soldat qui a signé son engagement. Que la passion politique m'entraîne ou m'égare, il n'en reste pas moins que je suis engagé dans ces problèmes d'en bas, pour des raisons d'en haut. ("Jeudi 1 avril 1954," BN I, 126–27)

> Pour moi, le voudrais-je, il m'est interdit de m'abstraire désormais, de me détourner de tout le sang répandu injustement, du fait de ceux qui

parlent et agissent au nom de la France. ("Vendredi 2 avril 1954," BN I, 127)[31]

[The horror in Indochina is at its peak. How much blood has been wrongly shed there! I feel suddenly nauseated, and am tempted to flee such a sight to escape from this "imbroglio of errors and violence," as Goethe defines politics. . . . I feel I have a right to focus on eternity, which at my age begins on this side of death. As in the theater, when we are early for a play and, behind the curtain that has not yet been raised, we hear the muffled sounds of what is happening . . . in the timeless realm. We are already into the play that has not yet begun. An old man has permission to turn his heart and mind away from what constitutes the absolute evil. In the political order, the war in Indochina is spiritually the absolute evil. Ah! I understand why Charles Du Bos loved so much Keats's verse: "The soul is a world in itself and has enough to do in its own realm." Yes, but it is too late: I have committed myself in the material sense of the word, as a soldier who has signed up for the military. Even if I let myself get carried away or led astray by political passion, the fact remains that I am committed to these problems here below for reasons from on high.

Even if I should want to, it is forbidden for me to disregard or turn away from all this unjust bloodshed, since those speaking and acting are doing so in the name of France.]

Horrified by the useless bloodshed, Mauriac first conjures up all the alibis he could plausibly give to remain aloof: disgust with politics, the endemic nature of violence, old age, spiritual aspirations, and the physical and moral quietude of a family dwelling. But in the end they all prove to be inadequate, both because Mauriac feels inextricably caught up in the human drama unfolding around him and because his "otherworldly" faith in "the kingdom of heaven" (cf. "raisons d'en haut" [reasons from on high]) compels him to engage in the struggle for peace and justice on earth (cf. "en bas" [here below]: "cette foi m'interdit de me désintéresser du combat pour la justice" ["Malagar, samedi 9 avril 1955," BN I, 259–60; this faith forbids me from being indifferent to the fight for jus-

31. Other passages offer an equally striking example of Mauriac's own situation with respect to history. See Appendix, Section B.

tice]). Mauriac thus finds and declares himself *engagé*, engaged by, committed to, implicated in history no less than did Sartre, Camus, Aragon, and Mounier (among others) at the outset of the postwar period.[32] With a notable difference, however: he is compelled not by the march of history to some new humanity, but rather by an orthodox Christianity. Contrary to what is often assumed, Mauriac's faith did not induce indifference to the hic et nunc, but on the contrary summoned him to responsibility for the well-being of his fellow human beings.

Mauriac's particular perception of history and his own stance vis-à-vis the events of his time appear rather paradoxical. While insisting that history is the fruit of human action and not blind forces, he continually foregrounds the chain of violence and injustice not only in France's past but in the universal story of humanity: "Les désastres jalonnent notre histoire, comme toute histoire . . ." ("Vendredi 14 décembre 1956," BN I, 419–20; Our history is strewn with disasters, as is every history. . .). While rejecting all forms of determinism (and Marx's dialectical materialism in particular), he points to large-scale political and social developments that cannot be attributed to any one person, that (as Aron observed in the above-cited remark) do not obey the reason or goodwill of the individual, that overtake private lives, and that force the individual to take a political stance.

Mauriac acknowledges that history in the sense invoked by Sartre et al. does often call the trumps. However, he denies it holds all the cards, even if in some instances historical developments outstrip not only the private world of the individual but also the prerogatives of entire nations. Writing at one of the most dramatic moments of the cold war, in early 1957, several years after the death of Stalin and shortly after the crushing of democracy in Hungary, Mauriac, like many of his compatriots, deplores the division of the world into two hegemonic blocks that deny traditional powers such as France their accustomed autonomy.

> Cette histoire, notre histoire, se déroule à l'intérieur d'une autre qui l'enveloppe et qui finalement décidera d'elle. ("Mardi 15 janvier 1957," BN I, 432)

32. See Ariane Chebel d'Appollonia, *Histoire politique des intellectuels en France 1944–1954* (Brussels: Éditions Complexe, 1991), 1:17–32.

[This history, our story of history, is unfolding within another one that is enveloping it, and that will ultimately determine its outcome.]

Here again history appears not as some stuffy collection of memorabilia, but as the gripping drama of humanity playing itself out before our eyes. In this case, however, history not only refuses to obey the conscious control of individuals, it also escapes the desires of entire nations. For France's role in the universal drama has now been scripted:

> Ainsi se déroule notre drame, tout enveloppé d'un plus grand qui le contient. Ainsi nos petits hommes s'agitent et cassent tout à l'intérieur de notre wagon particulier; mais il est entraîné, Dieu sait où, sur mêmes rails avec beaucoup d'autres.
>
> Cette histoire totale, je doute qu'elle soit la seule vraie. . . . Je crois qu'il existe une autre histoire que l'Histoire: la mienne, la vôtre—autant d'histoires que d'êtres humains. ("Mardi 15 janvier 1957," BN I, 433)
>
> [Thus our drama unfolds, all wrapped up in a larger drama that contains it. Thus our little men get all excited and break everything inside our private rail car; but it is being pulled away to God-knows-where on the same track along with many others.
>
> I doubt that this total history is the only true story. . . . I believe that there exists another story besides history: my story and yours—as many stories as there are human beings.]

Action thus seems to have been spelled out by a preexistent text; the train of events seems to be leading France over rails laid out by two superpowers. Nowhere in the *Bloc-notes* do we find more powerful images of historical developments totally unsubmissive to human thought and volition. But in the same breath, Mauriac goes on to posit the unfathomable autonomy of human beings and to deny that this history has the last word. History may be inescapable, but it is not the whole story: there exists for Mauriac a part of human being that cannot be subsumed by events, dissolved into some material process, or reduced to a chain of causes and effects. Each human being ultimately remains, to borrow a term from Lévinas, "other."[33] Here we find the crux of the par-

33. This repeated emphasis on the inalienable uniqueness and autonomy of the human

adox: the disjunction between history and the private world of the individual does not provide a pretext for dodging the demands of history, but on the contrary constitutes Mauriac's motive for plunging into the fray.

This complex position compelled him to pen one of his most powerful editorials; written for the 15 January 1955 edition of *L'Express*, it was one of the very first to publicly denounce the use of illegal detentions and torture by French authorities in Algeria.[34] The piece illustrates how the *Bloc-notes* conveys a fundamentally historical perception of current events, how Mauriac expresses the disjunction between the self and history, and how the text nevertheless spurs the reader to adopt Mauriac's political and ethical perspectives.

Mauriac establishes his historical frame of reference from the very outset, presenting his own original reflections on "La Question" some three years before Henri Alleg's famous book published under the same title in 1958, and supplying a double epigraph, one taken from Matthew 25.40, "C'est à moi que vous l'avez fait" (You have done it to me), and the other taken from Montaigne, "Je hais cruellement la cruauté, et par nature et par jugement, comme l'extrême de tous les vices" (Touzot, note 1, BN I, 237; By temperament and by judgment, I cruelly hate cruelty as the extreme of all vices). "La Question" being the archaic term for "torture," the title immediately places current abuses in North Africa in relation to medieval practices, and thus relates the issue to France's past. Moreover, the epigraphs ground Mauriac's condemnation of torture in two of the most venerable discourses of Christianity (Matthew) and French humanism (Montaigne).

The editorial takes the form of a dialogue between Mauriac and a lawyer. The dilemma posed by the disjunction of history and the self begins in the very first lines, as seemingly perennial violence and injustice are juxtaposed with the impossibility of remaining indifferent. Having

---

person throughout the *Bloc-notes* (as well as during the World War II period, as I explain in my article "Facing History: Mauriac and Lévinas on Nazism") seems to be completely overlooked or ignored by Malcolm Scott, who characterizes Mauriac's views as subservient to a Gaullism that supposedly absorbs all individuality in promoting France's national identity. See Scott, *Mauriac et de Gaulle*, 228.

34. Sirinelli, "Mauriac, un intellectuel engagé sous la IVe République," 153–54.

personally witnessed the effects of torture on his clients in Algeria, the lawyer enjoins Mauriac to avail himself of his prestige and moral authority and speak out:

> —Vous seul pouvez parler. . . . Vous seul.
> Je détourne la tête. ("Vendredi 14 janvier 1955," BN I, 237)
>
> ["Only you can speak out. . . . Only you."
> I turn my head away.]

When the reticent editorialist protests that he lacks the proof to back up such charges, the lawyer responds with a graphic description of the techniques employed:

> —A quoi bon [dénoncer la torture], puisque "ça" ne laisse pas de traces!
>
> —Ils n'ont pas renoncé aux coups de nerf de boeuf, vous savez! Mais la baignoire, ou plutôt le baquet d'eau sale où la tête est maintenue jusqu'à l'étouffement, mais le courant électrique sous les aisselles et entre les jambes, mais l'eau souillée introduite par un tuyau dans la bouche jusqu'à ce que le patient s'évanouisse. . . .
>
> —Ce n'est pas possible, dis-je.
>
> Mais oui: comme pour la Brinvilliers,[35] comme pour Damiens. . . .[36] (237–38)
>
> ["What for (why denounce torture), since 'it' doesn't leave any traces!"
>
> "They haven't stopped using bludgeons, you know! And how about the bathtub, or rather the bucket of filthy water in which the head is dunked to the point of asphyxiation, and the electric shocks under the armpits and between the legs, and the fouled water forced into the mouth with a pipe until the patient faints. . . ."
>
> "That's not possible," I said.
>
> "But it is, just as it was for la Brinvilliers and Damiens. . . ."]

35. Marie-Madeleine d'Aubray, marquise de Brinvilliers, was burned at the stake in Paris for having poisoned her father and brothers. See *Petit Larousse Illustré 1994*.

36. Robert François Damiens was quartered in Paris in 1757 for having stabbed Louis XV with a pocket knife. See *Petit Larousse Illustré 1994*.

The allusions to seventeenth- and eighteenth-century prisoners tortured by French authorities once again place the contemporary situation in a historical perspective whose full significance will become apparent in the final portion of the editorial:

—La détention en elle-même, quelle torture! On parle d'Oudjda. Si vous connaissiez la prison de Tizi-Ouzou! Les détenus y sont parqués à soixante et onze dans des pièces de cent cinq mètres carrés. Il leur est interdit d'ouvrir la bouche, fût-ce pour prier. Des "droit commun" les surveillent: l'école d'Himmler, quoi! Quel héritage!

Encore un silence et j'entends de nouveau l'éternelle parole: "Vous seul. . . . Si les gens savaient . . . vous, il vous croiront."

Je secoue la tête:

—Mais non! ils s'irritent au contraire de ce qu'on les oblige à voir ce qu'ils sont résolus à ignorer. Ils admettent que toute civilisation repose sur une horreur cachée: prostitution, traite des femmes, police des moeurs, maisons de correction, geôles pour les fous et les idiots, toutes les tortures; c'est le mal nécessaire. Malheur à qui ose en parler ouvertement! Les Aztèques scellaient des débris humains dans les pierres du temple élevé à la gloire du dieu Soleil.

—Mais nous ne sommes pas des Aztèques.

—Non, bien sûr! Nous sommes les Français de cette France dont les meilleurs fils, de génération en génération, ont mieux compris qu'aucun peuple et mis en pratique le Sermon sur la montagne. Nous sommes cette France qui a proclamé les droits de l'homme à la face d'une Europe enivrée.

—. . . Oui, et dire que pour la plupart de ceux que nous faisons souffrir, la France reste cette France-là!

—Les bourreaux n'auront donc même pas l'excuse des conquérants, car ce n'est pas par la force, c'est par son message humain que la France reste conquérante: en la déshonorant, ils la désarment. (240–241)

["And then, detention constitutes a torture in itself. People talk about Oudjda: if only you knew about the prison at Tizi-Ozou! Seventy-one detainees are penned up in rooms of one-hundred-five square meters. They are forbidden from opening their mouths, even to pray. 'Common law' criminals guard over them: these are methods worthy of Himmler! What a legacy to follow!"

After another moment of silence, I once again hear the incessant refrains: "Only you. . . . If people only knew . . . people will believe *you*."

I shake my head:

"They most certainly will not. On the contrary, they get upset when they are forced to see what they have resolved to ignore. They accept the fact that every civilization reposes on hidden horrors: prostitution, the sale of women, vice squads, reform schools, jails for the insane and the retarded, every kind of torture. It's a necessary evil. Woe to anyone who dares speak openly of these things! The Aztecs sealed away body parts in the stones of the temple built to the glory of the Sun god."

"But we aren't Aztecs."

"No, of course not! We are the French, and, from one generation to the next, the brightest and best of France's children have understood and put into practice the Sermon on the Mount better than any other people. We are the country that proclaimed human rights to a euphoric Europe."

". . . Yes, and to think that, for most of those suffering under us, France still remains that country of idealism and human rights!"]

On the one hand, the historical references, first to the ancien régime (the torture of Brinvilliers and Damiens), then to the Third Reich (Himmler's use of common-law criminals to police political detainees), and finally to the Aztecs, place the human rights abuses in France's colonial war in the context of history and of the seemingly endless chain of violence and injustice so often invoked in the *Bloc-notes.* This passage even presents these endemic political crimes as integral components of human society itself, since "toute civilisation repose sur une horreur cachée" (every civilization resposes on hidden horrors).

Mauriac formulates these remarks not as dispassionate philosophical meditations, but as a stinging indictment of the French Republic. The taking of the Bastille epitomized the revolt against arbitrary detention and human rights abuses, and the Republic prided itself in having replaced the arbitrary rule of the monarchy with a democracy based on *Liberté, Égalité, Fraternité.* Just a decade before, in 1944, the French Republic had reemerged from the nightmare of the German Occupation to reaffirm itself as the antithesis of nazism, although the tragedy would have it that many of those responsible for French policy in North Africa were former *résistants.* France had moreover always thought of itself as the torchbearer of enlightment and civilization (particularly in its colonies, where it claimed to be carrying out "la mission civilisatrice de la France" [France's civilizing mission]). In the unlikely event that someone might have missed these historical allusions the first time, Mauriac underscores them once again:

> Nous sommes cette France qui a proclamé les droits de l'homme à la face d'une Europe enivrée.
>
> . . . c'est par son message humain que la France reste conquérante. . . . (240–41)
>
> [We are the country that proclaimed human rights to an overjoyed Europe.
>
> . . . it is through its message of humanism that France will continue to conquer. . . .]

The use of torture by French authorities in Algeria takes on its full significance in the light of history: as depicted by Mauriac here, the very heritage that France has always proudly invoked to claim a preeminent role in international affairs accentuates the horror of its current actions.

Mauriac then models the response he hopes to evoke from his readers by portraying his own reaction to disturbing reports from the lawyer, who continues to implore Mauriac to intervene:

> Ce sont des chrétiens, vos frères [qui sont détenus comme prisonniers politiques par les autorités françaises à Madagascar]. Vous devriez. . . .
>
> Je réponds: "Oui . . . oui. . . ." Je l'accompagne jusqu'à la porte. Me voici seul. J'ouvre distraitement l'album des disques de Mozart, les Sonates pour piano interprétées par Gieseking, que J. m'a rapporté de New York. J'en choisis un. . . . Mais non: l'horreur de ce que j'ai entendu emplit encore la pièce. Cette musique n'est pas pour moi. Je suis comme un homme qui a pris part, sans le vouloir, à un crime et qui hésite à aller se livrer. (241)
>
> ["These [[political prisoners held by French authorities in Madagascar]] are your fellow Christians, you should. . . ."
>
> "Yes. . . yes. . . . ," I answer. I escort him to the door. Then here I am alone again. I absentmindedly open a record album of Mozart's piano sonatas performed by Gieseking, the album that J. brought back from New York for me. I choose one. . . . But no, it's impossible. The horror of what I have heard still fills the room. This music is not for me. I am

> like a man who has unwittingly taken part in a crime and now hesitates to turn himself in.]

The oppression manifest throughout the long history of civilization does not lead Mauriac to quietism: unable to seek solace in the ethereal music of Mozart, he instead considers himself irremediably implicated in the drama of history unfolding around him.

Returning to Mauriac's general approach to history in the *Bloc-notes*, we observe that, as an editorialist for *L'Express*, Mauriac aims to be an active party to events. For history is ultimately a narrative, a story of events written and told by one human being (or group of human beings) to another. Witnesses to the events (such as the lawyer here) and writers of the story (such as Mauriac) thus bear crucial responsibility for setting the record straight and placing the events before the public eye.

As is evident throughout the *Bloc-notes*, neither task can be taken for granted. For just as the Aztecs sealed away body parts in their most magnificent temple, so the official narratives of modern societies invariably gloss over violence and injustice. The *Bloc-notes* repeatedly exposes such obfuscation. In a series of editorials deploring France's brutal (albeit covert) deposition of the sultan in Morocco, Mauriac cites a famous French diplomat: "Talleyrand définissait l'histoire: 'La conjuration universelle du mensonge contre la vérité'" ["Mardi 18 août 1953," BN I, 95; Talleyrand defined history as "the universal conspiracy of lies against the truth"]. In a later article, he reviews various factors having allowed the bourgeoisie to keep the working class in check throughout the nineteenth and twentieth centuries, and then cites Simone Weil's incisive definition of history: "Simone Weil: 'L'histoire n'est pas autre chose qu'une compilation des dépositions faites par les assassins, relativement à leurs victimes et à eux-mêmes'" ["Lundi 29 mars 1954," BN I, 123; Simone Weil: "History is nothing but a compilation of the depositions given by murderers on the subject of their victims and themselves"]. Mauriac then proceeds to comment on the use of torture and capital punishment in Tunisia. On another occasion, reflecting on subsequent revelations having justified his condemnation of the bombing of Guernica as a premeditated fascist crime, Mauriac wryly observes:

> L'histoire nous justifie, mais tant de crimes ont recouvert les vieux crimes! C'est ce qui assure à la plupart des criminels de l'histoire l'impunité de l'oubli: une vague de sang innocent recouvre l'autre. ("Mercredi 14 juillet 1954," BN I, 190)
>
> [History proves us right, but how many [[new]] crimes cover up old crimes! That is what ensures that most of history's criminals will benefit from the impunity that comes with oblivion: one wave of innocent blood covers up another.]

Mauriac often presents such cover-ups as a virtually universal, ages-old basis of an unjust order. Such is the case in an editorial decrying the French public's indifference to the use of torture both in mainland France and in North Africa:

> Cette indifference ne doit pas étonner: nous la tenons d'héritage, nous l'avons dans le sang. Les honnêtes gens ont toujours donné leur consentement tacite aux abominations cachées qui fondent l'ordre. ("Samedi 29 janvier 1955," BN I, 246)
>
> [Such indifference should not surprise us: we have it by inheritance, it is in our blood. Good people have always given their tacit consent to the hidden abominations that are the basis of order.]

Nevertheless, Mauriac refuses cynical indifference precisely because he sees history not as some mechanical process but as a human drama: barbaric events, especially those involving so-called civilized peoples, always have a human face in the *Bloc notes*.

Thus underscoring the human, all-too-human, character of violence and injustice, Mauriac vigorously summons all who have directly or indirectly witnessed political crimes. Passive indifference is not an option, since they, like the protagonists, are subject to the judgment of history. For in the *Bloc-notes*, this judgment does not reside simply in the facts that will inevitably emerge from the historical record over time, but more importantly appears as the judgment of those who observe events and respond or remain indifferent.

Here again, the motif occurs throughout the *Bloc-notes*, as Mauriac repeatedly refers to the face of protagonists in the drama of history and to eyes of witnesses whose gaze delivers the verdict. Such was the case when he learned the truth of France's role in deposing the sultan of Morocco: "Je puis dire que ce matin d'août, *sur le visage bouleversé du médecin marocain, j'ai déchiffré le sombre avenir* qui est devenu notre sombre présent" ("Vémars, dimanche 18 avril 1954," BN I, 139; On this August morning, I can safely say that, on the distraught face of the Moroccan doctor, I have read the somber future that has become our somber present). Mauriac further describes how humans ultimately pronounce judgment on events in one of the passages decrying the seemingly endless cycle of violence:

> Obsédé de ce que j'ai entendu hier soir: ce drame de l'Afrique du Nord, je l'aurai vécu heure par heure. Cette chaîne sans fin des deux terreurs qui s'enfantent l'une l'autre, qui fait naître la répression de l'attentat, l'attentat de la répression, ce malheur a un aspect quotidien et que le journal nous rapporte: film policier monotone, film à épisodes. *Mais ce malheur a un autre visage, un visage caché.* Un suspect arrêté, interrogé dans des conditions souvent cruelles, même s'il est relâché, ne garde pas pour lui seul son ressentiment. Il a des amis, des compagnons, des frères, mais surtout il a des fils. Cette génération qui naît, s'instruit, grandit dans l'atmosphère empoisonnée des deux terreurs: *pour eux, ceux que nous appelons des bandits sont des martyrs.* Cette génération qui mûrira si vite, *ces enfants déjà adolescents, que sera la France pour eux*, cette France à qui leurs pères gardent à travers tout un reste de vénération? Mais eux, les enfants de colère, ils la haïssent déjà. ("Vendredi 14 mai 1954," BN I, 153)
>
> [I remain haunted by what I heard yesterday evening, and I have been living through North Africa's ordeal hour by hour. This unbroken chain of two forms of terrorism that give rise to each other, with the terrorist bombings engendering the repression, and the repression leading to more bombings. This tragedy has a routine everyday aspect, as related by newspaper reports: a monotonous detective film in several episodes. *But this woeful affair has another, hidden face.* Even if they are released, suspects arrested and often cruelly interrogated do not keep their resentment to themselves. They have friends, companions, brothers, and, above all, children. This generation is being born, schooled, and raised in a climate poisoned by these two forms of terror: for them, those whom we call thugs are martyrs. In spite of everything, their par-

ents still find France venerable to some degree. But what will France represent for this generation that is growing up so quickly, for these children who are already adolescents? These children of wrath already hate France.]

For Mauriac, the lessons of history are neither self-contained nor imposed from outside or above: the "moral of the story" will ultimately be formulated not by any omniscient narrator, but by "spectators" destined to become actors. At the end of the piece cited above, Mauriac bemoans the French authorities' failure to understand that the judgment of history ultimately consists of the judgment of others:

> Ils [les Français] ne la voient donc pas, cette immense foule d'enfants qui touchent à l'âge d'homme, chez les peuples protégés, et qui, tous ces temps-ci, *enregistrent ce qu'ils voient et ce qu'ils entendent, recueillent, au jour le jour, les leçons de l'histoire*—et pas seulement de celle qui se déroule à leur porte. . . . Pour la déchiffrer et pour l'interpréter, ils n'ont pas besoin de lire. (BN I, 154)
>
> [The [[the French]] therefore do not see this great crowd of children about to become adults in the colonies: all along, these children *have been taking in what they see and hear, and gleaning day by day the lessons of history*—and not only based on what is happening at their doorstep. They don't have to read in order to decipher and interpret it.]

The lessons of history are not meted out by the march of events toward some supposed end, nor are they inherent in the success or failure of human enterprise. They are instead dispensed by the human protagonists who observe events and draw the necessary ethical conclusions. It is this judgment of others that Mauriac always finds implacable, as confirmed in the *Bloc-notes* devoted to a photo exhibit on France's colonial war in Indochina:

> Terrible témoignage de la photographie, témoignage irrécusable. J'ouvre, j'écarte, je reprends cet album de Jean-Pierre Dannaud: *Guerre morte* (Revue d'Indochine, 20, rue La Boétie).
>
> *Toute la Guerre d'Indochine est ici racontée, mais par les visages.* Que ceux qui, de près ou de loin, se croient responsables de cette guerre (et qui de nous n'en a pris sa part, quand ce ne serait que parce qu'il s'est tu?) trouvent le courage et la force d'entendre *cette leçon qui s'adresse au*

regard d'abord pour atteindre plus sûrement le coeur et pour informer la pensée.

Oseraient-ils convenir qu'ils haïraient moins l'homme [Pierre Mendès France], qu'ils ont chassé du pouvoir, s'il avait une part de responsabilité dans cette histoire, s'il n'était pas, au milieu d'eux, l'Innocent? ("Mardi 1 mars 1955," BN I, 258–59)

[Photography provides devastating, unimpeachable testimony. I open, then put aside, then pick up again this album by Jean-Pierre Dannaud. *Guerre Morte.* (Revue d'Indochine, 20, rue La Boétie).

The entire Indochinese war is told here, only by the faces. May all those who believe themselves to be directly or indirectly responsible (and who among us has not taken part in some way, if only by keeping silent?) find the courage and strength to receive *this lesson addressed first of all to our eyes* in order better to reach our hearts and inform our minds.

Would they dare to acknowledge that they would not hate this man [[Pierre Mendès France]] so much if he had a share of responsibility in these historical events, if he were not the only one to stand innocent among them?]

Barbaric or civilized, history always has a human face, not just because it results from human action, but more importantly because these actions will ultimately be subject to moral judgment. To "put a face on events" as Mauriac indeed does here is not necessarily to name specific individuals or point out particularly moving incidents: the faces that recount the history of the war here are no mere images to contemplate, but human subjects whose gaze looks back upon the reader/spectator, bearing witness to what has happened, implicating the reader/spectator in their story, and summoning ethical conscience.

We are now poised to review the various senses of "history" so prominent in the *Bloc-notes* and draw some preliminary conclusions. We have seen that Mauriac invariably adopts a historical perspective by depicting contemporary issues as emerging from the sediment of the past. "Seeing the big picture" in the *Bloc-notes* means placing the present against the backdrop of history without which it cannot be fully understood; current conflicts thus appear as part of an ongoing saga of French and even world history. In stressing continuity while at the same time underscoring irreversible evolution, the *Bloc-notes* lends greater depth and richness to what otherwise would seem merely anecdotal or topical.

On the other hand, Mauriac's approach to history exhibits a pessimism that would at first glance seem to favor complacency or withdrawal. Numerous pages of the *Bloc-notes* refer to a seeming endless cycle of violence, while others express the disjunction of a self from political contingencies. We moreover find repeated rejections of the selective memory of events presented as official history. Notwithstanding these considerable misgivings, however, Mauriac's observations on current events remain centered on his notion of history.

Although aware of large-scale developments defying conscious control, Mauriac persists in viewing history as not only a human but in the final analysis a personal matter. History lies in human hands in the sense that it must ultimately be understood and communicated through narrative and therefore placed under the gaze of those who must suffer its consequences. Like so many of his counterparts on the French intellectual scene, Mauriac is compelled to *engagement* as a journalist. However, unlike Sartre, the team of *Les Temps modernes*, and other fellow travelers who joined in what they thought to be the irrestible march of history, Mauriac invokes the inescapable judgment of the other (as defined by Lévinas) that repeatedly summons moral conscience through the gaze of those directly exposed to violence and oppression.

Mauriac's stance as a narrator of history in the *Bloc-notes* is crucial. Reserving further exploration of his narration of history for Chapter 4, let us focus here on the fact that Mauriac does not posit himself as an omniscient narrator who would simply record the events of history as if from outside and above. Consequently, he avoids the pitfall so cogently described by Tzvetan Todorov. For when writers narrate history, they tend to depict their own social group or nation as either heroes or victims, as evident in the opposing perspectives of American and Japanese narratives of World War II. The Americans stress their role as innocent victims in the attack on Pearl Harbor, but portray themselves as triumphant heroes in the bombing of Hiroshima and Nagasaki.[37] The re-

37. Todorov, *Mémoire du mal*, 159.

cent (late Spring 2001) film *Pearl Harbor* is a case in point: as Ellen Goodman points out, the opening scene stresses American innocence by shooting the Japanese attack from the ground and detailing the suffering and destruction caused by the bombing; the later American bombing of Tokyo, on the other hand, is shot from the sky, with no view of the deaths and damage inflicted.[38] For their part, however, the Japanese are inclined to focus on the horrific human and material consequences of the Americans' use of atomic bombs, while at the same time glossing over Pearl Harbor and the atrocities committed by Japan's military forces in their aggressive prosecution of the war.

In leading readers of the *Bloc-notes* to view France's political policies and military (and police) operations through the eyes of those subjected to their consequences, Mauriac not only refuses such a one-sided narration of history, he makes it impossible to wipe injustice and violence off the historical slate. He continually stresses the contingency of his role as one who participates in events and highlights the moral dilemma resulting from his unwilling implication in the most dramatic episodes of France's contemporary history. This ability to narrate history from within as well as from without enables Mauriac not just to convey the pathos of events, but to place the burden of history squarely on his own and his readers' shoulders.

38. Ellen Goodman, "May All Wars Be Fought in the Movies," syndicated newspaper column, 4 June 2001.

3 AN UNCERTAIN IDEA OF FRANCE

Mais dans tous les camps la vérité et la justice éclatent moins à mon regard que l'erreur et l'injustice: il est injuste d'excuser chez les uns les crimes que vous condamnez chez les autres. ("Paris, dimanche 30 octobre 1960," BN II, 492)

[*But on all sides, truth and justice jump out at me less than error and injustice: it is wrong to condone the crimes of some people while condemning the same crimes committed by others.*]

The *Bloc-notes* emerged out of the relative obscurity of the rather exclusive literary readership of *La Table Ronde* and into the national limelight when Mauriac decided to join Jean-Jacques Servan-Schreiber and Françoise Giroud and the rest of the editorial team of the weekly news magazine *L'Express* in November 1953. Mauriac strongly supported Pierre Mendès France's efforts to conduct a peaceful decolonization of Indochina, Morocco, and Tunisia, then went on to speak out forcefully against torture and oppression in Algeria. The colonial conflicts touched his keen sense of national identity by calling into question the underlying notions of civilization and history. We must therefore explain how this moral and ideological crisis engaged both Mauriac's approach to the past and the national sentiment operative in his editorials.

Far from idiosyncratic, Mauriac's quandary is symptomatic of a larger upheaval: national liberation movements in several colonies challenged France's self-image and international stature, and the Algerian war drew French intellectuals of all persuasions into fierce polemical battles over what they claimed to be the true values and identity of their nation.[1] Raoul Girardet points out that, in the hearts and minds of those on all sides of the debate in France, nationalism heavily influenced both the inception and liquidation of the colonial enterprise that stretched from the regime of Jules Ferry in the 1880s to the signing of the "Accords d'Évian" in 1962.[2] Interestingly, Mauriac's life spans the entire period, whose beginning and end were each characterized by an acute crisis of his country's national identity and international stature: the France of Jules Ferry was still suffering from the humiliation of 1871, the ensuing civil strife, and the amputation of the Alsace-Lorraine regions, while the France of the 1950s had to confront both the bipolar hegemony of the cold war relegating it to the status of a secondary power and the bloody colonial conflicts leading to the disintegration of its empire.

In 1885, the year of Mauriac's birth, Jules Ferry was exhorting his compatriots to embark on a great enterprise of colonial expansion. Without reviewing the entirety of his often-cited speech before the Chambre des Députés (the national assembly) on 28 July 1885, we should observe that the nationalism infusing Ferry's exhortation was based on an acute sense of history and national identity, the latter deriving from the former. Simply stated, Ferry expresses the familiar notion of France as the torchbearer of civilization, a beacon of enlightenment, progress, and liberty that he—and he is of course hardly an exception—sees shining throughout France's illustrious past, legitimating its foreign conquests, and illuminating the path to the future, as France fulfills its "mission civilisatrice" (civilizing mission) and lives up to the grandeur that has always been its trademark. Thus it was obvious, at least to Ferry and doubtless to the great majority of his colleagues,

> . . . qu'on ne pouvait pas proposer à la France un idéal politique conforme à celui des nations comme la libre Belgique et comme la Suisse républicaine; qu'il faut autre chose à la France: qu'elle ne peut pas être seulement un pays libre; qu'elle doit être aussi un grand pays, exerçant

1. Jean-Pierre Rioux, "La guerre d'Algérie dans l'histoire des intellectuels français," in *La guerre d'Algérie et les intellectuels français* (Paris: Editions Complexes, 1991), 38–39.

2. Raoul Girardet, *L'idée coloniale en France* (Paris: La Table Ronde, 1972), 375–78.

> sur les destinées de l'Europe toute l'influence qui lui appartient, qu'elle doit répandre cette influence sur le monde, et porter partout où elle le peut sa langue, ses moeurs, son drapeau, ses armes, son génie.[3]
>
> [. . . that for France, one could not propose a political ideal that was similar to that of countries such as the free state of Belgium or the Swiss republic; France has to have something else. It cannot just be a free country. France must also be a great country, exerting all the influence that is rightly its own on the destiny of Europe, spreading this influence over the world, and carrying wherever it can its language, its *mores*, its flag, its arms, and its mind-set.]

Thus Ferry justified the imperial undertaking by invoking a powerful conception of national identity: France's place of eminence among the civilized nations of the world supposedly conferred upon it special rights and duties with regard to "inferior races."[4] This notion of national identity was in turn based on a sense of history: conceiving of history in general as a linear series of events leading to technical and cultural refinement, Ferry opposes the civilized nations of the West to the "barbarous" non-European peoples supposedly still mired in superstition and backward ways.[5] Ferry's view of the particular history of his country as the patrimony of noble and glorious deeds thus compels him to preach this new crusade of colonial expansion.

This is of course familiar terrain: we have chosen to tread over it once again because it will frame our study of Mauriac's sentiment of national identity as seen through his editorials on the colonial question. For many years, Mauriac's attitude did indeed stem largely from the sort of smug ethnocentrism implicit in Ferry's nationalistic missionary fervor. He condoned the Rif war by signing a "Manifeste des intellectuels aux côtés de la patrie" (Manifesto of intellectuals in support of the fatherland) in 1925,[6] and even in the late 1940s, after his politics had veered to the left during the Spanish civil war and the Occupation period, he greeted protests against French colonial policy with icy disdain.

3. Ferry's speech is cited in Girardet, *L'idée coloniale en France*, 86.
4. Girardet, *L'idée coloniale en France*, 83.
5. Cf. Furet, *L'atelier de l'histoire*, 10–14.
6. Jean-Pierre Biondi, *Les anticolonialistes* (Paris: Robert Laffont, 1992), 298.

This posture seems hardly surprising on the part of someone who avidly read the *Action Française* in the 1920s and 1930s and wrote novels in the most traditional narrative forms so often associated with a nineteenth-century eurocentric view of history. Indeed, up until the 1950s, Mauriac's editorials often refer either to great men having supposedly shaped history through their extraordinary exploits or to France's rich literary, artistic, and intellectual heritage. France is thus the country of the Crusaders, Jeanne D'Arc, Montaigne, Descartes, Racine, and Montesquieu. In a 1935 article deploring the absence of a strong national leader, Mauriac depicts the France that was nervously watching the rise of Nazi Germany as first a Minerva, goddess of civilization, horrified by Medusa (in Mauriac's view a symbol of barbarity), and finally as a Perseus, the hero who lops off Medusa's head. "Aujourd'hui," asserts Mauriac confidently, "le monde français sent profondément qu'il appartient au peuple civilisé par excellence" (Today, the French world feels deeply that it belongs to the civilized people par excellence).[7]

And yet, even during those years, Mauriac's adherence to the overbearing nationalism of the Third Republic was neither unconditional nor unequivocal. He denounced the cruelty of Mussolini's invasion of Abyssinia and harshly criticized the racism underlying the extreme right's enthusiasm for the Duce's adventure. Similarly, in "La Nation française a une âme" (The French nation has a soul) written in 1944, he unambiguously condemned Maurras and his "nationalisme intégral" (fanatical, uncompromising nationalism) as the root of French collaboration with the Nazis.[8]

As cataclysmic as the upheavals of the 1930s and the 1940s were, however, they really never called into question Mauriac's acute sense of national identity. The Spanish civil war was strictly speaking not a French matter, and was furthermore fought out with, if indeed not instigated by, heavy foreign intervention. Similary, World War II did not fundamentally challenge Mauriac's national sentiment, since France—Vichy and the Parisian "ultra-collaborationists" notwithstanding—found it-

7. Mauriac, *Mémoires politiques*, 37.

8. Mauriac, *Mémoires politiques*, 155–58. See also Scott, *Mauriac et de Gaulle*, 52–56.

self subjugated by an outside invader. As for other intellectuals writing resistance pieces for the *Lettres Françaises*, the most urgent task for Mauriac during the Occupation years was to rally large numbers of his compatriots around a consensual idea of the French nation and to exhort them to oppose the Nazis, whose stranglehold threatened France's very existence. During a national crisis of such magnitude, one could hardly expect writers to engage in soul-searching on the colonial question. As we have already observed, many Resistance heroes (including Georges Bidault and Jacques Soustelle) on both the right and the left became prominent hawks on the Algerian question.[9]

Add to that the fact that in the late 1940s and early 1950s Mauriac was engaged in an intensively polemical battle over the question of communism, and one is little surprised to find that his reaction to the Indochinese war in 1947 was nothing short of knee-jerk nationalism. The several articles that he wrote on the subject are worth examining at some length, for they will enable us to gauge the transformation of his concept of national identity as later articulated in the *Bloc-notes*. The first piece, "Le Bourreau de soi-même," was inspired by Mauriac's indignation at having heard France's policy in Indochina criticized by a Frenchman on the national radio, an act which for Mauriac borders on treason: hence the title (literally, "the one who executes [tortures] himself," reminiscent of Baudelaire's "L'Héautontimorouménos") presenting France as the victim.[10] The very notion that, as suggested by *Les Temps modernes*,[11] the presence of the French could be as offensive to the Vietnamese as was that of the Germans to the French Mauriac labels as "criminal." In the same breath, he peremptorily dismisses criticism of the colonial regime in Indochina as an affront to the "histoire glorieuse et le sacrifice de nos morts" (glorious history and the sacrifice of those who have died there).[12] Such criticism, he further contends, only serves to demoralize French troops and encourage France's enemies (both the Vietnamese rebels and the rival Soviet "empire").

9. Jean-François Sirinelli, "Les intellectuels français en guerre d'Algérie," in *La guerre d'Algérie et les intellectuels français*, 24.

10. Mauriac, *Mémoires politiques*, 443–45.

11. Biondi, *Les anticolonialistes*, 263.

12. Mauriac, *Mémoires politiques*, 444.

He continues along much the same lines in 1950, brushing aside suggestions of French oppression in Indochina with only the slightest concession to possible misconduct: for Mauriac, the colonial legacy is the story of the "les crimes de quelques-uns, . . . l'héroïsme et la sainteté de beaucoup" (the crimes of a few . . . the heroism and saintliness of many).[13] Shrugging off any suggestion of "mauvaise conscience" (bad conscience),[14] all he feels compelled to do in order to justify France's colonial heritage and continued domination in Indochina is to invoke the past:

> Bien sûr, "ces choses à faire frémir" qu'un orateur sacré dénonçait à la source de toutes les grandes fortunes se trouvent aussi dans les commencements des empires. Mais les erreurs, les fautes et même les crimes se perdent dans trop d'héroïsme, de sainteté, de travail, sont compensés par trop de victoires sur l'ignorance et sur la maladie pour qu'un peuple d'esprit aussi délié que le nôtre puisse de bonne foi douter de son droit à demeurer sur toutes les terres qu'il a trouvées dans son héritage et où il est d'ailleurs tenu par toutes les obligations qu'il y a assumées envers les indigènes comme à l'égard de ses nationaux.[15]
>
> [Of course, as once decried by a man of the clergy, "these things that make one shudder" can also be found in the beginnings of empires. But the mistakes, the faults, and even the crimes are absolved by a surplus of heroism, saintliness, and work. And a surplus of victories over ignorance and disease more than compensates for the negatives, to such a degree that no people with an intelligence as nimble as ours could in good faith doubt its right to remain on all the lands that it has inherited. Such a nation is moreover bound by all the obligations that it has taken on both toward the indigenous people and its own citizens.]

Beyond Mauriac's well-known initial support of the prosecution of the Indochinese war (which will continue right up to his involvement in the Moroccan crisis, beginning in 1953), these words confirm his strong sentiment of national identity and the sense of French history upon which it is based. His loyalty to the notion of France that we find expressed here is so strong that he depicts his nation not only as a victim, but even

13. Mauriac, *Mémoires politiques*, 445.
14. Mauriac, *Mémoires politiques*, 448.
15. Mauriac, *Mémoires politiques*, 448.

as a sort of Christ figure suffering the scorn and insults of those who condemn the colonial war in Indochina:

> Les gens de votre sorte me font penser à ce qu'écrit Pascal de la fausse justice de Pilate "qui ne sert qu'à faire souffrir Jésus-Christ, car il le fait fouetter par sa fausse justice et puis il le tue. . . ." Ainsi traitez-vous la grande nation mal relevée, mal guérie, encore titubante, chargée de cet héritage accablant qu'elle essaie de défendre contre vous et que ses bras affaiblis ont tant de peine à porter.[16]
>
> [People like you remind me of what Pascal wrote about the phony justice of Pontius Pilate, who "only makes Jesus Christ suffer, since he has him flogged according to his phony justice and then kills him. . . ." Such is the way you treat our great nation, which is not yet completely back on its feet but is still staggering, laden with this burdensome heritage that it is trying to defend against you and that it is struggling to carry in its weak arms.]

Mauriac's allusion to the ordeals of the defeat, the Occupation, the struggle for liberation, and the postliberation purge indicate that he is still thinking in the World War II/Resistance mode, presuming that France, her territory, and her heritage must be fiercely defended and restored to full strength.

Mauriac gives particular importance to "une certaine idée de la France," an expression which, if coined and made famous by de Gaulle, has long charactized French national sentiment. Only by staunchly defending its empire, insists Mauriac, can France remain worthy of the special destiny that history has reserved for it: abandoning the colonies would amount to nothing less than a failure of France's duty toward the free world as well as renunciation of its responsibility toward the underdeveloped peoples in the Union Française.

These notions lead Mauriac to take several rather embarrassing polemical stands that he himself will vigorously reject only a few years later in the context of the Algerian war. For example, he goes so far as to state that the liberty of the press must be sacrificed to the greater needs of the state.[17] Still more surprising, coming from the same author who,

16. Mauriac, *Mémoires politiques*, 446.

17. Mauriac, *Mémoires politiques*, 446.

in his *Cahier noir*, penned an impassioned indictment of Machiavellian tactics, is Mauriac's criticism of those who would apply the rules of individual morality to the struggle between rival empires.[18] The rigidity and insensitivity of these pieces are best understood in the context of Mauriac's continuing polemical skirmishes with the editorialists of *L'Humanité* and *Les Temps modernes:* up until 1953, Mauriac only approached the colonial question as a function of domestic and international confrontation with communism, in which he was willing to give no quarter. That period, however, represents the apogee of what can be termed Mauriac's "knee-jerk nationalism," and will very quickly give way to much more sensitive, soul-searching articles.

Indeed, after being awarded the Nobel Prize for Literature in November 1952, Mauriac begins marching to the beat of a different drummer. From the beginning of the Moroccan crisis in early 1953, he receives firsthand accounts from trusted witnesses, highly respected scholars, and fellow Catholics such as Louis Massignon and Robert Barrat, whose testimony he could hardly greet with dismissive "harrumph's."[19] In any event, Mauriac dramatically reverses his expression of national sentiment in his editorials, particularly when they portray civilization. Whereas his unblinking defense of French domination in Indochina had been based upon essentially the same smug ethnocentrism that made Ferry sure he was doing the "inferior races" a tremendous favor by introducing them to the marvels of French civilization, we find, beginning in the *Bloc-notes* of 1953, a whole series of unsettling reflections on the nature and origins of this "civilization."

After attending an exclusive gala highlighted by an outdoor ballet at the British embassy, Mauriac relates that such exquisite entertainment was not sufficient to make him forget the hatred displayed by some of his fellow French guests infuriated by his incisive criticisms of French policy in Morocco. The entire scene prompts an uncompromising assessment of such sumptuous entertainment:

> Les divertissements, que c'est court! Le monde en a vu le bout sous les rois. Versailles fut une perfection dans cet ordre: le décor sublime in-

18. Mauriac, *Mémoires politiques*, 447.
19. Cf. Jean Lacouture, *François Mauriac* (Paris: Seuil, 1980), 453–56.

venté pour masquer la misère et le désespoir permanent des deux tiers de l'espèce humaine. ("Jeudi 11 juin 1953," BN I, 78)

[Entertainment lasts such a short time! The world witnessed its ultimate manifestation under the reign of the kings. Versailles was the perfect embodiment of this order of things: its sublime decor was invented to mask the dire poverty and perennial despair suffered by two thirds of the human race.]

Mauriac's choice of the term "espèce humaine" (human race) where one might have expected "son royaume" (its kingdom) or "ses sujets" (its subjects) indicates that he is including non-Europeans in his remark. Moreover, any impression that this might simply be a Pascalian meditation on the grandeur and misery of the human condition should be dispelled by the fact that this severe judgment of both a monument and an epoch widely regarded as one of the summits of French civilization is reinforced by several others of the same tenor.

The link between this reflection on the nature of civilization and the crisis in North Africa is even more readily discernable in the piece Mauriac pens for Easter Sunday 1954. After a series of observations on the gravity of the Moroccan situation and on the intransigence of the privileged few who were blocking progress, Mauriac abruptly turns to his reading of Henry James's notebooks. The striking portrait of Victorian England that Mauriac finds in them inspires a commentary similar to the one about Versailles and reveals the relation to the crisis in Morocco. Let us return briefly to the beginning of this previously cited passage:

> Quel art de vivre! Quelle indifférence au prix que devaient payer les quatre cinquièmes des sujets de Sa Gracieuse Majesté pour les délices de ce petit nombre! Toute civilisation exquise repose sur l'esclavage. Sinon elle ne serait pas exquise. (BN I, 139)

> [What an art of living! What indifference to the price that four fifths of Her Gracious Majesty's subjects had to pay for the exquisite pleasures of these few! Every exquisite civilization reposes on slavery: otherwise it would not be exquisite.]

As we already noted in Chapter 2, Mauriac goes on to explain that the England that so enchanted Henry James was thus necessarily built upon social injustice, and finally confesses "à un rang infiniment plus modeste, je fus en France un de ces privilégiés-là" (139; on an infinitely more modest level, I was one of those privileged people in France).

But as the conflict intensifies and the specter of institutional torture raises its head in Algeria, Mauriac makes the link between these indictments of "civilization" and the crisis of decolonization in North Africa even more explicit. Returning to the powerful denunciation of torture penned in January 1955 and analyzed at length in the preceding chapter, we can observe all the pathos and the contradictions of his present sense of national identity:

> "Vous seul. . . . Si les gens savaient . . . vous, ils vous croiront."
>
> Je secoue la tête:
>
> —Mais non! ils s'irritent au contraire de ce qu'on les oblige à voir ce qu'ils sont résolus à ignorer. Ils admettent que toute civilisation repose sur une horreur cachée: prostitution, traite des femmes, police des moeurs, maisons de correction, geôles pour les fous et les idiots, toutes les tortures: c'est le mal nécessaire. Malheur à qui ose en parler ouvertement! Les Aztèques scellaient des débris humaines dans les pierres du temple élevé à la gloire du dieu Soleil.
>
> —Mais nous ne sommes pas des Aztèques.
>
> —Non, bien sûr! Nous sommes les Français de cette France dont les meilleurs fils, de génération en génération, ont mieux compris qu'aucun autre peuple et mis en pratique le Sermon sur la Montagne. Nous sommes cette France qui a proclamé les Droits de l'Homme à la face d'une Europe enivrée.
>
> —. . . Oui, et dire que pour la plupart de ceux que nous faisons souffrir, la France reste cette France-là! ("Vendredi 14 janvier 1955," BN I, 240)
>
> ["Only you. . . . If people only knew . . . people will believe *you*."
>
> I shake my head:
>
> "They most certainly will not. On the contrary, they get upset when they are made to see what they have made up their minds to ignore. They accept the fact that every civilization reposes on hidden horrors: prostitution, the sale of women, vice squads, reform schools, jails for the crazy and the retarded, every kind of torture. It's a necessary evil.

Woe to anyone who dares speak openly of these things! The Aztecs sealed away body parts in the stones of the temple built to the glory of the Sun god."

"But we aren't Aztecs."

"No, of course not! We are the French, and, from one generation to the next, the brightest and best of France's children have understood and put into practice the Sermon on the Mount better than any other people. We are the country that proclaimed human rights to an overjoyed Europe."

". . . Yes, and to think that, for most of those suffering under us, France still remains that country of idealism and human rights!"]

Any notion that Mauriac might have entertained as to the inherent superiority of "civilized" people over the "uncivilized" is exploded by the words he pronounces in the first part of this dialogue, which one could almost ascribe to Foucault. There the crimes that Mauriac had summarily discounted as incidental in his first few articles on the war in Indochina are referred to in a much more disturbing manner, for he now points out that such acts of violence and oppression have been perpetrated not only by a supposedly "civilized" people, but even by the men and institutions who have claimed to act in the name of the Christian faith.

This observation is indicative of a whole series of highly critical remarks concerning the role of the Church in history. Speaking before a conference of Catholic intellectuals in November 1954, Mauriac delivered a lecture focused on one of the supreme perversions of history: the fact that, from the time of the Crusades to present-day Algeria, so many violent and cruel undertakings have been spearheaded by those claiming to act on behalf of the one who suffered death by crucifixion.[20] Mauriac articulates an equally searing indictment of Judeo-Christian civilization in his "Bloc-notes" for Christmas Eve 1957:

> Les millions de bouchons de champagne qui sautent cette nuit dans tous les cabarets de l'Occident, en l'honneur d'un petit pauvre né en Galilée, il y a mille neuf cent cinquante-sept ans, ce malentendu résume toute l'histoire chrétienne. . . .

20. The lecture was later published in François Mauriac, *L'imitation des bourreaux de Jésus-Christ* (Paris: Desclée de Brower, 1984), 15–32.

> La plupart des politiques qui, au long de l'Histoire, se sont réclamés du petit Enfant de cette nuit, furent en réalité ses bourreaux. En son nom, les conquistadors du roi catholique détruisirent des races entières. Les rois très chrétiens ne l'ont été que par antiphrase et les mains qui hier encore lâchaient sur Hiroshima la bombe atomique, anéantissant d'un seul coup deux cent mille créatures de Dieu, étaient des mains puritaines. (BN I, 559)
>
> [In honor of a poor little child born one thousand and fifty-seven years ago, millions of champagne bottles are being popped open tonight throughout all the night spots of the Western world. This misunderstanding sums up all of Christian history. . . .
>
> Throughout history, most of the politicians who have claimed allegiance to the little Child of that night were in reality his executioners. In his name, the Catholic king's conquistadors destroyed entire races. The "most Christian" kings made a mockery of the term, and the hands that just recently dropped the atomic bomb on Hiroshima, annihilating two hundred thousand of God's children in one stroke, were the hands of Puritans.]

All that Mauriac had so smugly, even arrogantly, glossed over with his praise of "saintliness" in French Indochina and his depiction of France as a Christ figure publicly mocked and scorned by its accusers seeths forth here in a crescendo of rage against the criminal hypocrisy now decried as endemic in Western Christendom. Setting his contemporaries' sumptuous holiday feasts awash in champagne over against Jesus' lowly origins and humble life, Mauriac painfully underscores the disjunction if not the outright opposition between the fundamental precepts advanced by the life and teaching of a "poor little child born in Galilee" and the actions of those principalities and powers calling themselves "Christian." Here as in his address to Catholic intellectuals, the latter appear as nothing less than imitators of Christ's executioners. On the question of colonialism, Mauriac has come a long way in a very short time: he has not only ceased to proclaim the putative benefits of Christendom's civilizing influence, but he has begun to deliver an uncompromising assessment of its crimes.

Equally scathing but in a slightly different vein is Mauriac's commentary on Camus's famous plea for the abolition of the death penalty.

While quickly stating his own opposition to capital punishment, Mauriac insists on shifting the focus to what he considers to be the overriding question, one that he accuses Camus of dodging even while making an eloquent plea against capital punishment. For Mauriac, the real issue of the hour (we are in the summer of 1957; the "Bataille d'Alger" [Battle of Algiers] is raging, with terrorist bombings prompting mass arrests and systematic torture) is the question of European responsibility. The editorial first reels off a long litany of the crimes that have marked the last twenty years of European history: the Spanish civil war, the Holocaust, Vichy massacres, and the excesses of the postliberation purge. Mauriac then goes on to argue that Europe has lost any claim to moral authority:

> Vendredi 5 juillet 1957
>
> Ce qu'Albert Camus écrit dans la *N.R.F.* contre la peine de mort, je l'ai toujours pensé et cru. Alors pourquoi ce malaise que je ressens à le lire? Je mesure ici ce qu'il en coûte d'avoir vécu cette histoire, la nôtre depuis vingt ans—celle des hommes de la race blanche, chrétiens ou héritiers de la civilisation chrétienne. . . .
>
> . . . la race blanche ne détient plus le droit de s'interroger sur la peine de mort, puisqu'elle a bafoué et violé tous les principes qui pourraient servir, dans ce débat, de repère ou de norme. (BN I, 477)
>
> [Friday, 5 July 1957
>
> I have always thought and believed just what Albert Camus wrote in the *N.R.F.* in opposition to the death penalty. So why am I unsettled when I read it? I now gauge how hard it is to have lived through this story of history that has been ours over the last twenty years, the story of the white Christians who have inherited Christian civilization. . . .
>
> . . . whites no longer have the right to pore over the question of the death penalty, since they have mocked and violated every principle that could serve as a benchmark or standard in this debate.]

This stinging (and, it must be said, rather uncharitable and unfair with respect to Camus) rebuke represents a complete about-face from the haughty indignation with which Mauriac first greeted charges of Nazi-like repression of indigenous people by the French in Indochina. More importantly, Mauriac realizes that the lofty ideals of "civilization" can be a decoy used to give oneself good conscience while diverting attention away from the real issues:

> Vous ne réveillez le débat sur la peine de mort que pour vous donner l'illusion d'appartenir encore à une communauté digne de l'aborder, et pour échapper à l'évidence insupportable que toute notion de justice s'est obscurcie en nous, d'année en année, surtout depuis vingt ans. . . .
>
> Discuter de la peine de mort dispense, je le crains, les belles âmes d'aborder les problèmes plus brûlants. C'est feindre de croire que nous appartenons à un monde où la vie d'un être humain, quelle que soit la couleur de sa peau, demeure sacrée. . . .
>
> Le respect de la vie, même chez les coupables de grands crimes, quel raffinement pour l'espèce de gens que nous sommes devenus. . . .
>
> Abolir la peine de mort quand on rétablit la torture? Un peu de logique, voyons, Camus! (BN I, 478–79)
>
> [You are only rekindling the debate over the death penalty in order to give yourself the illusion of still belonging to a community worthy of taking up the issue and to escape the unbearably obvious fact that all our notions of justice have become murkier and murkier from year to year, especially over the last twenty years. . . .
>
> I fear that discussing the death penalty relieves noble souls from dealing with the most burning problems. It makes believe that we are part of a world in which the life of a human being, whatever the color of his skin, remains sacred. . . .
>
> What refinement for the type of people we have become to respect human life even when guilty of great crimes. . . .
>
> Abolish the death penalty when we are reinstating torture? Come on Camus, be a bit logical!]

This piece marks Mauriac's most extreme indictment of European civilization, the rhetorical hyperbole being perhaps explainable by the pleasure that Mauriac may have taken in outflanking his fellow Nobel laureate and author of *La Chute* on the terrain of moral self-irony. His actual position in this respect is better reflected by the last part of the January 1955 article quoted above. First putting the French on the same level as the Aztecs (a non-European people that most of his readers would surely have thought of as primitive), he then rejects the identification and summons up "une certaine idée de la France," the ideal of a Christian, democratic France showing the way to liberty and justice.

Nevertheless, Mauriac questions not only the ideal image of European civilization that had been habitually opposed to the "barbarity" of indigenous peoples, but also the history upon which the ideal was based. His critical reflection bears not only upon history in the sense of past events, as we have already seen, but also on "official history," the narrative through which a nation chooses to transmit its version of events to posterity.

Here too the context in which one finds these remarks in the *Bloc-notes* clearly eliminates the possibility of literary rumination or mere academic theorizing. Soon after having been lambasted with charges of insulting France and demoralizing the army in the Moroccan crisis—ironically, the very accusations that he himself had leveled at the opponents of the French presence in Indochina—Mauriac cites a passage from Maupassant's *Bel Ami* that sheds an interesting light on the legacy of French domination in North Africa while at the same time raising questions about the official memory of the colonial enterprise. Interestingly, notes Mauriac, the text had been published in 1885 only a few months before his birth (and at the very time, let us recall, when Ferry was exhorting his compatriots to set out on a major colonial venture). Specifically, Maupassant's novel contains shockingly candid allusions to the French soldiers' practice of ransoming Arabs for goods, gold, and sheer amusement. Maupassant's narrator frankly explains that such behavior was in a sense to be expected, ". . . l'Arabe étant un peu considéré comme la proie naturelle du soldat" ("Vendredi 24 juillet, 1953," BN I, 88; . . . since the Arabs [were] considered a bit like the natural prey for soldiers). These facts prompt Mauriac to question how such information might have been greeted in Maupassant's time:

> J'aimerais savoir si la direction du *Gil Blas* reçut des lettres pour protester contre l'insulte faite à l'armée et au drapeau—ou si au contraire, en 1885, ces choses étaient considérées comme allant de soi, comme le "petit fait vrai" rigoureusement interdit à l'histoire officielle mais qui appartenait de droit au romancier naturaliste. (BN I, 88)

> [I would love to know if the editorial board of *Gil Blas* received any letters of protest against the insult to the army and the flag—or if in 1885 such things were on the contrary taken for granted, like the "little factual detail" rigorously banned from official history but assigned to the domain of the naturalist novel.]

The musings about possible protests against "the insult to the army and the flag" recall the scandal of the Dreyfus affair and point to the dangerous affiliation between nationalism and racism both at the turn of the century and in the early 1950s. In an editorial cited in the previous chapter, Mauriac recalls Talleyrand's cynical definition of history as a universal conspiracy of lies and relates it back to the colonial crisis in Morocco where France is about to depose the sultan (see BN I, 95). These two queries made in the summer of 1953 usher in a whole series of references to history and more specifically to French history: in each case, Mauriac scrutinizes the unseemly social and economic forces that have doubtlessly decided the fate of many events.

As we have observed, Mauriac often borrows Goethe's characterization of history as nothing but "ce brouillamini d'erreurs et de violences" (this imbroglio of errors and violence), both in his Occupation-period writings and throughout the *Bloc-notes.* There can be no doubt that he now specifically ties the violence and injustice that he had long denounced in history to France's own past in general, and to its colonial past in particular. French history no longer appears as an epic of great men and illustrious deeds, but rather as a sordid tale of money and power. This may in and of itself hardly appear to be an earthshaking observation, but in the context of national sentiment expressed in Mauriac's editorials, it marks an important evolution for several reasons. First, the epic of great men and illustrious deeds that had been presented as the history of France in elementary-school manuals (such as Lavisse's text)[21] and which Mauriac had for so long virtually taken for granted and unreflectingly invoked to legitimate French colonial domination, has now become acutely problematical. Caught up in the intense political battles over the colonial question, Mauriac realizes that the insidious

21. Cf. Raoul Girardet, *Le nationalisme français* (Paris: Seuil, 1983), 80–84, and Laurence Wylie and Jean-François Brière, *Les Français*, 39–50.

disinformation campaigns and the tawdry coalitions of financial interests dominating French politics in the 1950s are precisely the same forces that have all too often written official history:

> Je regarde, j'écoute, je souris, je ne m'étonne pas. La France a eu souvent le spectacle de ces Restaurations: les fusils changent d'épaule, les vestes se retournent. C'est réglé comme un ballet que l'Histoire remet de temps en temps à l'affiche. La dernière reprise date de la Libération. La peur jouait alors: les dieux avaient soif.
>
> Aujourd'hui, la peur ne joue plus; un peuple furieux n'occupe pas la scène, du moins en France, et seuls les intérêts s'agitent. Que les hommes soient intéressés, voilà une belle découverte! Mais cela frappe dans des moments comme celui-ci. Les politiciens, surtout les politiciens d'affaires, leur métier exige qu'ils aient toujours des principes pleins la bouche. Regardez-les: les principes sont tombés d'un coup. On ne roule plus les yeux, on n'invoque plus l'honneur de la patrie. Ils ont mal joué, ils s'occupent de rétablir leur jeu et de repartir sur de nouveaux frais.
>
> C'est alors qu'il apparaît à l'oeil nu que l'Histoire de France est écrite avec l'active collaboration des hommes d'argent, des politiciens d'affaires. "Les affaires, c'est l'argent des autres." C'est surtout le sang des pauvres. . . . (BN I, 307)
>
> [I look, I listen, I smile, and I am not surprised. France has often had the spectacle of such restorations: people switch horses, turn their coats, and change their loyalties. It's all choreographed like a ballet that history restages from time to time. The last performance dates from the Liberation. At that time, fear was playing itself out, the gods were bloodthirsty.
>
> Today, the fear is gone; an enraged people no longer occupies the stage, at least not in France, and only the special interests are getting all worked up. People look out for their own interests: now there's a fine discovery! But it is striking at times such as the present moment. Politicians, especially those from the business world, are required by profession to mouth profusely their high-minded principles. Look at them now: all their principles have suddenly vanished. They no longer roll their eyes and invoke the honor of their country. Their performance was bad, and now they are busy putting their act back together and getting off to a fresh start.
>
> It is at times like this that one can see with a naked eye that France's

> history has been written with the active collaboration of men from the circles of money and politicians from the world of business. "Business is a matter of other people's money." It is above all a matter of poor people's blood.]

These incisive lines were written shortly after the restoration of Sultan Mohammed V to the throne in Morocco. Instead of trumpeting the victory of the cause he had defended, and which he might well have presented as the one truly representative of France's liberal heritage, Mauriac ponders the human cost of this chapter of history, particularly to the anonymous players who will remain absent from the public version. That is why, in ending this article, Mauriac offers his suggestion as to what to do with the powerful who had previously dominated the scene, and who had brutally repressed their opponents: ". . . j'en ferais des gardiens de cimetière, je les chargerai d'entretenir les fleurs et les fosses communes" (BN I, 308; . . . I would put them in charge of the cemetery and make them take care of flowers and mass graves).

In his first articles on the colonial war in Indochina, Mauriac cited the supposedly glorious legacy of France's past as a sort of guarantor of the present. Now, considering the mass arrests and systematic torture carried out by French forces in North Africa, he is compelled not only to protest the present state of affairs but also to reexamine the history of the colonial enterprise. We can see this interplay between current events and history in the editorial written in response to the problem of human rights in Algeria as posed by the cases of Maurice Audin ("disappeared" at the hands of French authorities in Algeria) and Henri Alleg (the author of *La Question*, tortured by the French):

> Vous avez beau vous taire, la vérité suinte à travers les proses anodines des journaux. Les éléments s'accumulent d'un effrayant dossier. Le procès tôt ou tard sera plaidé. En fait il est déjà ouvert.
>
> Et cela, loin de nous accabler, doit nous rendre courage, parce que ce débat sera porté au crédit de notre génération comme l'affaire Dreyfus fut l'honneur de la génération qui précéda la nôtre. Sous l'Empire, il n'y aurait pas eu d'affaire Dreyfus. Elle eût été étouffée dès le commencement. Elle a failli l'être en régime républicain.
>
> Ce qui nous inquiète ou nous indigne aujourd'hui, ce sont des pratiques qui pendant des années sans doute furent courantes, dans tous

> les "empires" et quelle que fût la métropole dont ils relevaient, et sans que l'opinion chez les peuples responsables en ait été avertie ou s'en soit émue. Le scandale d'aujourd'hui doit donc nous réconforter, bien loin de nous abattre. Le pire n'est pas que certains crimes légaux soient pratiqués, mais qu'ils soient acceptés ou approuvés. Tout le progrès humain tient dans ce réflexe—ou plutôt dans cette réaction de l'esprit—comme tout retour à la barbarie se mesure au mépris de la personne et à l'accoutumance bientôt mêlée de plaisir, qui entraîne des hommes, nés chrétiens et Français, à faire souffrir d'autres hommes. ("Vendredi 16 août 1957," BN I, 499–500)
>
> [You may try as you will to keep silent, the truth keeps seeping out through the innocuous prose of newspapers. Little by little, a frightful case is being built up. The case will go to court sooner or later. In fact the trial has already begun.
>
> Far from overwhelming us with despair, the matter should give us heart, because this debate will be to the credit of our generation just as the Dreyfus affair had been the honor of the generation preceding ours. Under Napoleon, there would have been no Dreyfus affair. It would have been snuffed out in its beginnings. And it almost was under the Rebublic.
>
> What worries and outrages us today are practices that had doubtless been commonplace for years in every "empire" of all colonial powers without the public opinion being informed or upset. Instead of getting depressed, we should therefore console ourselves over the present-day scandal. The worst is not for certain legal crimes to be perpetrated, but rather to be accepted or approved. The entire amount of human progress can be found in this reflex—or rather this reaction of the mind—just as each lapse back into barbarity can be gauged by the disregard for the human person and by a sort of conditioned indifference, which leads people born Christian and French not only to routinely make other people suffer, but soon even to take pleasure in the practice.]

These poignant reflections illustrate the close interrelationship between the sentiment of national identity, the idea of civilization, the sense of history, and the colonial crisis that called them into question in Mauriac's editorials. His frank confrontation of the present repression in Algeria leads him to reflect on the past, and thus to reassess the legacy of

French colonialism and to realize that the current state of affairs, far from representing a historical anomaly, rather is an indication of the way things have always been in *all* colonial regimes.

This reevaluation of French history leads to a certain anxiety about national identity, that is, about the moral mettle of "des hommes, *nés chrétiens et Français*" (people born Christian and French) who take pleasure in the suffering of fellow human beings. Significantly, we no longer find the opposition between the civilized European colonizers and the uncivilized colonized that was a presupposition of Mauriac's staunch nationalism. For instead of depicting France as bearing the torch of civilization to supposedly backward peoples, Mauriac now suggests that it is the French who need to rise above barbarity in dealing with the Algerians.

Mauriac has clearly come a long way since the sneers that he had directed toward the anticolonialists in his early editorials on Indochina. The distance might well be measured by this willingness to confront the barbaric behavior of his own compatriots. Whereas Mauriac was once shocked at *Les Temps modernes*'s contention that, for the colonized, France's face in Indochina was that of the Gestapo, the *Bloc-notes* frequently refers to French military authorities in Algeria as "fascists" in the late 1950s. In one article, Mauriac suggests sarcastically that the difference between repression in the Soviet bloc and repression in the West was that the former didn't have to worry about principles or public opinion ("Mardi 15 janvier 1957," BN I, 432–33).

The remark was of course hyperbolic, for as radically as Mauriac questioned French history and national identity, and as problematical as they become for him, he never collapses the difference between civilization and barbarity or between France and Nazi Germany. Nor did he ever abandon the ideal of "une certaine idée de la France," as he explains in his "Bloc-notes" of 5 July 1958, shortly after de Gaulle's return to power, when he wonders

> . . . si la France est réellement telle que Péguy et Bernanos l'ont vue, telle que de Gaulle exige qu'elle soit. Ou est-ce leur amour qui a inventé, recréé (comme fait de son objet tout amour) une France à sa mesure?
>
> Au long de ces dix dernières années, je le confesse, il m'est arrivé de

croire qu'aucun trait ne correspondait plus, dans le réel, à cette idée héroïque de la France, qu'elle n'avait existé que dans la passion de quelques-uns qui retouchaient l'Histoire pour lui faire signifier ce qu'ils exigeaient d'elle, biffant et effaçant tout ce qui contredisait cette série d'images d'Épinal à la gloire de la grande nation.

C'est ce qui rend si pathétique, cette dernière "expérience de Gaulle." . . . De Gaulle croit en la France de son histoire de France. Il agit comme s'il y croyait, et par là il la tire de la fiction: elle devient vraie, grâce à lui. (BN II, 94–95)

[. . . if France is really the way that Péguy and Bernanos saw it to be, and the way that de Gaulle demands that it be. Or has their love (as does all love with the beloved) invented and re-created France in their love's own image?

I must confess that throughout these last ten years, I have at times believed that in the real world not a single trait corresponded to that heroic idea of France, and that such an idea had only existed in the passion of those few individuals who touched up history to make it mean what they demanded, and who crossed out and erased everything that contradicted this set of quaint images glorifying the great nation.

That is what makes de Gaulle's latest "experiment" so moving . . . De Gaulle believes in the France of his own French history. He acts as if he believed in it, and, in so doing, he lifts it up out of the fictional: it becomes true, thanks to him.]

This article marks a turning point in Mauriac's struggle to come to terms with the idealized image of France and French history that had informed his sense of national identity since childhood, since he fully acknowledges that the official version of French history as an epic of civilization and democracy represents not a record of the past but rather a fanciful construction based on countless exclusions and denials. Yet he refuses to consider this ideal as a sham. Refusing to deny or excuse oppression with this fanciful version of the past, he instead uses it as a standard by which France's behavior must be rigorously and honestly judged, and as a basis for holding civil and military authorities accountable. Albeit on a much more modest level as a polemicist, Mauriac thus emulates de Gaulle in trying to make France conform to his ideal image of the nation.

The return of de Gaulle corresponds to an important transition in Mauriac's articles. After a bit of initial hesitation, Mauriac becomes one of the general's most enthusiastic supporters: it is indeed his staunch defense of de Gaulle against severe attacks from the Left that will lead to his split with Jean-Jacques Servan Schreiber and *L'Express.* Two pieces written only a few weeks after de Gaulle's return in June 1958 illustrate both the latter's ideological attractiveness and Mauriac's preoccupation. Mauriac defends the general, first against the Left's accusations of setting up a dictatorship, and then against the army's fears of seeing the French nation weakened:

> La grandeur de De Gaulle, c'est qu'. . . il n'a jamais essayé de mutiler cette France que les siècles ont faite, la France des Croisades, mais celle aussi des droits de l'homme. Ce n'est pas un crime (si c'est une erreur) que de vouloir supprimer les partis,—mais c'en est un que de prétendre détruire ce qui s'exprime à travers eux: cette exigence de justice que tout homme né chrétien et Français garde au-dedans de lui et que vous n'étoufferez pas. ("Vendredi 27 juin 1958," BN II, 91–92)

> Vouloir une France grande, c'est vouloir une France juste. La civilisation d'un peuple se mesure à l'état de sa justice. On peut dire qu'une justice sommaire le disqualifie. Ces vérités, les jeunes chefs de l'armée en pourraient être persuadés. Et de quelques autres. Et par exemple de celle-ci: la belle affaire que de s'emparer les armes à la main d'un État démantelé et qui n'est plus défendu! Mais une fois maîtres de la place, qu'auriez-vous fait? Qu'auriez-vous fait face à cette université, à ces syndicats, à ces libéraux innombrables, à tout ce que vous flétrissez du nom de "progressistes" et de "défaitistes"? Ces étiquettes recouvrent, vous le savez bien, non une erreur absolue ni une volonté de trahison, mais une certaine conception de l'homme et qui a participé au rayonnement de la France; vous ne nierez pas qu'elle fait partie de ce patrimoine spirituel pour lequel vous vous êtes battus, vous avez souffert, et pour lequel tant des vôtres ont donné leur vie. ("Dimanche 29 juin 1958," BN II, 93)

> [De Gaulle's grandeur stems from the fact that he has never attempted to cripple this France that has been wrought by the centuries, the France of the Crusades, but also the nation of human rights. It is not a crime (even if it is a mistake) to want to eliminate political par-

ties, but it is criminal to set out to destroy what is expressed through them: the demand for justice that all persons born Christian and French keep within themselves and that you will not snuff out.

To yearn for a France that is great is to yearn for a France that is just. Any people's civilization can be gauged by the status of its justice. The young leaders of the army might be won over to these truths. As well as to a few others. Take this one for example: with armed force, you might indeed seize power in a state that is dismantled and no longer defended. But once in control of things, what would you have done? What would you have done, faced with this university, these labor unions, these countless liberals, and everything that you brand as "progressives" and "defeatists"? You know very well that these labels designate not some egregious error nor any will to betray, but a certain conception of humanity, one that has been an integral part of France's international influence and prestige. You won't deny that this ideal of humanity is part of the spiritual heritage for which you have fought and suffered, and for which so many of your men have given their lives.]

While insisting on justice and human rights, Mauriac seems to take it for granted that these ideals are inherently French, that is, characteristic of "tout homme né chrétien et Français" (BN II, 92; all people born Christian and French). Although Mauriac's denunciations of oppression and injustice do not cease, they henceforth yield more and more ground to this theme of "grandeur" that only de Gaulle can restore to France. Contrary to what Malcolm Scott would have us think,[22] however, this "grandeur," as problematical as it may be, does not constitute an absolute contradiction of the Sermon on the Mount. For Mauriac conceives of "grandeur" in terms of France's "rayonnement," that is, as a function of the prestige of French language and culture and of the influence of its democratic humanism: France thus achieves "grandeur" by virtue of moral and intellectual leadership, moreover affirmed in the face of the hegemony increasingly exerted over world affairs by the two superpowers, the United States and the Soviet Union.

Intent on defending the general, Mauriac seems unwilling to say anything that might weaken his position vis-à-vis either the right-wing mil-

22. Malcolm Scott, *Mauriac et de Gaulle*, 30–31.

itants intent on ousting or assassinating him or the leftists resentful of his authoritarian approach to government. This major shift did not escape the attention of Mauriac's readers, to whom he feels obliged to answer:

> Des lecteurs m'écrivent: "Rien n'est changé, on torture plus que jamais. Ce que vous dénonciez hier, vous le supportez aujourd'hui." Non, je le hais comme au premier jour, mais maintenant, mon attention se détourne des fruits empoisonnés, parce que, grâce à de Gaulle, la cognée est à l'arbre même qui les produit: la guerre des partisans. Le terrorisme, la torture naissent d'elle, inévitablement. Aucun ordre ministériel, aucune circulaire n'y a jamais rien pu changer et n'y changera jamais rien. . . . le Général de Gaulle . . . détruira la torture en détruisant la guerre. . . . ("Dimanche 9 novembre 1958," BN II, 162–63)
>
> [Some readers have written to me: "Nothing has changed, they are torturing more than ever. You are presently tolerating what you were formerly denouncing." No, I hate it as much as I did on the first day, but now my attention has turned away from the poisoned fruit, because thanks to de Gaulle, the ax is chopping down the very tree that bears them: guerilla warfare, which invariably engenders terrorism and torture. No ministerial order nor any memorandum has ever managed to change this order of things. . . . General de Gaulle . . . will do away with torture in doing away with the war. . . .]

The rather disingenuous suggestion that no high governmental authority could really stop terrorism or torture indicates to what degree Mauriac has placed himself in a highly paradoxical, if not contradictory, position. On the one hand, he must denounce the injustice and oppression that have made a mockery of the image of France as a torchbearer of enlightenment and liberty to non-European peoples. On the other hand, however, it is largely his own personal attachment to "une certaine idée de la France" that compels him to speak out against French abuses in North Africa, and it is often largely through that patriotic ideal that he will appeal to his readers.

This is obviously no easy task. For in order to preserve any claim to the dignity, honor, and prestige of his and de Gaulle's "certaine idée de la France," he knows that the problem of France's treatment of the non-

European peoples in its colonies must be confronted honestly and ultimately resolved in the political arena. Mauriac's basic strategy is to subject his compatriots to the scrutiny of their racial and cultural "others" and thus give the French a sense of what image they and their government were creating in the eyes of the indigenous peoples that had for so long been under French domination. The following excerpt from one of his early (April 1953) articles on the Moroccan affair shows to what extent this question of national image raised issues of national identity, "civilization," and "barbarity": ". . . il y a longtemps que nous avons perdu la face. Le Marocain nous considère comme un barbare" ("Lundi 6 avril 1953," BN I, 63; We lost face a long time ago. Moroccans consider us to be barbarians). In a similar vein, other articles point out that the militant opponents to France's domination have after all been inspired by the French ideals of liberty and equality:

> A tous ceux qui voudraient nous y aider, nous demandons un premier effort: c'est de ne plus penser à certains jeunes hommes de l'Istiqlal comme à des ennemis de la France, ni même comme à des adversaires, mais comme à des interlocuteurs dont nous pouvons certes, et à bon droit, récuser telle exigence. Ils n'en méritent pas moins quelque respect, ces fils de notre esprit, ces nationalistes de style français, farouchement hostiles au stalinisme et que, par la prison et par l'exil, nous avons trop souvent punis du crime de nous ressembler.[23]
>
> [We ask all who would like to help us to make this initial effort: think of certain young men in the Istiqlal no longer as France's enemies or even as adversaries, but as interlocutors whose demands we might in some instances rightfully deny. These intellectual sons of France, these French-style nationalists, are fiercely opposed to Stalinism: in condemning them to prison or exile, we have too often punished them for the crime of being like us.]

Without sharing all the political ideas of the Istiqlal or the FLN, nor approving of their methods, Mauriac nevertheless denounces the harsh treatment that France has reserved for its spiritual sons and daughters, and he warns his readers against demonizing their adversaries. Mauriac

23. Mauriac, *Mémoires politiques*, 455.

thus expresses his hopes for what will happen if his editorial is heeded: "Nous ne condamnerons plus toute une jeunesse parce qu'elle a cru aux idées que leur ont enseignées des professeurs venus de France" (We will no longer condemn an entire generation of youth because they have believed in the ideas taught to them by teachers from France).[24]

As was the case for French intellectuals of the 1950s in general, the Algerian war probably had a much greater impact on Mauriac than did his editorials on the course of the conflict.[25] The painful struggles of decolonization nevertheless called into question his interrelated notions of civilization, history, and national identity. And since Mauriac cannot dissociate himself with what has been accomplished or perpetrated in France's name, the conflicts in North Africa engage him on a personal level, for what is ultimately at stake in the colonial crisis is nothing less than France's and indeed Mauriac's own moral honor and political "salvation":[26]

> . . . je persiste à penser que le combat politique rejoint aujourd'hui le combat spirituel et ne s'en distingue pas, qu'il engage le salut de la France et du monde, que les heures qui viennent vont décider de notre avenir africain et de notre avenir tout court. . . . ("Belle-Ile, mardi 13 juillet 1954," BN I, 187–88)
>
> [. . . I persist in thinking that today the political struggle is linked to the spiritual struggle and is not distinct from it, that it involves the well-being (literally "salvation") of France and of the world, and that the coming hours are going to decide our future in Africa and our entire future. . . .]

If some commentators have abusively labeled Mauriac as a sort of neo-Maurrassian nationalist,[27] it is doubtless due to such patriotic appeals that, along with a fervent Gaullism to which we shall return in Chapter 5, came to permeate the *Bloc-notes* of the mid- and late 1960s.

24. Mauriac, *Mémoires politiques*, 467.

25. Cf. Jean-François Sirinelli, "Les intellectuels français en guerre d'Algérie," 27–28.

26. Cf. Etienne Fouilloux, "Intellectuels catholiques et guerre d'Algérie," in *La guerre d'Algérie et les intellectuels français*, 101–2.

27. Cf. Malcolm Scott's chapter on "Mauriac, Christian and patriot," in his *Mauriac* (Edinburgh: Scottish Academic Press, 1980), 127–40.

Mauriac's sentiment of national identity, however, combines enthusiastic adhesion to de Gaulle's idealistic view of France's historical destiny with uncompromising denunciations of the country's criminal policies. While paradoxical, this sentiment can be better understood without recourse to stigmatizing labels. The best explanation for such inconsistencies as his waffling on the issue of the state's responsibility for torture in Algeria is that de Gaulle offered Mauriac the chance to have his proverbial cake and eat it too—in other words, to preserve his ideal of France as a torchbearer of civilization and human rights even while chastizing specific policies and behaviors of the French both in history and in Algeria. If not without its own problems and contradictions, the national sentiment informing the *Bloc-notes* of the Algerian war period was of the open, generous, self-critical variety, decidedly opposed to the xenophobic, fearful, suspicious, and aggressive nationalism of Maurras and Le Pen.[28] For instead of confining his thought to a traditional, dogmatic notion of history and civilization, Mauriac subjected France's actions past and present to the most severe moral scrutiny, realizing that the very concept of "civilization" was problematical and admitting that the "certaine idée de la France" that he as much as de Gaulle cherished was not a historical fact, but an idealistic construct, and a very contingent, uncertain one at that.

28. Cf. Michel Winock, "Nationalisme ouvert et nationalisme fermé," in his *Nationalisme, antisémitisme et fascisme en France* (Paris: Seuil, 1990), 11–40. It is interesting to point out, as does Sirinelli, that along with Sartre and Camus, Mauriac was one of the three intellectuals "governing France" that Le Pen, using a scurrilous sexual slur, designated as his prime enemies; see "Mauriac, un intellectuel engagé sous la IVe République," 149.

4 THE LESSONS OF HISTORY

S'il y avait un écrivain *vivant* en 1956, c'était bien François Mauriac. . . . L'écrivain catholique et bourgeois, embicorné [dans l'Académie Française] avant que nous ne soyons nés, nobélisé avant que nous ne soyons bacheliers, gavé d'honneurs qui déshonorent (pour dire comme Flaubert), c'était beau de le voir saisi d'une nouvelle fièvre juvénile, retourné contre ses pairs, l'épée d'académicien à la main, pour crier justice dans le désert d'une France assoupie. Il était sur toutes les bouches, détesté où il était né, admiré où il renaissait. . . .

Mauriac avait soixante-dix ans. Il n'y avait guère en France d'écrivain plus jeune que lui, cette année-là. (Michel Winock, *La République se meurt.*)[1]

[If any writer was really *alive* in 1956, it had to be François Mauriac. . . . This Catholic bourgeois writer had become ensconced in his seat in the French Academy before we were born, and was laden with honors that dishonor (as Flaubert would say). What a fine sight it was to see him caught up in a youthful fury, whirling about to face his peers with his academician's sword in hand, crying out for justice in the desert of a somnolent France. His name was on everyone's lips; he was hated in his native milieu, but admired there where he was springing back to life. . . .

Mauriac was seventy years old. That year, there was hardly a writer younger than he in all of France.]

1. Paris: Gallimard (Folio-Histoire), 1985, 40, 45.

Winock's pithy sketch admirably summarizes the astonishing role that Mauriac assumed as France's premier editorialist of the 1950s: throughout the *Bloc-notes* we find Mauriac passionately engaged by history, that is, by the universal drama unfolding since the dawn of humanity as well as by day-to-day developments shaping and reshaping the contemporary world. Using frames of reference decidedly different from those of Sartre, Mauriac constantly "situates" events past and present all while "situating"[2] himself and his readers with respect to history, as he chronicles political developments, recounts tumultuous moments of the past, and pronounces judgment on the humanity or inhumanity of protagonists of every stripe. In so doing, he becomes a narrator of history. In order to understand how he uses the past to teach lessons for the present, we must further analyze historical narration in the *Bloc-notes.*

Here again, we would do well to keep ready-made assumptions at bay: many would be immediately inclined to discount such a narration of history as the most tendentious, arbitrary, biased rhetoric heavily informed by the writer-journalist's social position and written in view of a predetermined political agenda. However, a close textual study of the *Bloc-notes* will reveal a coherent, reasoned approach whose basic tenets have withstood the test of time much better than the Marxist paradigms dominating the discourse of Sartre and the Parisian intelligentsia in the 1950s.[3]

Mauriac's frequent plunges into the past are admittedly not "innocent" in that they do not stem from some dispassionate antiquarianism: as we emphasized in commenting on his own preface to the *Bloc-notes*, Mauriac writes in response to contemporary events, and to the traumatic events of the Algerian war in particular. But we must not assume that such motivation disqualifies him as a narrator of history or even sets him apart. On the contrary, French intellectuals and political figures alike are fond of invoking some venerable figure or momentous

2. I have of course chosen these terms to ironically echo Sartre's insistence that writers "situate" themselves with respect to history by "situating" their novels. See "Qu'est-ce que la littérature?," in *Situations II* (Paris: Gallimard, 1948), 55–330.

3. Pascal Ory and Jean-François Sirinelli, *Les intellectuels en France de l'Affaire Dreyfus à nos jours* (Paris: Armand Colin, 1992), 155–68.

event of the past as a basis of ideological legitimacy. Antoine Prost has pointed out that since the nineteenth century history has always been the foundation for democratic institutions and political ethics in modern France. Throughout the tumultuous succession of regimes that characterized France's political life from the Revolution to de Gaulle's instauration of the Fifth Republic, one thus finds French presidents of the Republic as well as monarchs and authoritarian figures striving to follow in the footsteps of some noble lineage or heroic past.[4]

Such was already the case for the young Third Republic into which Mauriac was born: France had just emerged not only from a humiliating defeat leading to the amputation of the Alsace-Lorraine region from its national territory, but also from the ordeal of the Commune, a violent insurrection whose brutal suppression had claimed some thirty thousand victims. In that context, it is hardly surprising that in the public schools of Jules Ferry, Ernest Lavisse's history of France was designed to instill a fervent patriotism that would bind its young citizens to the French nation, to the new democratic institutions of the Third Republic that now embodied it, and to their compatriots throughout the country. In order to overcome both the regional differences of culture and language that still existed in the late nineteenth century and the divisive forces that had led to violent conflict between the proponents of democratic reform and the defenders of authority and tradition, Lavisse depicted modern France as the product of a long series of difficult achievements and painful ordeals. National cohesion was thus to be forged out of historical continuity: the proverbial reference to "nos ancêtres les Gaulois" (our ancestors the Gauls) was intended to create a link to a supposedly common past visible throughout the varied experiences of bygone generations.[5]

This often-cited interplay between past and present in French politics explains why history occupies such a prominent place in French culture and intellectual debates, and rightly so. Tzvetan Todorov re-

4. Cf. Tony Judt, *The Burden of Responsibility* (Chicago: University of Chicago Press, 1998), 6. Cf. also Nathan Bracher, "Timely Predications: The Use and Abuse of History in Contemporary France," *Soundings* 81, nos. 1–2 (Spring–Summer 1998): 238–40.

5. Antoine Prost, *Douze leçons sur l'histoire*, 24–28, and Wylie and Brière, *Les Français*, 39.

minds us that history is never a matter of "pure" or disinterested "scientific" knowledge: since historians by virtue of their own humanity find themselves implicated in the object of their study, value judgments and interpretation invariably play a vital role in the narration of the past.[6] As long as the narrator remains scrupulously faithul to the facts (even or especially if the resulting narrative is damaging to the narrator's own social group) and gives a balanced presentation open to several perspectives, these historical assessments fulfill a crucial need: the reconstitution of past events independent from any practical application remains a valid and noble enterprise, maintains Todorov, since the attainment of knowledge is an eminently human endeavor. In the case of history, knowledge of the past enables humans to constitute individual and social identities and transmit the experience of the past to succeeding generations.[7] For to be human, contends Todorov, we must go beyond ourselves and transcend our own particular situation: we must know not only other people and other places, but other moments of history.[8]

The examination of the past should thus ideally give us access not only to the history of our own group but also to the patrimony of humankind. What we find more typically, however, are narratives in which the narrator's own nation, culture, or ideology appear as agents of heroic achievements or as victims of iniquities perpetrated by rival nations, cultures, or ideologies. Even in cases where narrators denounce the misdeeds of their own group, they tend to recount the past according to a Manichaean scheme of good and evil, systematically attributing unjust and criminal behavior to their compatriots. In the final analysis, such narrators actually pursue their own advantage by displaying their supposed moral superiority.[9]

Mauriac succumbs to none of these hazards of historical narration. A quick return to the preface to his collected *Bloc-notes* reveals his desire to present the reflections on the various issues of the day as a Montaigne-

6. Cf. Tzvetan Todorov, *Mémoire du mal*, 140–47.

7. Tzvetan Todorov, *Face à l'extrême* (Paris: Seuil, 1994), 35, 104. Cf. also his *Mémoire du mal*, 140–59.

8. Tzvetan Todorov, "Ten Years without Primo Levi," *Salmagundi* 116–17 (Fall Winter 1997): 5.

9. Todorov, *Mémoire du mal*, 151–52.

like quest for knowledge of the universal human condition. The raison d'être for his editorials thus bears citing again:

> . . . quelqu'un est là, avec ses idées, ses goûts, ses humeurs, les conditions d'une vie ordinaire, et chaque semaine, il réagit à l'histoire telle qu'elle se fait sous son regard. Cet affrontement de l'individuel et de l'universel, c'est tout le *Bloc-notes.* (BN I, 37)
>
> [. . . someone is there amid the circumstances of an ordinary life with his ideas, his tastes, his moods, and each week, *he reacts to history being made under his very eyes.* This confrontation of the individual with the universal is what the *Bloc-notes* is all about.]

Mauriac repeatedly declares himself engaged, implicated, caught up in history, and the narration of the past draws together a whole constellation of issues in the *Bloc-notes.* In closely studying his editorials on the Algerian war, we find that the relation to the past is inseparable from the question of personal and social identity for Mauriac, and that this question of identity touches at the same time on the question of humanity, which in turn can only be posed in terms of history and therefore through a lucid assessment of the great crimes of the past, particularly those of the twentieth century.

Even on the level of world history, Mauriac confronts monstrous crimes that could never leave him indifferent. Genocide, concentration camps, enslavement, and torture summon him to interpret the times that produced them and judge their perpetrators: he points back to such horrific events in hopes that his compatriots will not repeat them.[10] Throughout the *Bloc-notes,* but particularly in the pages devoted to North Africa, his revisitations of specific events in the past are motivated by his desire to shed light on the present.

Given this openly didactic use of history, we must give closer consideration to the questions that Todorov pointedly raises with respect to the narration of the past. Is it possible for Mauriac to conduct such moral assessments without falling into the trap of ideology, that is, without systematically rearranging the facts in favor of some predetermined personal prejudice or political agenda? How can he hope to es-

10. Cf. Todorov, *Face à l'extrême,* 35.

cape the old foil of "selective memory," which pushes narrators to pick and choose among various facts to create a perception of past events that in some way or another suits their needs and confirms what they "knew" all along. Can Mauriac use the past to teach a lesson while at the same time respecting historical truth? And since the story of the past is so intimately tied to the constitution of identity, what universal intellectual validity can we now claim for editorials aimed at driving home the morals of history? Can an editorialist transcend an ethnocentric or self-serving reading of the past?

These issues may seem particularly pressing when dealing with an editorialist with such an ostensibly marked identity as Mauriac. Many might expect this fervently Catholic Frenchman to construct pious images for some sacred history of his church and state, or for this bourgeois to defend "l'ordre," the status quo, and the army, or for this conspicuously Gaullist member of the French Academy to indulge in hagiography.

All such misgivings, however, can be dispelled by a close reading of the *Bloc-notes.* Far from leading to a partisan, tendentious presentation of events, the ethical, political, and metaphysical concerns informing Mauriac's frequent incursions into the past engage him in a series of critical reflections on history, humanity, and identity that remain richly instructive for our own current interrogations. When we analyze his own observations on the narration of history, we see that such writing was neither self-evident nor unproblematical for him. As we noted in Chapter 2, Mauriac not only wrestles with the momentous questions of injustice, oppression, and torture in the context of an ugly colonial (and, considering the damage inflicted by the putchists and the OAS, civil) war, but also with his own reluctance to jump into the fray. In a sense, suspicions that Mauriac's sensibilities might hold some sway over his approach to history are not totally unfounded, for as France's colonial conflicts lead to increasing political turmoil and violence, his first inclination is to withdraw from the secular scene to an inner realm of pure spirituality. Yet Mauriac invariably recognizes that such aspirations are illusory and ethically untenable, both because as a French citizen he is implicated in politics and because as a Christian he is called to be accountable for the plight of his fellow human beings.

In March 1957, at the height of the Battle of Algiers, we find just such a confluence of Christianity and humanism in the ethical tide sweeping Mauriac off the strands of personal isolationism and back into the stormy seas of history:

> Malagar, fin mars 1957
>
> J'avais résolu d'échapper à la politique durant quatre semaines. Mais écouter un disque entre deux lectures, épier le premier rossignol, le premier coucou, c'eût été créer du bonheur à trop bon compte. J'ai nourri toute ma vie cette illusion. Comme si aucune amarre pouvait jamais être coupée, qui nous lie au "malheur des temps"! Comme si je ne l'avais pas toujours su!
>
> L'instinct de conservation inspire les gens, lorsqu'ils protestent de leur horreur pour la politique et jurent qu'ils n'en veulent rien entendre. C'est qu'ils sentent que, derrière la politique, il y a le crime.
>
> La politique et ses crimes, durant des siècles, n'ont concerné que les Grands. Elle est devenue notre affaire aujourd'hui. Quand nous en avons à l'individu qui répond au nom de Mollet,[11] au nom de Lacoste, nous nous dressons contre une émanation de nous-même: la conscience de Caïn est devenue la nôtre. (BN I, 443)
>
> [Malagar, late March 1957
>
> I had made up my mind to get away from politics for four weeks. But it would have been too easy for me to create happiness by listening to records while pausing between two readings or by catching sight of the first nightingale or the first cuckoo. I have nurtured this illusion all my life. As if any of the moorings tying us to the "woes of our time" could ever be severed! As if I had not always known it impossible!
>
> When people protest, claiming that they despise politics and swearing that they do not want to hear anything, they are led by the instinct of self-preservation. The fact of the matter is that, behind politics, they sense the presence of crime.
>
> For centuries, politics and its crimes were matters only for kings and nobles. Today, they have become our concern. When we deal with the individuals who answer to the names of Mollet and Lacoste, we are standing up against emanations of ourselves: the conscience of Cain has become our own.]

11. The Socialist Guy Mollet was "Président du Conseil," in other words, France's premier at the time. Robert Lacoste was the French governor of Algeria in 1957.

What could be more natural than for the seventy-two-year-old novelist to retreat momentarily from the sound and fury of history and to savor the pleasures of nature, literature, music, and memory in the shelter of his country estate near Bordeaux? Yet it is because of, and not in spite of, his humanism that Mauriac cannot remain an island unto himself even during vacation, and that, as far as he would put himself from the madding crowds of Paris and Algiers, nothing human can be alien to him. Instead of fostering quietism or aesthetic rumination, Mauriac's human, French, and Christian identity provides a threefold moral imperative for political commitment: he feels compelled to answer for the politics of France's premier Guy Mollet as well as for the policies of the French governor of Algeria Robert Lacoste not only because a common humanity ties him to the suffering of his time, but also because as a citizen in a democracy he must answer for the deeds of those who act in the name of the French Republic. Most important of all is the prodding from his "conscience de Caïn" (Cain-like conscience). Summoned by God to explain what had befallen his brother Abel, Cain found he could not escape his responsibility as his "brother's keeper."[12] Mauriac declares himself similarly beckoned by the image of the divine in each of his fellow human beings, whose gaze summons him to take heed of their plight.

We find Mauriac's most powerful refusal to climb above history's "brouillamini d'erreurs et de violences" (imbroglio of errors and violence) to some ethereal realm of "ordre et beauté, / Luxe, calme et volupté" (order and beauty, / Luxury, calm, and voluptuousness) in response to the publication of Henri Alleg's *La Question*, in which the French communist recounts the torture that he personally endured at the hands of French forces in Algeria. The temptation to turn away from history is here voiced by a sophisticated cynic who reviews the sinister parade of crimes marking France's past and argues for enlightened detachment as the most logical response to history's horrors:

> Samedi 22 mars 1958
>
> Je voudrais bien me désintéresser de la France, des Français, me déclarer comme Lamartine "concitoyen de tout homme qui pense." Je

12. See Genesis 4.1–15.

ne puis: ce peuple est mon peuple, son histoire est mon histoire. L'avouerai-je? Comme Français, je ne me supporte plus. Je ne crois certes pas que notre droite soit la plus bête du monde, comme le prétend M. Guy Mollet, ni notre police la plus féroce. Je ne crois pas qu'un Anglais moyen d'Afrique du Sud appartienne davantage à l'élite humaine que le Français moyen d'Oran ou d'Alger, mais le comportement des uns m'engage et pas celui des autres.

Quelqu'un me dit: "Vous êtes fou, l'Histoire a toujours été criminelle, ce qui n'a jamais empêché les honnêtes gens, et les autres, de vaquer à leurs affaires, de se donner toutes les petites satisfactions auxquelles ils avaient droit, ou que leur tempérament exigeait, et à l'article de la mort, ils n'ont jamais songé à se confesser du massacre de la Saint-Barthélemy, de l'incendie du Palatinat, des guillotinades, noyades, fusillades, terreurs rouges ou blanches, et encore moins des manières un peu rudes dont toutes les polices du monde ont toujours usé dans leurs rapports avec les malappris qui ne répondent pas quand on les interroge. Vous nous assommez à la fin! Mme de Sévigné raconte à sa fille, dans une lettre, que les soldats, en Bretagne, se sont amusés à mettre un petit enfant à la broche et à le faire rôtir. Elle n'ameute pas l'Europe pour si peu. Vous voulez changer le monde, c'est une grande folie qui passera aux marxistes comme elle a passé aux chrétiens. Elle commence déjà à leur passer." . . .

Ces propos ont cela de bon que je sens mieux qu'il est vain d'essayer de rendre les gens sensibles à ce qui me tourmente. Ce n'est pas de sentir ce que je sens qui est fou, mais de l'exiger d'autrui et de ne pouvoir souffrir qu'il supporte ce qui m'est devenu insupportable. (BN II, 48–49)

[I would very much like to turn away from France and the French and declare myself, like Lamartine, to be the "fellow citizen of every thinking human being." I cannot: these people are my people, their history is my history. Shall I confess that I can no longer bear my position as a French citizen? I certainly do not believe that our right wing is the dumbest in the world, as Monsieur Guy Mollet claims, nor that our police is the most ferocious. I do not believe that the average English subject in South Africa belongs to the elite of humanity any more than the average French citizen in Oran or Algiers. But the behavior of the latter engages my responsibility, while the behavior of the former does not.

Someone tells me: "You're mad, for history has always been a criminal affair. That hasn't stopped decent people as well as the others from

> going about their business and indulging in all the little satisfactions to which they were entitled or which their temperament required. On their deathbed, they never dreamed of saying their confession for the Saint Bartholomew's Day massacre, or the Palatine fire, or the executions by guillotine, drowning, and firing squad, or for red or white terror, and even less for the rather rough methods that every police force in the world has always used in dealing with the uncouth individuals who don't answer when interrogated. You're going to bore us to death with this stuff! In a letter to her daughter, Madame de Sévigné tells of soldiers in Brittany who put a small child on a skewer and roasted it for fun. She didn't stir up a riot in Europe for a trifle like that. You want to change the world, and it's a grand folly: the Marxists will get over that urge just as the Christians did. They are already starting to get over it." . . .
>
> The one thing good about such talk is that it makes me sense how useless it is to try to make people sensitive to what is tormenting me. It is not madness to feel what I feel, but it is to demand that others feel the same way, just as it is madness to refuse to accept the fact that they can bear what has become unbearable for me.]

The enumeration of historical crimes accumulates into a sweeping flood of violence that leaves our imagination awash, and then the unbearable anecdote from Mme de Sévigné delivers the coup de grâce. The rapid-fire references to some of the darkest chapters of French history amply demonstrate that the folly and vanity of human endeavors notwithstanding, Mauriac plunges into the past in hopes of sensitizing his readers to the suffering brought about by French oppression in Algeria.

Intent on modeling the reader's response, Mauriac grapples with his own resistance to historical involvement while at the same time pointing out all the factors that make the passive bystander's position untenable. The complacency and indifference of the "great silent majority" of his compatriots indeed constitute the most serious obstacles to teaching the lessons of history. As familiar as the issue may be, it should not be underestimated, for, as Todorov reminds us, humans tend to prefer comfort to knowing the truth. Societies' proverbial sweeping of their unseemly (not to say criminal) past under the rug of course creates self-images most conducive to the functioning of their political institutions. When we recall that the great crimes of the twentieth century were carried out with little opposition and amid widespread indifference, we realize that we cannot revoke our responsibility as witnesses, interpreters, and judges of history.[13]

As a narrator of history, Mauriac must thus confront a twofold "banality of evil." In the first place, a quick survey of events past and present teaches that the "great silent majorities" of all nations and of every epoch prefer to remain passive, ignoring if not condoning the historical crimes committed in their name. In the second place, the perpetrators turn out in most cases to be "ordinary men,"[14] even if numerically only a minority. So it is with the practice of torture in Algeria, "cette torture confiée autrefois à des spécialistes, mais devenue le violon d'Ingres de citoyens pas plus méchants que d'autres" (BN I, 478; this torture formerly entrusted to specialists, but now the hobby of citizens no more wicked than others). In reality, both "banalities" are merely two different aspects of the same human capacity for carrying out the most unspeakable acts of violence, which is why Mauriac repeatedly presents one in conjunction with the other.

We find just such a conjunction in Mauriac's response to widely publicized reports about the use of torture by the French in Algeria and by the British in Cyprus. Returning to this previously cited passage, we see that the first paragraph speaks to the public authorities who would stifle such reports:

> Vous [members of the French National Assembly who wanted to dismiss accusations of torture and general abuse of human rights by the French in Algeria] avez beau vous taire, la vérité suinte à travers les proses anodines des journaux. Les éléments s'accumulent d'un effrayant dossier. Le procès tôt ou tard sera plaidé. En fait il est déjà ouvert.
>
> Et cela, loin de nous accabler, doit nous rendre courage, parce que ce débat sera porté au crédit de notre génération comme l'affaire Dreyfus fut l'honneur de la génération qui précéda la nôtre. Sous l'Empire, il n'y aurait pas eu d'affaire Dreyfus. Elle eût été étouffée dès le commencement. Elle a failli l'être en régime républicain.

13. Todorov, *Face à l'extrême*, 175–88, 274.

14. See Christopher R. Browning, *Ordinary Men: Reserve Police Battalion 101 and the Final Solution in Poland* (New York: HarperCollins, 1992).

Ce qui nous inquiète ou nous indigne aujourd'hui, ce sont les pratiques qui pendant des années sans doute furent courantes, dans tous les "empires" et quelle que fût la métropole dont ils relevaient, et sans que l'opinion chez les peuples responsables en ait été avertie ou s'en soit émue. Le scandale d'aujourd'hui doit donc nous réconforter, loin de nous abattre. *Le pire n'est pas que certains crimes légaux soient pratiqués, mais qu'ils soient acceptés. Tout le progrès humain tient dans ce réflexe—ou plutôt dans cette réaction de l'esprit*—comme tout retour à la barbarie se mesure au mépris de la personne et à l'accoutumance, bientôt mêlée de plaisir, qui entraîne des hommes, nés chrétiens et français, à faire souffrir d'autres hommes. (BN I, 499–500)

[You [[members of the French National Assembly who wanted to dismiss accusations of torture and general abuse of human rights by the French in Algeria]] may try as you will to keep silent, the truth keeps seeping out through the innocuous prose of newspapers. Little by little, a frightful case is being built up. The case will go to court sooner or later. In fact the trial has already begun.

Far from overwhelming us with despair, the matter should give us heart, because this debate will be to the credit of our generation just as the Dreyfus affair had been the honor of the generation preceding ours. Under Napoleon, there would have been no Dreyfus affair. It would have been snuffed out in its beginnings. And it almost was under the Rebublic.

What worries and outrages us today are practices that had doubtless been commonplace for years in every "empire" of all colonial powers without the public opinion being informed or upset. Instead of getting depressed, we should therefore console ourselves over the present-day scandal.

The worst is not for certain legal crimes to be perpetrated, but rather to be accepted or approved. The whole of human progress can be found in this reflex—or rather this reaction of the mind—just as each lapse back into barbarity can be gauged by the disregard for the human person and by a sort of conditioned indifference, which leads people born Christian and French not only to routinely make other people suffer, but soon even to take pleasure in the practice.]

These strident injunctions activate several essential components of Mauriac's historical narration. First, the key political battle is to be waged on the terrain of ethical conscience, and against the common inclination to acquiesce and accept the banality of violence and oppression, particularly when carried out by official agents of one's own nation. Second, in pursuing his quest for the hearts and minds of the French public, Mauriac adopts a universalist perspective: he grounds his narration of events in the common humanity shared by people of all races, nationalities, and social groups, and moreover posits the intrinsic, absolute value of each person.[15] Finally, as is the case in the *Bloc-notes* cited above, Mauriac most often approaches events on a comparative, analogical basis, discerning the lessons of human history in general and applying them to a specific situation in France and Algeria.

He does not function as a lawyer or archivist delving into the particular dossiers of France's rule of Algeria. Such a role would involve not only the specific current abuses of human rights that receive prominent attention from Mauriac, but also such issues as land confiscation, political inequality, and corruption. Instead, he writes in the vein of "moralists" such as Pascal and Montaigne. That is to say that events are related not on the basis of any direct historical causality or continuity—though that important aspect of history is, as demonstrated in our study of Mauriac's references to the Dreyfus affair, by no means absent from the *Bloc-notes*—but rather inasmuch as they pose the question of humanity. The first part of the editorial cited above, for example, refers to such apparently disparate historical occurrences as the gruesome practices of torture by the British in Cyprus, similar practices by police under Stalin and Hitler, concentration camps, the September massacre in the French Revolution, the repressive politics of Napoleon III's Second Empire, and the Dreyfus affair. None contain any specific factual link that could introduce new evidence bearing directly on the political situation in Algeria. Mauriac nevertheless relates them all back paradigmatically to the crucial issues of the identity and destiny shared by individual members of a common humanity. He points out that such crimes "sont les pratiques qui pendant des années sans doute furent courantes, dans tous les 'empires' et quelle que fût la métropole dont ils relevaient" (are practices that had doubtless been commonplace for years in every "empire" of all colonial powers), and moreover defines progress in terms of a

15. Cf. Finkielkraut, *L'humanité perdue*, 15, 86.

heightened sense of humanity compelling people to expose and condemn torture and oppression, particularly when perpetrated by those presuming to be "civilized":

> Tout le progrès humain tient dans ce réflexe—ou plutôt dans cette réaction de l'esprit—comme tout retour à la barbarie se mesure au mépris de la personne et à l'accoutumance, bientôt mêlée de plaisir, qui entraîne des hommes, nés chrétiens et français, à faire souffrir d'autres hommes. (BN I, 499–500)
>
> [The whole of human progress can be found in this reflex—or rather this reaction of the mind—just as each lapse back into barbarity can be gauged by the disregard for the human person and by a sort of conditioned indifference, which leads people born Christian and French not only to routinely make other people suffer, but soon even to take pleasure in the practice.]

Mauriac denounces French misdeeds in Algeria by comparing them with a wide range of historical events that pose the question of human identity precisely because the abuses committed constitute a lapse into barbarity, the very negation of humanity that results from the failure to respect the intrinsic value of each person as unique, irreplaceable, and irreducible.[16]

Narrating history from this perspective of a common humanity entails neither the denial nor the renunciation of personal identity. Quite the contrary, Mauriac invokes the responsibilities incumbent on his compatriots and his coreligionists in view of both their lofty claims and their historical record, and calls them to task by holding their crimes up against universal human values. The following editorial, also written shortly after Henri Alleg's *La Question* had provided incontrovertible testimony on the widespread use of torture by the French military and police in Algeria, denounces the banality of evil with incisive commentary on Alfred Jarry's Ubu, who for Mauriac personifies the silent majorities ultimately responsible for the crimes committed for "the love of country":

16. Cf. Finkielkraut, *L'humanité perdue*, 86, 110–11.

Sa tranquille certitude qu'il n'en coûte jamais trop de vies humaines pour se remplir la panse et pour ne rien perdre de ce dont on a bourré ses poches, c'est un trait commun à notre espèce, et fort répandu, non parmi les tribus primitives, mais chez un vieux peuple chrétien comme le nôtre, moraliste en diable et révolutionnaire à ses heures.

Il n'empêche que le père Ubu, stupide, cruel et lâche, est moins stupide, moins lâche et moins cruel que certains inspirateurs de la politique française en 1958. Je ne vois à aucun moment de la pièce que la couleur de la peau des gens lui inspire de la haine ou du mépris, ni qu'il prenne plaisir à faire souffrir personne. Sa machine à décerveler manque d'invention, après tout. Et Henri Alleg pourrait lui donner des conseils.

Le vrai Ubu, celui de l'Histoire, ce n'est pas Hitler, ni Mussolini, ni Staline: ils ont des parties d'Ubu, ces monstres, mais ils étaient constructeurs et organisateurs. Ils avaient une idée. Si terrifiante qu'elle fût, c'était une idée, et il la modelaient en pleine pâte humaine. Ubu ne pense pas, il dévore et conserve. Et pour conserver, il massacre.

. . . En démocratie, il pullule. . . . Et s'il n'avait que des pinces! Mais Ubu a des principes: l'amour de la patrie lui sort par tous les pores. (BN II, 47–48)

[His smug certitude that it never costs too many human lives to fill his belly and keep a tight fist over everything that has been stuffed into his pockets is a trait that is common in our species, and widespread, not only among primitive tribes, but even among an old Christian people like ours, fiercely moralistic and at times revolutionary.

As stupid, cruel, and cowardly as he may be, the fact remains that old man Ubu is not as stupid, cruel, and cowardly as some of the people behind French political policy in 1958. At no time during the play do I see him hate or despise people because of the color of their skin, nor take pleasure in making somebody suffer. His machine for debraining people is after all not very original: Henri Alleg could give him a few pointers on the subject.

The real, historical Ubu, is neither Hitler, nor Mussolini, nor Stalin: these monstrous figures have a few of the same components as Ubu, but they were builders and organizers. They had an idea. As terrifying as it may have been, it was an idea, and they shaped it into the form they desired using humans as clay. Ubu does not think, he devours and stores away. And to store away, he massacres.

. . . In democratic regimes, he proliferates. . . . And if all he had were his pincers! But Ubu has principles: he literally exudes the love of country.]

Here again, Mauriac brings the past to bear on the current situation in Algeria through paradigmatic references to three of the twentieth century's most infamous dictators, whose barbarous deeds constitute an affront to the notion of humanity. But most surprising—and doubtless most unsettling—is that rather than presenting Jarry's quintessentially grotesque king as the archetypal head of evil empires (as it would be so easy and tempting to do), Mauriac cruelly underscores the traits likening Ubu to the smug, sententious middle-class patriots fiercely devoted to ensuring their own material and moral comfort.

Here as throughout the *Bloc-notes* we find that Mauriac relates specific events past and present back to the overarching framework of the common human destiny shared in history. He thus undermines the ethnocentric presumptions which, as Alain Finkielkraut points out, have always served as a pretext for plunder and destruction of indigenous peoples by "civilized" Europeans.[17] Mauriac's stunning portrayal of Ubu as the bourgeois "everyman" of liberal democracy thus reaffirms the common human identity that compels him to assume the role of historical narrator. Whereas pretensions of "superior humanity" have often been invoked in attempts to justify barbaric oppression, the concept of universal human destiny posits the dignity and worth of all persons, and can be the basis for defending the autonomy and well-being of all peoples, and in particular of indigenous populations. The sense of a common humanity shared by peoples throughout the world also provides a means for condemning violence and injustice. By repeatedly invoking a common human identity found in history, Mauriac challenges the claims of the very groups whose own particular identity he, as a bourgeois French Catholic European, shares.

Mauriac penned his most stinging indictment of European arrogance at the height of the Battle of Algiers, as he ironically chides fellow Nobel laureate Albert Camus, who had just used the forum of France's most prestigious literary review to argue for the abolition of capital

17. Finkielkraut, *L'humanité perdue*, 13–28.

punishment, as we saw in Chapter 3. Returning to this passage, we find a detailed indictment of Mauriac's compatriots and fellow Europeans:

> Je leur refuse le droit de se prononcer pour ou contre la peine de mort. Ils n'en sont plus là. Seules les formes de la justice subsistent chez eux. Les attentats contre la personne se multiplient partout derrière les façades vermoulues des vieilles lois. Il s'agit bien de la peine de mort!
>
> La race qui a fourni à la guerre civile espagnole ses protagonistes, qui a traqué, torturé et brûlé des millions de Juifs pour les punir du crime d'être juifs, des centaines de milliers d'enfants, la race qui utilise encore le régime concentrationnaire et dont les pendus de Nuremberg demeurent, en plus d'un point de la planète, les maîtres et les inspirateurs, la race qui a multiplié les Oradour, qui a rétabli la torture—cette torture confiée autrefois à des spécialistes, mais devenue le violon d'Ingres de citoyens pas plus méchants que d'autres—, la race familiarisée avec la notion de crime politique, et qui l'utilise, en Russie surtout, chaque fois qu'il importe de faire place nette—mais nous avons montré sous Vichy et aux jours de l'Épuration ce dont nous sommes capables nous-mêmes sur ce point—, la race blanche ne détient plus le droit de s'interroger sur la peine de mort, puisqu'elle a bafoué et violé tous les principes qui pourraient servir, dans ce débat, de repère ou de norme. (BN I, 477–78)
>
> [I deny them the right to declare themselves for or against the death penalty. They are no longer on that level. Only the forms of justice subsist in their society. Human rights abuses are proliferating everywhere behind the worm-eaten facades of old laws. As if the issue were really that of the death penalty!
>
> The white race has provided the protagonists of the Spanish civil war; it hunted down, tortured, and burned to death millions of Jews, including hundreds of thousands of children, in order to punish them for the crime of being Jewish; it is still using the concentration camp regime; in more than one place on the planet, those executed at Nuremberg remain its leaders and inspirations; it has reestablished torture, and the practices formerly entrusted to specialists have now become the hobby of citizens no more wicked than others; it has familiarized itself with the notion of political crime and is using it, especially in Russia, every time that it needs to make a clean slate (and we [French] have shown under the Vichy regime and during the purge what we are capable of in this area). The white race no longer holds the right to reflect on

the death penalty, since it has flouted and violated all the principles that could serve as reference point or norm in this debate.]

Mauriac's universalist perspective, his valorization of each and every human life, and his paradigmatic references to major crimes of the past (with a specific focus on the twentieth century) compose the narrative matrix of this lesson on the war in Algeria. And it is precisely in the context of France's treatment of the Muslims revolting against European domination that we can best understand the hyperbolic indictment of the "hommes de la race blanche, chrétiens ou héritiers de la civilisation chrétienne" (BN I, 477; men of the white race, Christians or heirs of Christian civilization). We might express serious reservations about assigning collective guilt along systematically racial or cultural lines, but such is not actually Mauriac's point here. At a time when some of the most ardent supporters of an "Algérie française" (a "French Algeria," the term used by French nationalists fiercely opposed to decolonization) were invoking the supposed defense of Christianity and Western civilization as a justification for a totally unfettered use of force by the French military and police forces in Algeria,[18] Mauriac is intent on stripping away any and all such claims to moral authority along with any attendant pretext for political and economic domination. The outburst of indignation that he directs against his own race, culture, and religion stems from his deep sense of implication in a common history, as he gauges "ce qu'il en coûte d'avoir vécu cette histoire, la nôtre depuis vingt ans" (BN I, 477, what price must be paid for having lived through this story of history that has been ours for the last twenty years).

Mauriac once again enumerates this recent history of white European Christians so profoundly marked by the "attentats contre la personne" (criminal attacks against the human person) in a numbing crescendo of horrors that, aside from its rhetorical power, illustrates several crucial aspects of his historical narration. Throughout this litany of historical crimes, Mauriac pointedly refuses to assign guilt along the

18. See Anne-Marie Duranton-Crabol, "Du combat pour l'Algérie française au combat pour la culture européenne. Les origines du Groupement de Recherche et d'Etudes pour la Civilisation Européenne (GRECE)," in *La Guerre d'Algérie et les intellectuels français*, 59–78.

lines of any national or even political category, as he recalls atrocities committed by the "protagonistes" of the Spanish civil war (and thus implicitly even the Republican forces that he himself had vigorously supported but which were not exempt from criminal acts), the Nazis, the Soviets, and even the French (including not only Vichyites but Resistance forces implicated in the excesses of the purge). Particularly cruel for Mauriac's readers is the reference to Oradour, which even today is commemorated as an emblem of the terrible suffering gratuitously inflicted on innocent women and children by the Nazis in France.

Here again, it must be stressed that Mauriac is most decidedly *not* suggesting that "all are guilty": in myriad other instances, he clearly delineates the criminal responsibility of Franco, Nazi Germany, and Vichy. His point in denouncing the crimes marking "cette histoire . . . des hommes de la race blanche" (BN I, 477; this history of white men) is to strip away all moral pretensions based on race, culture, or religion. In so doing, he refuses the systematic, biased attribution of guilt or innocence according to social, national, or ideological a priori's. Rather than invoking the past to claim some special moral or political privilege for one specific group, Mauriac often uses the particular pretensions of the French as the basis for subjecting their history to severe scrutiny.

An editorial written later in 1957 targets more specifically France's World War II heritage by highlighting the complicity of a significant portion of the French population with their Nazi occupiers. Once again the question of humanity provides the matrix for Mauriac's interrogation of France's historical heritage as well as his denunciation of the crimes committed by French military forces in Algeria. This remarkable piece illustrates the full depth and complexity of Mauriac's use of the past to understand the present, and bears citing at length.

> Vendredi 27 septembre 1957
>
> L'armée . . . au vrai, c'est le problème de l'homme qui se pose; car enfin ceux qui se spécialisent dans ces sortes d'interrogatoires "un peu poussés" ne sont pas des monstres. Ils appartiennent au "tout-venant." Ils n'auraient sans doute rien fait de pire, sans cette guerre qui les a révélés à eux-mêmes, que de s'amuser pendant la classe à arracher les pattes d'une mouche. (BN I, 516)

[Friday, September 27, 1957

The army . . . in fact, we are dealing with the question of humankind; for after all, those specializing in these kinds of interrogations "that get a little rough" are not monsters. They belong to the category of everyday people. Had it not been for this war that led them to discover their true nature, they would doubtless have done nothing worse than to tear the legs off a fly in order to keep themselves entertained in class.]

Mauriac thus begins by relating the specific crisis in Algeria to the larger question of human identity, reflecting on what type of person could be capable of practicing torture. The answers he finds are neither flattering for the French nor reassuring for humankind.

Je remâchais ces pensées, au long d'une journée lumineuse et brumeuse, faisant admirer à des amis les petites villes fortifiées qui entourent Malagar. Nous pénétrions dans des églises romanes, merveilles inconnues qui se délitent. Sur la plus haute colline, le château de Benauge dressait, dans la lumière de la cinquième heure, des murs orgueilleux qui se souviennent de la guerre des Anglais et qui ont vu peut-être passer le Prince Roi dans sa lourde armure. Il y a des heures où mon pays, je ne puis plus l'aimer que physiquement. J'éprouvais cela, à Paris, durant l'Occupation: les arbres et les balustres des Tuileries, le reflet des arches dans la Seine m'étaient plus sacrés que la plupart des humains autour de moi, que tous ceux qui s'enrichissaient alors, qui s'engraissaient: ce couple affreux du *Bon Beurre* dont on oublie trop qu'il demeure une des composantes essentielles des majorités électorales d'aujourd'hui. Ces fortunes issues de l'Occupation nous occupent à leur tour et nous tiennent. (BN I, 517)

[I kept chewing over these thoughts during a bright, hazy day, while letting my friends take in the ancient ramparts of the little towns surrounding Malagar. We went inside some Romanesque churches, unknown marvels of architecture now crumbling. On the highest hill, in the light of the fifth hour, stood the Benauge chateau with its proud walls that recall the Hundred Years' War with the English and that perhaps saw King Edward, Prince of Wales, pass by in his heavy armor. There are certain moments when I can only love my country physically. That was my experience in Paris during the Occupation: the trees and balustrades in the Tuileries and the reflection of arched bridges off the

Seine were more sacred to me than most of the humans in my vicinity, particularly those who were then getting rich, really getting fat [[off the black market]], for example the horrible couple depicted in *Au Bon Beurre.* People too often forget that such people are still one of the essential components of today's electoral majorities. These fortunes that were heaped up during the Occupation now hold and occupy us in turn.]

In sum, those carrying out torture in Algeria appear to Mauriac just as much "ordinary men" as were the collaborators and black-market profiteers of the Occupation era, and moreover constitute a major component of the "silent majority" now tacitly supporting the actions of French authorities. Most remarkable, however, are Mauriac's concluding comments:

> Aimer physiquement sa terre, c'est tout de même aimer cette face à l'image de l'homme qu'au long des siècles lui ont imposée ceux qui torturaient et massacraient, mais aussi qui peinaient obscurément, rendaient témoignage à la vérité, donnaient leur vie—de sorte que croyant ne plus chérir qu'une certaine lumière sur des coteaux et sur des cimes, qu'une certaine odeur de feuilles mouillées et de brume, que les tuiles anciennes devenues violettes sous la pluie, c'est tout de même l'homme de mon pays que je chéris. Oui, le même, car la brute qui torture est de tous les temps. En revanche, les meilleurs parmi ceux qui nous ont précédés n'étaient pas plus saints que ne le sont encore des vivantes et des vivants, et je connais les noms de quelques-uns. (BN I, 517–18)

> [After all, to love one's land physically is to love this face made in the image of humanity, the face imposed on the land by those who, over the centuries, tortured and massacred, but also by the obscure people who painfully struggled, testifying to the truth and giving their lives. And so even when I believe that I no longer cherish anything but a certain light on the hills and mountain tops, or a certain smell of wet leaves and mist, or the old roof tiles turned violet by the rain, I nevertheless cherish my country's humanity. Yes, the same humanity, for the brutes that torture have lived in every time. On the other hand, the best among those who have gone before us were no more saintly than the men and women still living today, and I know the names of a few.]

This conjunction of uncompromising scrutiny of his own nation's historical crimes with passion for its historical, cultural, and even geographical heritage eminently defines Mauriac's own "certaine idée de la France." And it is precisely this complex, self-critical notion of national identity that sets Mauriac apart from Sartre and his "porteurs de valises" (literally, "suitcase carriers," who smuggled funds from France to rebels in Algeria) but also from the self-appointed defenders of Western culture who would turn a deaf ear to the Algerians' plea for justice and dignity.

Let us recapitulate the exceptional scope of this editorial. Mauriac first relates the problem of torture in Algeria back to the question of human (vs. inhuman or barbarian) identity, and then explores the question of humanity in the context of French history, approaching the past from the perspective of the *longue durée*[19] to point out the rich sediment of events deposited on ancient churches and châteaux in the vicinity of Malagar, his country estate. The vivid connection of idyllic rural and urban French landscapes to the dramatic events having transpired there testifies once more to the intensely historical perception informing Mauriac's narration of daily events. But neither the melancholic beauty of crumbling Romanesque village churches and medieval fortresses, nor the graceful charm of Parisian esplanades and bridges lead him to ignore the violence of the Hundred Years' War or the brutality of the Occupation. As we observed in Chapter 2, Mauriac displays a strong sensitivity to the "historicity" of the everyday world of both public and private life even though he does not trumpet it in philosophical terms (as does Sartre in his *Carnets de la drôle de guerre* and many subsequent writings).[20]

Above all, Mauriac's strong attachment to his compatriots' past and present and to the human habitat they have so painstakingly fashioned over time does not prevent him from decrying the violence and injus-

19. The concept of the *longue durée* (long duration or timespan) was introduced by Marc Bloch and Lucien Febvre and widely used by the *Annales* school of historians, who insisted on going beyond great events and political figures in order to understand rich and complex economic, social, and cultural processes that evolve slowly and are not defined by timelines and standard chronological divisions into historical periods. See Jacques Le Goff, "L'Histoire nouvelle," and Michel Vovelle, "L'Histoire et la longue durée," in *La nouvelle histoire*, ed. Jacques Le Goff (Paris: Editions Complexe, 1988), 54–55, 77–96.

20. Cf. Sirinelli, *Sartre et Aron*, 153–58.

tice they have inflicted on each other as well as on peoples of other races, cultures, and religions. Nor does the beauty of the architecture and the countryside in this part of France obscure the vulgar materialism of a certain segment of the bourgeoisie and their complicity with the Germans during the Dark Years as well as with the torturers in Algeria. Mauriac's strong sense of national identity in no way prevents him from presenting a truthful, balanced narration of France's historical crimes: refusing to use one to obfuscate or deny the other, he instead holds his sentiment of national identity and his nation's crimes in stark juxtaposition.

Equally noteworthy in Mauriac's use of the past to define the ethics of the present is his narration of a history to which he is even more deeply attached, namely, that of Christianity and of the Catholic Church. At the end of 1957, Mauriac begins his Christmas Eve editorial by focusing on the subject of most immediate concern to his readers, the gastronomical festivities surrounding the customary feast, "le réveillon." He then links it to momentous events past and present through the matrix of humanity and history:

> Mardi 24 décembre 1957
>
> Cette nuit, l'Occident s'empiffre. En l'honneur de qui et de quoi, tous ces bouchons qui sautent? Il y a eu ce moment de l'histoire, cette nuit entre les nuits, la naissance d'un enfant mâle entre des milliards d'autres. (BN I, 557)
>
> [Tuesday, December 24, 1957
>
> Tonight, the Western World is stuffing itself. In whose honor and for what reason are all these champagne corks popping? There was this moment in history, this night among all nights, this birth of one male child among billions of others.]

As in the 27 September 1957 editorial cited above, Mauriac draws out the full historical significance of the evening's merrymaking. For whether or not all the revelers eager for an insouciant evening are cognizant of the fact, their celebrations commemorate the event that for Mauriac holds the key for approaching human history in general as well as the current situation in Algeria:

> Du petit être vagissant de cette nuit, il ne restera, au soir du vendredi saint, qu'un cadavre adulte, un cadavre torturé pareil à tous les cadavres torturés avant lui et après lui, dans tous les corps de garde et par toutes les polices, avec la permission de tous les Pilates, au milieu du silence approbateur des scribes. (BN I, 558)
>
> [Of the squealing little creature of this night, nothing will remain on the evening of Good Friday but the dead body of an adult, a tortured body similar to all bodies tortured before and after him, tortured by all guards and police forces, with the permission of all the Pontius Pilates, and in the midst of the scribes' approving silence.]

The passion story of Jesus thus figures the plight of all persons arrested and tortured by oppressive regimes with the tacit support of the "scribes," that is, the highly educated teachers, intellectuals, and journalists whose intelligence and rhetorical skills should compel them to protest.[21] Chiding the escapism of pleasure seekers and the failings of intellectuals and journalists, Mauriac reserves his most forceful condemnation for rulers and politicians who have throughout history claimed to be inspired by the original Christmas story. The devastating words that Mauriac reserves for this perversion of Christ's teachings bear citing again.

> Les millions de bouchons de champagne qui sautent cette nuit dans tous les cabarets de l'Occident, en l'honneur d'un petit pauvre né en Galilée, il y a neuf cent cinquante-sept ans, ce malentendu résume toute l'histoire chrétienne. Aujourd'hui comme aux premiers jours, le Royaume de Dieu se ramène à quelques mesures de levain dans la pâte.
>
> La plupart des politiques qui, au long de l'histoire, se sont réclamés du petit Enfant de cette nuit furent en réalité ses bourreaux. En son nom, les conquistadors du roi catholique détruisirent des races entières. Les rois très chrétiens ne l'ont été que par antiphrase et les mains qui hier encore lâchaient sur Hiroshima la bombe atomique, anéantissant d'un seul coup deux cent mille créatures de Dieu, étaient des mains puritaines. (BN I, 559)

21. Scott points out that Christ appears as the "archetype of all victims of political oppression and legalized violence" already in Mauriac's *Vie de Jésus* published in 1936; see *Mauriac et de Gaulle*, 29.

[In honor of a poor little child born one-thousand-fifty-seven years ago, millions of champagne bottles are being popped open tonight throughout all the night spots of the Western world. This misunderstanding sums up all of Christian history. Today as in the first days, the Kingdom of God comes down to a few measures of yeast in the dough.

Throughout history, most of the politicians who have claimed allegiance to the little Child of that night were in reality his executioners. In his name, the Catholic king's conquistadors destroyed entire races. The "most Christian" kings made a mockery of the term, and the hands that just recently dropped the atomic bomb on Hiroshima, annihilating two hundred thousand of God's children in one stroke, were the hands of Puritans.]

Few could formulate a more stinging indictment of Western Christendom's historical legacy. Even fewer could express such a seething condemnation while in the same breath professing a profound veneration for the Christ child present throughout the ages. Moreover, in emphasizing the disparity between the hedonistic *soirées* most characterisic of a French Christmas Eve in 1957 and the event supposedly being commemorated—the humble birth of a poor child destined for torture and execution—Mauriac points out a much more dramatic contradiction, since some of the most egregious crimes in history were committed by Christians claiming to act in the Christ child's name.

Mauriac then invites his readers to take this historical paradigm of the violence and oppression perpetrated by regimes claiming to represent Christianity and transpose it onto the current situation in France and Algeria:

> Et ici même, et aujourd'hui, et au moment où j'écris. . . . Mais à quoi bon parler! Chacun de nous sait bien qu'il assume une part de tout ce qui s'accomplit et qu'en démocratie il n'existe pas d'irresponsables. (BN I, 559)

> [And today, right here and now as I write. . . . But what good is it to talk! All of us know that we each take our share of responsibility for what is being done, and that no one is exempt from responsibility in a democracy.]

Just as Mauriac finds himself compelled to narrate France's history past and present, and to situate himself ethically and politically with respect to these events, so he indicates the ethical and political responsibilities incumbent on his readers as citizens of the French Republic.

Mauriac thus uses the story of Jesus not only to assess the events of history but also to urge his readers to strip away the pretensions of their leaders and fight against the torture and injustice perpetrated by French Christians in Algeria. For Mauriac, the story of Jesus does not reveal the march of human events: as we have already observed, he pointedly rejects the notion that history embodies divine will. Nor does he try to suggest that the story of Jesus furnished the principle guiding those who shaped the past, as might an ideological narrator of history intent on arranging events to illustrate the virtues of Christianity. His references to the conquest of the Americas, absolutist monarchy, and Hiroshima instead shatter any such claims on the part of a Christian narrator who would champion the cause of a specific group.

Yet the story of Jesus constitutes Mauriac's basic and ultimate reference in that it gives him a moral gauge by which the events of history are to be assessed and a paradigm for situating himself and his reader in relation to history. Through the sacred memory of Christ's suffering and death, the Catholic author of the *Bloc-notes* affirms that he and his French Christian readers are connected to the victims of violence and oppression throughout human history, both here and now and in all times and all places. History is neither an arbitrary construction nor a random collection of unconnected incidents, but rather a cohesive ensemble of interrelated events, the ongoing story of the universal drama of humanity: the question of personal and collective identity must accordingly be approached through the perspective of history. Mauriac's commitment to Christianity ultimately compels him to eschew the comfort of aestheticism and spiritual quietism in favor of the struggle for peace and justice in and through history:

> Me voilà retombé de haut, et les pieds joints, dans la politique. L'autre monde ne détourne pas de ce monde le chrétien engagé. Il l'y ramène, au contraire, et l'y rattache, il lui interdit toute évasion. C'est dès maintenant et c'est ici-bas que ce chrétien doit chercher le Royaume de Dieu

et sa justice—le chercher, bien qu'il le possède déjà dans son coeur, ce royaume du petit Enfant qui est né ce soir. (BN I, 559–60)

[So you see that I have tumbled back down from the lofty heights and jumped feetfirst into politics again. The other world does not lead committed Christians away from this world. On the contrary, it leads them back here, ties them to this world, and forbids any and all escapes. Such Christians must seek the kingdom of God and its justice right here and now on this earth: they must seek the kingdom, even though they already possess in their hearts this kingdom of the little Child who was born this evening.]

This conclusion to Mauriac's Christmas Eve 1957 "Bloc-notes" reaffirms the role he has assumed as a narrator of history.

It is clearly history that binds the various moments and theaters of the human drama into one ongoing story for Mauriac. The numerous passages already cited in this chapter have shown how the *Bloc-notes* often relates seemingly disparate episodes paradigmatically, through the question of universal humanity (and inhumanity) as well as through the story of Christ, whose life and death provide Mauriac the standard by which to judge events. But Mauriac also narrates history through the mode of continuity and linear causality. Such is even the case when he foregrounds his Christian identity as the motive for jumping into the fray.

In late March 1958 the seizure of Henri Alleg's *La Question* coincided with the beginning of the liturgical week commemorating the arrest, trial, torture, and execution of Jesus. This dramatic juncture provided Mauriac an occasion just as momentous as the one that prompted his forceful editorial on the preceding Christmas Eve. In this case, Mauriac not only denounces the French governor of Algeria's attempts to dismiss and discredit the repeated, documented reports on the practice of torture detailed in Alleg's book, but also emphasizes the historical responsibility he feels obligated to assume precisely as a French citizen and a Christian. He lashes out at Robert Lacoste's attempt to label serious abuses of human rights as "errors":

> . . . Mais ils restent des crimes et qui atteignent, à travers ceux qui les commettent, le corps d'élite dont ils portent l'uniforme, et à travers

l'armée, nous-mêmes, notre peuple, monsieur Lacoste, dont vous êtes l'élu. . . . J'ose écrire ici cette vérité qui ressemble à un blasphème: "En Algérie, monsieur Lacoste, vous êtes la France." La France, c'est vous. Hélas!

Pour moi, je me sens associé étroitement à tout ce que vous faites, ou laissez faire, à tout ce que vous couvrez. Je voudrais durant cette semaine sainte entrer, par la basse porte du crime politique, dans le mystère si souvent médité, de ce poids des péchés du monde qui écrase les épaules d'un seul homme. Et puisque le dernier des chrétiens doit chercher, ces jours-ci, à se conformer au Christ, c'est à cette conformité-là que je voudrais tendre, et je souhaiterais d'en éveiller le désir chez les croyants qui me lisent: nous ne nous laverons plus les mains, nous ne nous proclamerons plus innocents du sang d'aucun juste. . . .

Lui n'avait eu aucune part aux crimes qu'il assumait: nous, ce ne sont pas seulement nos péchés qui nous chargent, ce n'est pas seulement cette pauvre vie personnelle que nous avons tissée jour après jour, mais tout ce que notre peuple aura tenté contre sa vocation. La politique française n'est pas le fait de quelques-uns. De grands partis au service d'intérêts puissants, et au premier rang la démocratie chrétienne, presque toute la grande presse y ont collaboré. Quel Français, s'il est chrétien, oserait dire qu'il n'est responsable en rien de ce qui s'accomplit? (BN II, 52–53)

[. . . But they remain crimes that, by virtue of the uniform worn by those who commit them, besmirch the special forces, and therefore the army, and therefore ourselves and our nation, which you have been elected to represent, Monsieur Lacoste. . . . I shall boldly write this truth that sounds like blasphemy: "In Algeria, Monsieur Lacoste, you are France." You yourself embody France. Alas!

For my part, I feel closely associated with everything that you do or allow to be done, and with everything that you condone. During this Holy Week, I would like to use the back door provided by crime and enter into the often-meditated mystery of [how] the crushing weight of the world's sins [were] placed on one man's shoulders. And since all Christians without exception must seek to live in conformity with Christ, I would like to strive toward such conformity; I should hope to stir up a similar aspiration among the believers reading these lines: no longer shall we wash our hands of the matter, no longer shall we proclaim ourselves innocent of the blood of any blameless person. . . .

As for Christ, he had had no part in any of the crimes that he bore

> on his shoulders. We, however, are burdened not only by our own sins and by the tawdry personal life that we have woven together day after day; we are also burdened by all that our nation has attempted to do in contradiction with its true calling. France's political policies are not the doing of just a few people. Major political parties—and first and foremost the Christian Democrats—along with the major newspapers have all collaborated on these policies. What French citizens, if they are Christians, would dare say they are in no way responsible for what is being done?]

Mauriac thus exhorts himself and his readers to answer for Lacoste's actions in Algeria. He issues his summons not only through the ethical paradigm of their human and Christian identity, in other words not only through historical analogy, but also through the historical continuities emphasized at the outset by the preposition "à travers" (through) and toward the end by the verb "ont collaboré" (have collaborated). Mauriac moreover links the social and political roles of French Christians to the past and present policies of their official representatives: hence the allusion to Louis XIV's famous (if apocryphal) pronouncement "L'État, c'est moi" (I am the state).

We can appreciate the full significance of such continuities by returning to his references to the Dreyfus affair: those traumatic events of the past illuminate the crisis in Algeria and clearly situate Mauriac as both a Frenchman and a Catholic compelled to narrate a shameful chapter of history. Two preliminary observations are in order. First, it is hardly surprising that Mauriac should hark back to the Dreyfus affair in commenting on the Algerian war, for the turn-of-the-century scandal marked the advent of the intellectual as a major player in French politics, one whose courage and journalistic eloquence could participate decisively in the political struggle for truth and justice.[22]

Mauriac's many references to the Dreyfus affair also confirm the crucial role of his paradigmatic perspective on history. There were salient analogies between the tumultuous events of the turn of the century and the Algerian war, and Mauriac often depicted the latter as a sequel to the

22. See Pascal Ory and Jean-François Sirinelli, *Les intellectuels en France*, 5–10. Cf. Winock, *Le siècle des intellectuels*, 18–27.

former. As was the case at the turn of the century, France in the late 1950s was sharply divided. On the one side were those willing to defend the interests of the army and the French nation at all costs, even if it meant trampling the fundamental principles of justice and subjecting innocent people to severe punishment in the process. On the other side were the proponents of universal justice and equal rights. Just as the upper echelons of the army were involved in a conspiracy to frame Dreyfus and cover up the truth, so high-ranking military officers in Algeria were organizing abusive arrests and detentions, conducting systematic torture of suspects, and pressuring soldiers to suppress their knowledge of what they had seen. Once again, those (especially intellectuals) who raised their voices in protest were threatened with reprisals (including death) for supposedly betraying the nation and dishonoring the army. The French army moreover posed an even greater problem during the Algerian conflict than during the Dreyfus affair: while nostalgia for Boulanger led Déroulède to attempt to plot a military coup in the Dreyfus affair,[23] the threat of a military takeover—which very nearly occurred on several occasions—loomed constantly on the horizon during the late 1950s and early 1960s. And during the conflicts in North Africa, as had been the case throughout France at the turn of the century, ethnic prejudice once again fueled the violence and tended to make large sectors of the public indifferent toward persecutions and injustices inflicted on members of another race or followers of another religion.

Although there was no direct causal connection between the Dreyfus affair and the Algerian war in terms of a linear sequence of events, Mauriac perceived a distinct ideological and ethical continuity. To encourage those who would resist intimidation and arouse public conscience against torture and oppression in North Africa, he holds up intellectuals such as Émile Zola, who relentessly assailed government and military officials for abusing their power and obfuscating the truth. In the following lines, Mauriac exhorts his readers to reject the notion that journalists and intellectuals are traitors and defeatists responsible for the catastrophes at Dien Bien Phu and in Algeria:

23. Winock, *Le siècle des intellectuels*, 57–58.

Les intellectuels: c'est pour eux que La Fontaine a écrit "Les animaux malades de la peste."[24] Les intellectuels! Quelle basse envie se soulage dans ce vocable devenu une injure, qui, du temps de Dreyfus, servait déjà à ameuter les foules furieuses et qui, hier encore, pour les S. S. et pour les chemises noires, désignait le premier ennemi. C'est encore l'intelligence et l'usage de l'intelligence qu'il s'agit aujourd'hui de disqualifier. (BN I, 357)

[As for intellectuals, it was for their sake that La Fontaine penned "The Animals Stricken by the Plague." What dubious urge do people satisfy when they use the term "intellectuals" as a slur? In the days of the Dreyfus affair, the term was already being used to agitate riotous crowds. It was used more recently by the SS and the Black Shirts [[of Mussolini]] to designate the enemy. Now as before, the term is once again being used to disqualify thinking and the use of the mind.]

Beyond such analogies that discredited and shamed Mauriac's adversaries while bolstering the morale of colleagues fighting for the same cause, the continuity between the Dreyfus affair and the Algerian conflict also compelled readers to rethink France's historical heritage and question their assumptions, as we pointed out in Chapter 3. In a long article decrying the mediocrity and shortsighted conservatism that prevented the Fourth Republic from engaging on courageous paths toward social justice and international peace, Mauriac repeatedly calls the dominant interests of the early 1950s "les féodalités qui tiennent l'État" (the feudal powers that control the state), traces the fears of the bourgeoisie back to the phobias of the Dreyfus era, and concludes:

L'histoire ne pardonne pas, parce qu'elle ne s'interrompt jamais, parce qu'elle développe sans arrêt, dans tous les sens et sur tous les plans, les

24. The fable depicts the entourage of the king (a lion) as a group of servile flatterers. Convinced that the plague decimating his subjects has been sent as a chastisement for some offense, the king suggests that all confess their misdeeds. Led by the fox and the wolf, the counselors assure the lion that he is blameless for having devoured both sheep and shepherd, and urge him to execute the donkey to expiate the "crime" of having grazed a few blades of grass. The explicit moral of the tale is that royal justice will be tailored to each according to the criteria of power, money, and social status. Implicitly, the fable mocks the moral cowardice of prominent figures who fail to speak out against injustice and abuse of power.

conséquences d'un acte une fois posé, mais celles aussi de nos dérobabes et nos refus. (BN I, 111–12)

[History is unforgiving because it continues without interruption and because, in every direction and on all levels, it ceaselessly develops the consequences of a deed once it has been committed, just as it develops the consequences of our refusals and our attempts to dodge the issues.]

For Mauriac, virtually every issue raised by the crisis of decolonization in North Africa could be connected to the Dreyfus affair: again and again, he presents the struggle for human rights and justice in Algeria as its continuation.

Such is the case in the following passages. The first points to the principles opposing Mercier, the army's fiercest accuser of Alfred Dreyfus, and Picquart, who championed the Alsatian Jew's innocence; similar ideological differences pitted the officers condoning or denying torture in Algeria against Bollardière, who requested to be relieved of his command in solidarity with Jean-Jacques Servan-Schreiber's denunciation of the army's abuses (Touzot, BN I, 445n, 516n).

> Ah! Philippe Barrès! Philippe Barrès! c'est toujours la même question posée aujourd'hui à la conscience française qu'il y a soixante ans. Qui donc alors mettait en péril l'honneur de l'armée: le général Mercier ou le lieutenant-colonel Picquart? Et aujourd'hui, est-ce le général de Bollardière ou les hommes qui pratiquent ces méthodes déjà dénoncées par le rapport de la Commission internationale contre le régime concentrationnaire et que confirmera, vous n'en doutez pas, puisque le gouvernement ne l'a pas rendu public, le rapport de la Commission de sauvegarde? (BN I, 516)

> "Le beau courage d'être Dreyfus aujourd'hui!" me dira-t-on. Mais oui, le beau courage. L'affaire Dreyfus dure toujours et les Bureaux de Guerre sont éternels. (BN II, 351)

> Nous savons aujourd'hui que l'Affaire ne fut pas un accident, que les deux familles d'esprit qu'elle avait dressées l'une contre l'autre n'ont pas cessé de s'affronter. . . . (BN II, 447)

> [Let me tell you, Philippe Barrès: the question that is being put before our national conscience today is still the same as the question

posed sixty years ago. Just who was it that was jeopardizing the honor of the army at that time, General Mercier or Lieutenant Colonel Picquart? And today, is it General Bollardière or the men who apply the methods already exposed and condemned by the report of the International Commission? This report protested against the use of concentration camps, and it will be corroborated by the Safeguard Commission's report. There can be no doubt about it, since the government has not made this report public.

"What great courage it takes for you to be Dreyfus nowadays!" people will scoff. What great courage, yes indeed: the Dreyfus affair is still happening and the War Offices will never be closed.

We now know that the Affair was no accident, that the two mindsets pitted against each other then have not ceased their clash . . . .]

Over and over, Mauriac leads his readers to see the crisis in Algeria as an extension of the Dreyfus affair, for two fundamental reasons: first, he believes such historical parallels are key to understanding the true nature of the conflict, and second, he intends to jolt the "silent majority" out of the indifference that leads to tacit approval of political crimes.

Nowhere is the stress on historical continuity between the Dreyfus affair and the later ordeals of the Dark Years and the Algerian war more striking than in the piece written on 3 August 1957. Reading the *Journal* written by Ernst Jünger in Paris during the Occupation, Mauriac finds that the early 1940s as well as the late 1950s can be illuminated by the divisive tumult that shook France at the turn of the century. In fact, Jünger's observations spur Mauriac to unsettling reflections on a sort of "banality of evil" present not only among those who perpetrate violence against members of a certain race and against intellectuals, but also among all those who tacitly or overtly approve of such brutality. The passage bears citing at length. First, Mauriac compares his own situation as a writer in Paris in 1957 to that of Jünger in 1942 and 1943:

"Le tremblement de terre passe, on s'en prend au sismographe. On ne peut pourtant pas faire expier les typhons au baromètre, si l'on tient à se distinguer des primitifs." Cette note d'Ernst Jünger dans la préface de son *Journal* des années 1942–1943 (il fut à Paris l'un des "occupants") marque très exactement le niveau moyen qu'a atteint l'intelligence politique française en 1957—si nous en jugeons d'après une certaine presse.

Les nazis ne pouvaient que haïr cet écrivain qui les connaissait. Après quatorze ans, ils continuent de haïr tout écrivain qui les connaît—car les nazis sont là toujours. (BN I, 491)

["Once the earthquake is over, people blame the seismographer. But if they are intent on distinguishing themselves from primitives, they cannot make the barometer atone for typhoons." This remark by Ernst Jünger in the preface of his *Journal* of the years 1942–1943 (he was one of the "occupiers" in Paris) very accurately indicates the average level of French political thought in 1957, judging from certain newspapers.

The Nazis could only hate this writer who knew them. Fourteen years later, they still hate any writer who knows them, for the Nazis are still there.]

In condemning the use of torture in Algeria and Morocco by his own countrymen in the 1950s, Mauriac had encountered hostility similar to that feared by Jünger when recording Nazi atrocities. Mauriac thus depicts as Nazis those wishing to suppress the truth about torture. We would be wrong to dismiss his charge that "les nazis sont là toujours" (the Nazis are still there)—that is, not among the Germans, but in France's own political and military institutions—as mere rhetoric. Mauriac goes on to drive home a point even harder for the French to countenance, as he articulates the lessons to be learned from the history of nazism:

Le 18 octobre 1943, Jünger note que "Kniebolo (c'est Hitler qu'ils appellent ainsi) est un phénomène européen." Ce que nous comprenons mieux aujourd'hui, c'est que Kniebolo est un phénomène humain. Son avènement, son ascension, son triomphe ont déchaîné partout à la fois une bête féroce qui n'a pas été ensevelie avec lui sous le béton de la Grande Chancellerie. Elle erre librement désormais dans les ruines des partis et des idéologies.

Ce qu'Ernst Jünger a bien vu et a osé écrire dès 1943, c'est cette vérité insoutenable et qu'il faut pourtant regarder en face: pour une certaine race d'hommes, très répandue, et à laquelle peut-être, si peu que ce soit, chacun de nous est lié, les idées ne sont que des prétextes dont la férocité se couvre. (BN I, 491)

[On 18 October 1943, Jünger notes that "Kniebolo (as the Germans called Hitler) is a European phenomenon." What we understand better today is that Kniebolo is a human phenomenon. His political debut, his rise to power, and his triumph unleashed everywhere a ferocious beast that was not buried with him under the concrete of the Great Chancery. This beast is roaming about freely among the ruins of parties and ideologies.

What Jünger saw so clearly and dared to write already in 1943 is the following unbearable truth, a truth that we must nevertheless face squarely: for a very widespread breed of people, to which we are perhaps all linked to a slight degree, ideas are only pretexts used by the ferocious to mask their true nature.]

Mauriac thus contends that the systematic use of violence and cruelty is not just an aberration that can be ascribed to "Nazi barbarity" but a practice that can be found to some degree in all societies, including France. As evidence, he points to the French who willingly participated in Nazi crimes during the Occupation, to his contemporaries who torture in Algeria, and to those who would hush up the matter.

Et maintenant osons arrêter notre pensée, nous autres Français, sur ce que Jünger écrit dans son *Journal* le 8 février 1942. Il vient de recevoir sur les intentions de Kniebolo [Hitler], sur ses projets de massacre, des renseignements qui le terrifient. Et il ajoute: "Il faut aussi que l'on sache que nombre de Français approuvent de tels projets et sont avides de prendre du service comme bourreaux." Cette parole est dure et comment la supporter? Mais cette parole se vérifie depuis quatorze ans, chaque jour, moins peut-être par des attentats contre la justice, comme celui dont s'est fait l'écho le dernier *Express* en publiant la lettre de Mme Henri Alleg, que par le consentement d'une part de l'opinion, par le silence de la presse, par l'exaspération qu'éveillent ceux qui protestent: "Mais taisez-vous donc, imbéciles!" C'est ce que nous entendons gronder autour de nous. (BN I, 492)

[And now we French people must dare to ponder what Jünger wrote in his *Journal* on 8 February 1942. He has just received some terrifying information on Kniebolo's [[Hitler's]] intentions and on the Führer's plans for massacre. And Jünger adds: "People should also know that a number of the French approve such plans and are eager to take on jobs as executioners." These words are harsh: how can we bear to hear them?

> But they have been proven to be true every day for fourteen years, perhaps less by the crimes against justice such as those reported in the latest edition of *L'Express* containing the letter from Madame Alleg, than by the consent from a segment of public opinion, by the silence of the press, and by the exasperation aroused by those who protest: "When are you going to shut up, you idiots!" That is what we hear people muttering all around us between clenched teeth.]

And just as Mauriac refuses to confine historical examples of endemic brutality and injustice to certain nations, he cites the Dreyfus affair to refute the notion that such abuses might simply be exceptions or excesses brought on by the harsh circumstances of war or occupation.

> La pensée m'est venue, en lisant le *Journal* d'Ernst Jünger, que l'affaire Dreyfus ne nous a pas fait connaître des événements étranges ni des êtres exceptionnels. . . . Le même homme qui, il y a soixante ans, faisait des faux pour maintenir un innocent au bagne, menaçait l'autre jour un lieutenant français de le salir et de le perdre s'il ne se taisait sur ce qu'il avait vu. (BN I, 492)
>
> [It occurred to me while reading Ernst Jünger's *Journal* that the Dreyfus affair confronted us neither with strange events nor with unusual people. . . . The same man who was forging documents sixty years ago in order to keep an innocent man in the pen was just the other day threatening to smear a French lieutenant and ruin him if he did not keep silent about what he had seen.]

A quick recall of the context of the late 1950s reveals Mauriac's audacity here. Little more than a decade had passed since the end of World War II, and according to the chronology of memory laid out by Henry Rousso, France had just turned its attention from the healing and rebuilding during the years of "Unfinished Mourning" to glorifying the Resistance (while suppressing the memory of Vichy) during the phase of "Repressions." Mauriac was not alone in portraying as fascists the French ultranationalists willing to use any and all means in order to keep Algeria in France's possession, nor was he the only one to see the sharp political divisions occasioned by the Algerian war as reminiscent of the Dreyfus affair.[25] The tendency, however, was to claim the heritage

25. Henry Rousso, *The Vichy Syndrome*, trans. Arthur Goldhammer (Cambridge,

of the Resistance as a model for opposition to the war in Algeria while at the same time using the specter of fascism to demonize political adversaries.[26]

Mauriac follows a different tack. By conspicuously drawing his lessons on political violence from the writing of one of the German soldiers occupying France in 1942 and 1943, he makes any such conveniently Manichaean divisions impossible. In the second paragraph cited above, the potential for barbarity is clearly not limited to any ideology or national group, but rather remains latent in all human beings, since "si peu que ce soit, chacun de nous est lié" (to a slight degree, we are all linked) to the category of men—moreover "très répandue" (very widespread)—capable of such atrocities (which as we know from Christopher Browning were indeed often committed by "ordinary men"). That is why Mauriac, once again following Jünger, sees Hitler not as a sort of freak or monster arising out of the depths of some supposed "Teutonic barbarity" (as would be so tempting for the French narrator of history in portraying the "Führer"), but as a disturbingly human phenomenon to be understood in the context of European history and culture. Hitler represents not only a "phénomène européen" (European phenomenon), as Jünger suggested, but also a "phénomène humain" (human phenomenon) still lurking "dans les ruines des partis et des idéologies" (amid the ruins of parties and ideologies). As if all that were not enough, Mauriac suggests that even such Nazi tendencies are to be situated in the continuity of French history. Even in the extreme examples just cited, we would be wrong to reduce them to the status of rhetorical expedients, particularly since the parallels drawn between the Dreyfus affair, on the one hand, and the Occupation and the Algerian war, on the other hand, go against the grain of convention, which in France typically uses the past to legitimate political power and galvanize public support.

Far from legitimating any party or individual or bolstering some dominant ideology, the historical continuity underscored in Mauriac's editorials turns out on the contrary to be deeply disturbing. Instead of

Mass., and London: Harvard University Press, 1991), 75–76. Cf. also Jean-Pierre Rioux, "La guerre d'Algérie dans l'histoire des intellectuels français," in *La Guerre d'Algérie et les intellectuels français*, 35–44.

26. Rousso, *The Vichy Syndrome*, 81–82.

stirring up his compatriots' ire against a common exterior enemy, Mauriac seeks to deflate the national hubris of France's racist, oppressive practices in Algeria. Even when the crimes committed by Nazi sympathizers and collaborators could easily have been considered a foreign import and thus an aberration, Mauriac relates them back to the mainstream of French history by connecting them to the Dreyfus affair.

Mauriac continually confronts the darkest episodes of France's past. Yet, in the long run, he is no iconoclast and remains attached to "une certaine idée de la France" and thus a certain idealism. Understood from the perspective of history, the present is not isolated, nor autonomous, nor disconnected, but rather appears as another episode in a larger drama that has been unfolding for generations. Now it may well be that the Algerian conflict prompted Mauriac to "remember" the affair as prophetic, since he indicates that the experience of current events can shed new light on the past. In a long reflection on the persistent threat that the army posed to democratic institutions in France, Mauriac points to such reciprocity between the intelligence of the past and his understanding of the present:

> Que faut-il donc faire pour que l'armée ne soit plus une nation dans la nation? Je n'ai pas lu *L'Armée nouvelle* de Jaurès. J'ignore ce qu'il conseillait pour remédier aux maux que l'affaire Dreyfus venait de révéler au monde. . . .
>
> . . . Ces soixante premières années du siècle, l'événement d'Algérie les éclaire, en montre le courant profond. C'est l'histoire dont les hommes de mon âge auront été les témoins, et nous ne saurions mieux faire que de la reprendre et de la méditer, et d'en tirer, chacun à notre place, l'amère leçon. (BN II, 380–81)
>
> [So what must we do in order that the army might no longer be a nation within the nation? I have not read *The New Army* by Jaurès. I do not know what he was recommending to remedy the evils that the Dreyfus affair had just revealed to the world. . . .
>
> . . . The events in Algeria shed light on these first sixty years of the century and show their underlying current. People of my age have witnessed this history, and the best thing we could do is to go back over it, meditate it, and, each according to our own station, draw its bitter lesson.]

The Dreyfus affair offers Mauriac a paradigm for understanding the conflict in Algeria, but at the same time the events of the Algerian war (and of the Occupation years) lend an even wider significance to the affair that had rocked France over a half a century earlier. For Mauriac, French history constitutes an ongoing story, a saga of narratives and experiences handed down from one generation to the next. The many references to the Dreyfus affair thus serve not only as filter through which contemporary events and issues are to be interpreted but also as one of the "lieux de mémoire" (places of memory) that have come to constitute the fabric of France's collective memory and even of its very identity, as we shall see in greater detail in Chapter 5.

In the broader context of narrating the past, the *Bloc-notes* represents, as Mauriac himself insists, the writings of an informed observer and French citizen assuming his responsibilities as a protagonist in history. Instead of attacking or abandoning the very notions of history, morality, and national identity as arbitrary social constructions inherently determined and skewed by some political agenda, Mauriac clearly affirms his French Christian identity as his point of departure, stating in his 15 December 1955 editorial that "ce sont des faits d'histoire jugés par une conscience chrétienne" (BN I, 311; these are facts of history judged by a Christian conscience], and in his "Bloc-notes" of 4 January 1957 that "je l'observe [l'histoire] en chrétien, c'est-à-dire en homme partial" (BN I, 423; I observe [history] as a Christian, in other words, as someone who is partial). As for being French, admits Mauriac, ". . . ce peuple est mon peuple, son Histoire est mon Histoire" (BN II, 48; this people is my people, its history is my history). He even goes so far as to exclaim: "Mais à mon âge, en fait d'aventure, il n'arrive plus guère que ce qui arrive au pays, et je n'ai plus d'autre histoire que la sienne" (BN II, 41; But as far as adventures go, at my age the only thing that happens to me is what happens to this country, and I have no other history besides that one). Mauriac's integrity as a narrator of history resides to no small degree in his recognition that his own national and religious identity implicates him willy-nilly in events past and present. When situating himself as French and Catholic, however, Mauriac avoids the pitfalls of Manichaeanism and selective memory, which, as cogently argued by

Tzvetan Todorov, undermine the authority of many narrators implicitly or explicitly dispensing lessons on the past.

As dramatically evident in the above-cited commentary on Jünger, Mauriac manages to transcend the perceptions and political agenda of his own group without renouncing or denying his identity as a member of it. He therefore offers a singular exception to Todorov and Sartre's contention that the lesson that the French should have learned as victims of Nazi atrocities during the Occupation was totally lost on them ten years later, when they became perpetrators of similar crimes in Algeria.[27] Mauriac's editorials prove that a narrator of history can articulate the lessons of the past in a non-self-serving, nonideological, nonnationalistic way by viewing the past from the perspective of humanity.

In many cases, Mauriac summons his readers to greater humanity by pointing out the extreme inhumanity of those claiming to champion the causes of Christianity or French civilization. However, his invocation of humanity is not limited to the denunciation of barbaric acts committed by his compatriots or coreligionists. He rather goes on to affirm the humanity of others, and in particular the humanity of France's adversaries. Here again, he does not confine himself to the kind of negative example we find in his commentary on Jünger, where he argues that the barbaric practices of the Nazis were ultimately the doing of human beings who are sadly to be found among all peoples of all times, including the French of the late 1950s. He instead points out the fundamental humanity of the Algerians' desire to affirm their identity through their own historical narrative.

The twofold recognition that France's narrative of its past will be subject to the scrutiny of other peoples and that other peoples are writing their own story constitutes one of Mauriac's greatest assets as a narrator of history. Both find powerful expression in a "Bloc-notes" written to protest the execution of two pro-FLN militants, whose case is all the more poignant in view of their status as European and Muslim schoolteachers married to each other:

27. Todorov, "Ten Years without Primo Levi," 6; *Mémoire du mal*, 182. I shall not address the obvious fallacy of attributing one common behavior to all the French either in the context of the Occupation or of the Algerian war.

Lundi 27 janvier 1958
Le curé d'Uruffe [convicted for a nonpolitical double murder, according to Touzot, 24 n1] ne montera pas sur l'échafaud. Abdelkader et Jacqueline Guerroudj, instituteurs d'Algérie, condamnés à mort, y monteront s'ils n'obtiennent pas leur grâce. Pour quel crime? Cette Française, cette mère de famille (elle a cinq enfants), cet Algérien sont communistes et affiliés au FLN. Cela est vrai comme il est vrai qu'elle a remis à Iveton la bombe qu'il déposa dans l'immeuble du Gaz d'Algérie. Mais l'engin avait été réglé de telle sorte qu'il ne pût éclater qu'après la sortie du personnel. Il n'y a pas eu de victime, il ne pouvait y avoir aucun. Le Tribunal a admis qu'il ne s'agissait pas d'une tentative d'homicide volontaire: ces singuliers criminels avaient prémédité de ne pas verser le sang. Alors pourquoi un verdict impitoyable, sinon parce qu'Iveton, lui, a été exécuté? Comme si ce malheureux eût exigé d'être rejoint par les deux instituteurs et qu'il fallût apaiser son ombre!

Que leur acte mérite une dure sanction, qui le nierait? Mais la mort! La très noble déclaration de Guerroudj devant ses juges témoignait de ce même déchirement entre la race et la culture que naguère encore, dans *Le Monde*, nous confiait Jean Amrouche. La guerre d'Algérie peut tenir tout entière dans un seul être. Le couteau de la guillotine ne constitue pas une réponse valable à la question posée au peuple français par un de ces hommes qui ont appris notre histoire, mais ce n'était pas la leur; et ils ont résolu d'en avoir une. Ils l'écrivent en ce moment. Et nous devrions y tenir un rôle qui n'est pas celui dont la politique de M. Robert Lacoste nous impose le masque horrible. (BN II, 24–25)

[Monday, 27 January 1958
The parish priest of Uruffe [[who was convicted for a nonpolitical double murder, according to Touzot, 24 n1]] will not be sent to the scaffold. Abdelkader and Jacqueline Guerroudj, the two elementary-school teachers from Algeria who were condemned to death will be sent to the guillotine unless they obtain a pardon. For what crime? This French woman, this mother of five children, and this Algerian man are communists affiliated with the FLN. That is true, and it is equally true that she gave Iveton the bomb that he placed in the Gaz d'Algérie building. But the device had been set in such a way that it could only go off after the personnel had left. There were no victims, and it was not possible for there to have been any victims. The Court admitted that this was not an attempted murder: these strange criminals had premeditated not to shed blood. So why such a pitiless verdict, unless it was because

> Iveton was for his part executed? It is as if this miserable fellow had demanded that the two schoolteachers join him and that it were necessary to appease his ghost!
>
> Who would deny that their deeds deserved severe punishment? But the death penalty! Guerroudj's own noble declaration before his judges was a testimony to the agonizing split allegiance [[of a man]] torn between race and culture, the same dilemma that Jean Amrouche confided to us. The entire war in Algeria can fit inside one single person. The cutting edge of the guillotine does not constitute a valid answer to the question posed to the French people by one of these men: they have learned our history, but it wasn't theirs, and they have resolved to have one. They are writing it at this very moment. And the role that we should play in it is not the one whose horrible mask we are made to wear because of Robert Lacoste's policies.]

Even while condemning the bombing of an administrative building, Mauriac does not dismiss the perpetrators as criminals, as was so easily and commonly done by the French when dealing with the Algerian rebels. The author of the *Bloc-notes* instead points out the alienation of an Algerian obliged to learn the dominating power's history and his concomitant attempt to compose the saga of his own people by liberating them from the colonial regime. At the same time, Mauriac deplores the role that the Algerians are seeing the French play in this history.

Acknowledging his identity as a French Catholic approaching history through humanity, Mauriac nevertheless affirms a multiplicity of perspectives in pointing out that the role the French assign themselves in their narrative of history is not necessarily the one that will be assigned by others. They cannot unilaterally impose their version of events, but must take into account the experience, perceptions, and aspirations of the Algerians. As Mauriac contends, the French must situate themselves with respect to the image that Algerians and other peoples have of them.

We can now better measure the importance of the changing, often self-reversing, point of view already identified in Chapter 2. Many pages of the *Bloc-notes* compel the reader to heed the gaze of others and consider France's history past and present "from the outside" as in the following lines prompted by the widely published testimony of Algerian refugees:

Lundi 3 mars 1958
X. est arrivé cette nuit de Tunis dans le même avion que M. Murphy. Il a encore dans le regard l'horreur des camps réfugiés algériens qu'il a visités sous la neige, dans les oreilles les récits, horribles pour nous, qu'ils ont faits aux journalistes du monde entier. X. protestait: "Ce n'est peut-être pas vrai!," mais, en ce qui nous concerne, le monde entier désormais croit le pire.

Des pharisiens? Oui, certes. Dans mon courrier, ce matin, je trouve l'article découpé d'un journal de Stockholm: sous une caricature insultante, une main rageuse a écrit: "Et nous qui avons aimé la France!" Je ne jette pas ce papier. Il me concerne, et chacun de nous. Il faut nous familiariser avec le visage qu'une politique butée nous impose aux yeux des autres nations. (BN II, 40)

[Monday, 3 March 1958
Mr. X arrived from Tunis tonight on the same plane as Mr. Murphy. His gaze still reflects the horror of the Algerian refugee camps that he visited in the snow. His ears still echo with the stories that these refugees told to journalists from around the world and which give us a horrible image. Mr. X kept on protesting: "Maybe it's not true!" As far as we are concerned, however, the whole world believes the worst.

Are they self-righteous? Of course they are. In my mail, this morning, I found an article clipped from a Stockholm newspaper. Under an insulting political cartoon, a furious hand had written: "And to think that we loved France!" I am not throwing this paper away. It concerns me and every one of us. We need to familiarize ourselves with the face that our dogged intransigence has given us in the eyes of other nations.]

Instead of relating the details of the military abuses alluded to here, Mauriac focuses on the impact that they have visibly made first on a personal friend, and then on world opinion as evidenced by the Swedish newspaper clipping: the French find themselves subjected to the judgment of observers reading a historical narrative that escapes France's control.

In the *Bloc-notes*, standing in the judgment of history ultimately means submitting to this outside scrutiny. Such is the case in the editorial penned by Mauriac shortly after the publication of Henri Alleg's *La Question:*

Dimanche 23 février 1958
La Question, de Henri Alleg, aux Éditions de Minuit. Il n'y a plus rien à dire. Tout ce qui a été dénoncé reçoit ici, d'une des victimes, un témoignage sobre, qui a le ton neutre de l'histoire. Car cette histoire sera écrite, elle est déjà écrite. (BN II, 36)

[Sunday, 23 February 1958
La Question, by Henri Alleg, has been published by the Éditions de Minuit. There is nothing more to say. In this book, all that has been exposed and condemned is confirmed in the sober testimony of one of the victims who speaks in the neutral tone of history. For this story of history will be written. It has already been written.]

Here again, Mauriac presents the specific event not as an isolated incident but as part of a story that is being composed. This story of history will escape the designs of its protagonists, and in particular the French, who will not be able to simply "edit out" the facts that are not to their liking. In the end, "the facts" will be disclosed and incorporated into a history of the Algerian war based on the accounts of others and subject to the judgment of humanity, including those who have suffered injustice and oppression from the French.

As we saw when analyzing "1er mars 1955" in Chapter 2, Mauriac places himself and his readers under the judgment of history, in that they are summoned to assume responsibility for events to which all are a party as protagonists or witnesses. In the conclusion to that same "Bloc-notes," Mauriac goes on to underscore the idea that France will not be able to mold the judgment of history according to the self-images it has stamped on its coins and printed in its history texts:

Coïncidence: reçu ce matin la lettre d'un confrère de race kabyle, qui fait écho à ce que j'écrivais hier au sujet des nouvelles générations de son pays: "Rien n'est perdu, me dit-il, quand il s'agit des hommes de mon âge: la France est en eux, qu'ils ne sauraient renier sans périr. Mais il y a ces garçons et ces filles pour qui la France n'a point le visage de Marianne ou de cette Semeuse qu'on voyait sur les pièces d'argent, mais une trogne de flic." (BN I, 154)

[What a coincidence: this morning I received a letter from a fellow editorialist who is a Kabyle. He echoes what I was writing yesterday about

> the younger generations in his native region: "It is not a lost cause," he told me, "when we are dealing with men of my age: France is within them, and they would not be able to renounce France without perishing. There are, however, these young men and women for whom France is emphatically not represented by the face of Marianne or by the woman sowing grain as seen on coins, but rather by the ugly mug of a cop."]

The outside perspective on events is made even more vivid here by the fact that Mauriac has given the final word in this editorial to a non-European observer.

Mauriac vigorously rejects the one-sided narration of events, and instead leads his readers to view France's military operations through the eyes of those who suffer their consequences, as we observe in his vigorous indictment of the bombing of Sakhiet written for the 13 February 1958 edition of *L'Express.* In response to antiaircraft fire coming from a little Tunisian village just across the border from Algeria, the French army carried out a ferocious bombing raid that killed seventy-eight people and created an international outcry (Touzot, BN II, 29n). Shortly after, Mauriac lashed out against the French press and political leadership for attempting to discount if not totally ignore the brutality of the bombing:

> . . . les conséquences politiques d'une bagatelle comme un village détruit avec son école et ses enfants ne leur apparaissent pas toujours [aux généraux]. Certains de ces grands chefs ignorent que des petits cadavres alignés d'écoliers—fussent-ils arabes—cela ne passe pas inaperçu. Non qu'ils soient insensibles, mais leur sensibilité est particulière. . . .
>
> S'il n'y avait le reste du monde, cette aventure se liquiderait sans histoire. J'ignore si nous sommes un peuple léger, mais nous ne sommes pas un peuple tendre. Sauf lorsque ce sont des Hongrois qui sont tués et des Russes qui les tuent. Alors tous les crocodiles de la presse ruissellent. Il faut éponger dans les salles de rédaction.
>
> *France-Soir* le notait dès dimanche: le bombardement de Sakhiet a causé beaucoup de satisfaction dans les milieux français d'Algérie. Du côté musulman, selon notre confrère, on se serait montré plus réservé. Nous l'aurions juré. Mais enfin l'important est que M. Lacoste soit satisfait, s'il l'est, et que le général Salan le soit plus encore, et que les Français d'Algérie se sentent un peu détendus. . . .

Et pour ce qui est de l'opinion en France, M. Félix Gaillard [the French premier] est tranquille. La presse connaît son métier. Ce titre qui me saute aux yeux, ce matin, quelle merveille! "La riposte française de Sakhiet!" Riposte française, cela sonne clair: quel joli cliquetis! On pense à des mots cinglants à la Cyrano—et pas du tout à des cadavres de pauvres. C'était nous en effet qui ripostions—mais non à ce qu'avaient dit ou fait ces paysans, ces écoliers. Ils ne nous avaient rien dit ni rien fait. Ils resteront éternellement étonnés de ce sommeil dans lequel le général Salan et M. Lacoste, qu'ils ne connaissent pas, les ont précipités sans crier gare. (BN II, 29–31)

[. . . the political consequences of a trifle such as the destruction of a village along with its school and its children are not always apparent to them [[the generals]]. Some of these great leaders don't know that, even if they are Arabs, the little bodies of schoolchildren lined up in a row will not escape public attention. Not that these men are insensitive, but their sensitivity is of a very particular kind. . . .

If the rest of the world were not there, this escapade could be liquidated without any fuss. I don't know if we are a frivolous people, but we are not tender, except when it is Hungarians who are being killed and Russians who are killing them. Then tears stream from all the crocodiles in the press. They have to mop the offices of the editorial board.

[[The newspaper]] *France-Soir* made such an observation Sunday already: the bombing of Sakhiet provided great satisfaction among the French in Algeria. According to our colleagues, the reaction was much more reserved among the Muslim population. We would have presumed as much. But, after all, the main thing is for Monsieur Lacoste to be satisfied, if indeed he is, for General Salan to be even more satisfied, and for the French in Algeria to feel a bit more relaxed. . . .

As for public opinion in France, Monsieur Félix Gaillard [[the French premier]] rests assured. The press knows its job. What a marvelous headline jumped out at me this morning! "France Strikes Back at Sakhiet!" France strikes back: what a crisp sound, with a nice ring to it! It reminds us of Cyrano [[de Bergerac]]'s words, and not at all of the bodies of poor people. We did indeed strike back, but not at what these peasants and these schoolchildren had said or done. They shall remain forever surprised in this sleep into which General Salan and Monsieur Lacoste precipitated them without warning.]

Mauriac first points out that not everyone will find it as easy as did General Salan (the commander of French military forces in Algeria) and his colleagues to wipe the death of these Arab children off the historical slate. He then proceeds to denounce the selective sensitivity that allows his compatriots to remain indifferent to the suffering inflicted on Muslims in North Africa while at the same time moving them to a flood of tears over the brutal suppression of Hungarians by the Soviets. The irony directed against *France-Soir*'s smug reports of "satisfaction" among the European population of Algeria and its French governor virtually seethes with outrage at such callous indifference to Muslims. A similar irony dismantles the rhetoric of *Le Figaro*'s headline, "La riposte française de Sakhiet" (The French Strike Back at Sakhiet), which would have the French public view the bombing as a deft maneuver in a sort of gentlemen's duel. Mauriac thwarts this verbal slight of hand, however, first by calling attention to the headline's specific linguistic character, then by referring the clever formula back to the totally incongruous context of the burlesque *Cyrano de Bergerac*, and finally by pointing to the bodies of the civilians killed in the incident.

Although Mauriac does not explicitly invoke the past in this piece, he nonetheless obliges us to read the bombing of Sakhiet as a page in the ongoing narrative of history being written within and without France. He thus casts a harsh light on the French military's brutality and subjects the ethnocentric presumptions of the French press, government, and military officials to the uncompromising judgment that will inevitably be rendered by those who are witnesses to this historical violence both on-site and throughout the world.

Throughout the *Bloc-notes*, Mauriac not only conveys the pathos of such events as the bombing of Sakhiet decried here, he provides a truly human view of history by narrating from the perspective of the French protagonists as well as from the perspective of those who experience the event as victims or outside observers. Thanks to these multiple perspectives, he communicates the lessons of events past and present, but nevertheless avoids the instrumentalization of history we find in narratives arranged according to the ideological or political agenda of some particular nation or social group. Such narratives might offer interesting illustrations of their authors' convictions, but will ultimately teach us little beyond what was planted in them to begin with. For history to be instructive, it must lead us out of our own immediate context, beyond the presumptions of our own group, and past our own experience. It must not be a mere construction mirroring our own values and principles, however noble or just they may be. It must be "other," opaque to our acquired knowledge and intellectual analysis. It must engage us in a dialogue that calls our own values, experience, and ideas into question (though not necessarily invalidating them). It must in short lead us to assess ourselves, our group, and our time from another perspective not beholden to pious self-images, self-interested agendas, or ideological a priori's.

Such is the history narrated in the *Bloc-notes*. Mauriac's narration of the past is certainly motivated by the issues of (in)justice and (in)humanity, particulary during the Algerian war. But as many historians have often pointed out, knowledge of the past is always grounded in the present: we are always driven to study the events of history in order to understand some aspect of our own current situation,[28] if only to realize that the present is radically different from the way things used to be and therefore not a given but the fruit of a long, complex evolution of human society over time.

But Mauriac's narration of history is distinctive with respect to the French intellectual milieu of the 1950s and 1960s. Unlike his counterparts among the Parisian intelligentsia dominated by Sartre and *Les Temps modernes*, he does not seek to legitimate his views by invoking history as an immanent process driving events toward some ultimate end. Nor does he seek to ground the axioms of political doctrine in some putative "historical" necessity, either in that of maintaining an "Algérie française" or in moving toward a classless society. He instead refuses to encapsulate history in terms of ideology. His "Bloc-notes" rather relate concrete human experiences and explore issues raised by particular developments: history is not merely the interplay of ideas, it is the flesh-and-blood drama of human beings as engaged by specific events.

28. See Richard J. Evans, *In Defense of History* (New York and London: W. W. Norton, 1999), 72–75. See also Henry Rousso, *La hantise du passé* (Paris: Les éditions Textuel, 1998), 23–25; Prost, *Douze leçons sur l'histoire*, 88–97; and Furet, *L'atelier de l'histoire*, 30–31.

We have studied Mauriac's narration of history in great textual detail precisely because one must follow the specific contours of events as well as his references to the past in order to appreciate his general approach. However, if Mauriac is not driven by theoretical paradigms, neither does he limit his narration of history to what Todorov has called "literal memory." He does not simply reiterate some narrative of a supposedly self-contained past presented as the subject of commemoration or incantation. We find him on the contrary engaging in a continual dialogue with the past; comparing one historical figure, event, context, or epoch with another; analyzing, assessing, and judging through the common denominator of humanity. He does indeed focus on the past that bears most on his identity as bourgeois, French, and Catholic, but far from pleading his cause by championing the deeds of his own group over those of others, he subjects the history of France, Europe, and even Christian civilization to severe scrutiny from without, on the basis of a shared humanity (though most strongly affirmed through the life and death of Jesus). As such, the "Bloc-notes" of the 1950s provide both an eloquent plea for justice and human rights in the context of the Algerian war and a model for engaging pressing issues of the present in reference to salient events of the past. The return to power of Charles de Gaulle and the end of the colonial crisis, however, bring about a major shift in Mauriac's perspective, as he thereafter shows less interest in articulating the lessons of history than in ensuring the continuity of France's heritage.

5 IN SEARCH OF TIMES PAST

> Il s'est produit un séisme, une coupure énorme entre hier et aujourd'hui, alors qu'il n'y en avait eu aucune entre hier et tout ce qui avait précédé. . . . ("Samedi 2 juillet 1966," BN IV, 289)
>
> Ainsi je recherche avidement les moindres signes d'une permanence des temps d'autrefois, ce qui a résisté, ce qui résistera encore un peu à l'homme fou de technique. ("Jeudi 13 septembre 1962," BN III, 228)
>
> [There has been an earthquake, an enormous break between the past and the present, whereas there had been none between the past and everything that had come before. . . .
>
> Thus I eagerly seek out the slightest signs of a permanence of times past: what has withstood the years, what will hold up a little longer against a humanity crazed with technology.]

It is now a commonplace to observe that throughout the 1940s, 1950s, and 1960s, Mauriac's intense activity in the French press largely eclipsed the literary production that had established his renown as a novelist depicting stark sexual, social, and spiritual conflicts among the bourgeois Catholics of the Bordeaux region. Weighing in on the side of the Spanish Republicans fighting against Franco, Mauriac quickly appeared as a prominent voice in French politics and culture during the last years of the Third Republic and went on to become the most widely read editorialist of the Fourth Republic.[1]

While his detractors attributed this major career shift to waning inspiration, if not diminishing talent, Mauriac himself presented his move from aesthetics to politics in a much different light. Speaking to *L'Express* (the venue of his own *Bloc-notes* at the time of this April 1957 interview), he characterized his turn from art to history in the following terms:

> . . . J'ai commencé à me détacher de la fiction au moment de la Guerre d'Espagne, par exemple. Je vivais jusque-là dans une espèce de rêve, de monde fictif, et la guerre d'Espagne a révéillé le garçon silloniste[2] que j'étais à vingt ans. . . . Je me suis débattu et puis il y a eu l'occupation, la Libération. Je me suis évadé le plus que j'ai pu entretemps: n'empêche que, depuis la guerre d'Espagne, je ne peux plus me détourner de la condition humaine telle qu'elle est imposée aux hommes par d'autres hommes. Joubert disait que "la révolution avait chassé son esprit du monde réel en le lui rendant trop horrible." Pour moi, c'est le contraire: l'horreur du monde réel m'a chassé de la fiction.[3]
>
> [. . . I began to move away from fiction, particularly at the time of the Spanish civil war. Up until then, I had been living in a sort of dream or fictitious world, and the Spanish civil war revived the aspiration to Christian piety and social justice that I shared with the *Sillon* at the age of twenty. . . . I struggled with these questions and then came the Occupation and the Liberation. I found as many escapes from reality as I could in the meantime: the fact remains that, ever since the Spanish civil war, I can no longer turn away from the human condition such as it is imposed on some people by others. Joubert used to say that "the [French] Revolution had driven his mind out of the real world by making the world so horrible." The opposite is true in my case: the horror of the real world has driven me away from fiction.]

Although couching his remarks in the unpretentious terms of personal ethics instead of some full-blown philosophical system, Mauriac traces

1. Sirinelli, "Mauriac, un intellectuel engagé sous la IVe République," 146–53.
2. Led by Marc Sangnier, "Le Sillon" was a movement of young Catholics seeking to regain the focus on social justice and unpretentious spirituality.
3. "Le Métier d'écrivain," *L'Express*, 5 April 1957, pp. 17–20, p. 19.

a path not at all unlike the one Sartre followed in abandoning his aloof skepticism (moreover maintained throughout the Spanish civil war) in favor of political commitment and attention to history: for Sartre as for an entire generation, World War II and the Occupation had starkly demonstrated that the human condition was to be understood and decided not within the confines of literary narrative but rather in the arena of history. And we have amply seen that Mauriac engaged the questions of human psychology, identity, and destiny through the pressing issues of injustice, oppression, and torture posed concretely by the Algerian war that was raging at the time of the statements quoted above.

Yet if Mauriac pointedly refused any unilateral, uncritical narrative of France's past as a pretext for avoiding the vexing political questions of the present, neither did he see the events of the political arena as exhausting the drama of history. The "horreur" of historical reality may have dissipated aesthetic presumptions, but it did not lead Mauriac to abandon the questions of personal and religious identity that had always infused his novels, nor did it ultimately lead him to abandon the strong sense of national identity that had always informed his politics.

The transition from literary creation to editorial commentary acknowledged by Mauriac at the height of the Battle of Algiers in 1957 undeniably represents a major turning point, but hardly constitutes the last development or the unique focus of the *Bloc-notes.* In unswerving support of de Gaulle and in protest of his colleagues' virulent attacks on the general's politics, Mauriac parted company from Jean-Jacques Servan-Schreiber and *L'Express* in 1961. As the bloody Algerian conflict ended in 1962, the editorialist now writing for *Le Figaro littéraire* directed increasing attention to the disappearance of "la vieille France" (old France) in the wake of France's belated but rapid industrialization, the advent of a consumer society, and the Americanization of French culture.

Indeed, the *Bloc-notes* provides an eloquent, firsthand account of what we now understand as the radical transformations of "Les Trente Glorieuses" (The Thirty Glorious Years) experienced by a Frenchman who had come of age in a society whose institutions and *moeurs* still belonged to the nineteenth century. In this context, Mauriac pens editorials not so much to teach the lessons of history, but rather to revive it, to preserve from oblivion the seemingly ephemeral experiences of times past, to reveal the rich legacy of humanity inscribed on the countrysides, landscapes, and edifices testifying to both the triumphs and the crimes of previous generations. In focusing on this aspect of the story of history, Mauriac strives to capture the unique human identity constituted on a personal, social, and national level precisely by the accumulation of experience over the years.

Mauriac's many references to the past thus serve not only as a filter through which contemporary events and issues are to be interpreted but also as one of the "lieux de mémoire" (places of memory) that have become an integral part of French identity. For the tendency to project the controversies of the present into the past, and vice versa, is not specific to the writing of François Mauriac but on the contrary widely cited as a distinctive trait of contemporary French culture. As the industrialized, urban France of the twentieth century moved farther and farther from the time-honored traditions, rituals, and gestures that had structured everyday life in a largely rural, agrarian, Catholic France, the French turned to the past with ever-increasing frequency and passion, seeking to retrieve what had virtually disappeared. Hence the emergence of the "lieux de mémoire": "la raison d'être fondamentale d'un lieu de mémoire est d'arrêter le temps, de bloquer le travail de l'oubli, de fixer un état de choses, d'immortaliser la mort, de matérialiser l'immatériel pour . . . enfermer le maximum de sens dans le minimum de signes . . ." (the fundamental reason for being of a place of memory is to halt time, block the process of forgetting, freeze one state of things, make the mortal immortal, make the immaterial material in order to . . . enclose the greatest amount of meaning in the least number of signs . . .).[4]

Such is eminently the case with the *Bloc-notes*, as Mauriac voices his alarm over the sweeping changes transforming daily life in France. First and foremost among these are the upheavals of the agrarian world in the wake of urbanization and unbridled technology. Ironically, it is precisely Mauriac's keen sensitivity to this profound historical evolution that alienates him from the contemporary age, as we see in the following protest against the destruction of the rural habitat:

4. Nora, "Entre mémoire et histoire," xxxv.

> Tout ce qui touche à la civilisation de l'atome, je le reçois du dehors, ou plutôt je ne le reçois pas, rien n'en pénètre ma pensée. Je mourrai sans avoir franchi le seuil de cette terre promise qui, en réalité, me fait horreur et me rejette vers le royaume au-dedans de moi. Je hais ce monde où les poissons crèvent, où les grillons se sont tus, où tel oiseau ne chante plus que dans mon souvenir, où le silence des espaces infinis est violé même la nuit, où tous les peupliers et tous les ormes des routes de la vieille France ont été abattus. Il n'y a pas de vérité à laquelle je serai demeuré plus étranger qu'à celle que formulait Etienne Gilson: "Mieux nous connaîtrons la nature, mieux nous pourrons connaître Dieu!" Mais la nature aujourd'hui succombe à un attentat multiforme et je me sens devenu l'ennemi de ce monde tel qu'il est dans le temps que j'y respire. ("Vémars, août 1965," BN IV, 119–20)
>
> [As for everything concerning the civilization of the atom, I get it from without, or rather, I don't get it at all. None of it penetrates into my thinking. I shall die without having crossed over the threshold of this promised land that in reality repels me and throws me back toward the kingdom within me. I hate this world in which the fish die, the crickets have grown silent, certain birds no longer sing except in my memory, the silence of infinite space is violated even at night, in which all the poplars and all the elms along the France of yesteryear's roads have been cut down. There is no truth that has remained more alien to me than that formulated by Etienne Gilson: "The better we shall know nature, the better we will be able to know God!" But today nature is succumbing to a multifaceted attack and I sense that I have become the enemy of this world as it is at this time when I live and breath in it.]

Though one might be tempted to discern a precocious environmentalism in this impassioned outcry against human encroachment upon nature, these lines actually testify to Mauriac's deep-seated humanism; as indicated by his lament for Pascal's "silence des espaces infinis" and his reference to "la vieille France," he deplores the violation of the natural world as a violation of the humanity inextricably tied to it through history.

The venerable landscapes of Mauriac's family dwellings were indeed undergoing radical transformation in many places, as "la vieille France" experienced the throes of a rapid modernization that often sacrificed natural beauty and human memory to pressing economic needs. Such is the context for Mauriac's concern for the rich sedimentation of the past that he fears will be devastated by the construction of the Roissy airport:

> . . . c'est de cette maison et de ce jardin [Mauriac's own at Vémars] qu'il s'agit, voués à la destruction, comme d'ailleurs la campagne qui les entoure, dont les traits se sont lentement effacés depuis cinquante ans que je la connais: il y avait autrefois dans la plaine des avenues de vieux poiriers qui ont fini par être tous abattus. Et puis l'autoroute vient de surgir.
>
> Mais une campagne a la vie dure: il faut beaucoup d'années pour qu'elle meure de sa belle mort. Celle-ci eût tenu le coup longtemps encore si sa fin n'était inscrite dans la volonté des hommes et dans ce projet d'aéroport à Roissy-en-France. *Aménager le territoire, c'est atteindre son âme*, même dans cette banlieue nord de Paris, dans ces paroisses mortes où Péguy entendit sa dernière messe.
>
> Je me réponds à moi-même qu'après tout ce futur aéroport, avec ces avions supersoniques, de jour et de nuit, manifestera la vie des hommes à ce moment de la durée et n'effacera aucune trace d'*une histoire dont rien ne subsiste visiblement sur cette plaine nivelée par la grande culture.* ("Samedi 16 juillet 1966," BN IV, 295)
>
> [. . . at stake here is this house and garden [[Mauriac's own at Vémars]], which are doomed to destruction, as is moreover the case for the countryside surrounding them. Over the fifty-some years that I have known this landscape, its traits have slowly worn away: on the plain, there used to be avenues of old pear trees that all wound up getting cut down. And now the superhighway has just sprung up.
>
> But the countryside is tough: it takes many years for it to die of old age. This one would have held up even longer if its demise had not been willfully inscribed in the plans for the airport at Roissy-en-France. *To remodel the land is to wound its soul*, even in this northern suburb of Paris, in these dead parishes where Péguy heard his last mass.
>
> I reply to myself that after all, this future airport with its supersonic airplanes will testify day and night to human life at this moment in the duration of time and will not erase one single trace of *a story of history that is no longer visible on this plain leveled by the intensive growing of crops.*]

Speaking of the soon-to-be razed landscape in terms of a person whose facial features have slowly faded away ("dont les traits se sont lentement effacés"), who is long-lived ("a la vie dure"), who dies of old age ("qu'elle meure de sa belle mort"), and whose very soul is being violated (see emphasized words) by the designs of technocrats, Mauriac underscores the humanity painstakingly etched into the rural habitat over the course of time. The references to Péguy and to "une histoire dont rien ne subsiste visiblement" (a story of history that is no longer visible) clearly illustrate Mauriac's fervent desire to preserve the fabric of history woven into the countryside. This passion for a "lieu de mémoire" is articulated even more explicitly in the concluding lines:

> "Aimez ce que jamais on ne verra deux fois. . . ." Je sens bien ce que cette exigence a d'absurde quand il s'agit de mes paysages familiers et de ma pauvre destinée personnelle. Je la crois légitime quand ce n'est plus de moi qu'il est question, ni de la trace de lièvre que j'aurai un instant laissée dans le sable, mais de la France, mais de son illustre histoire. Et même sans sortir de Paris: tout ce qui y a été détruit du temps d'Haussmann et même depuis que nous y sommes venus! L'année de mon arrivée, le morne boulevard Raspail achevait de détruire l'Abbaye-aux-Bois dont ma femme fut une des dernières couventines.
>
> Dire que c'est sous le règne de De Gaulle que les pires attentats auront été médités contre cette France dont il ne se faisait une certaine idée que parce qu'enfant il s'en était fait une certaine image—peut-être comme moi-même d'après les illustrations d'Alphonse de Neuville dans l'*Histoire de France* de Guizot.
>
> Chaque pierre durant l'Occupation nous en semblait précieuse: les parapets de ces ponts de Paris, les seuls que la débâcle n'eût pas détruits, ces anciens parapets auxquels s'étaient accoudés Baudelaire et Rimbaud dans ces aubes d'autrefois. Il n'est pas une pierre en Ile-de-France et pas un arbre qui puisse être touché sans respect. Mais surtout il y a des zones de silence aux abords de Versailles qui ont été miraculeusement préservées, comme si l'histoire avait intimidé ceux dont le métier est d'en effacer les traces pour y substituer la laideur morne des grands ensembles et pour s'enrichir. Voici qu'ils surmontent leur timidité, que l'histoire ne leur fait plus peur . . . (BN IV, 296–97)

> ["Love that which you will never see a second time. . . ." I sense quite well what is absurd about this demand when it is a question of my own humble destiny and the landscapes familiar to me. But I believe that it is legitimate when we are no longer dealing with me, nor with the foot-

> prints that I have left in the sand at one certain moment, but with France and its illustrious history. Even within the confines of Paris: think of everything that has been destroyed there at the time of Haussmann and even since we have come there! The year of my arrival, the dismal Boulevard Raspail was finishing off the Abbaye-aux-Bois convent, where my wife was one of the last to attend school.
>
> And to think that it is under the reign of de Gaulle that people have concocted the worst criminal attacks against this France of which he maintained a certain idea only because he had formed a certain image when he was a child, perhaps just as I myself had done, led on by Alphonse de Neuville's illustrations in Guizot's *Histoire de France.*
>
> Each stone seemed precious to us under the Occupation: the balustrades of the bridges in Paris, the only ones not destroyed by the catastrophic defeat of June 1940, were the old parapets that Baudelaire and Rimbaud used to lean on at dawn. There is no stone nor any tree in the Paris region that may be touched without respect. But above all, there are zones of silence around Versailles that have been miraculously preserved, as if history had intimidated those who make it there business to erase the traces of the past, replace it with the gloomy ugliness of high-rise public housing, and get rich. Now they have surmounted their timidity, and history no longer scares them. . . .]

Since they are integral parts of the history that has fashioned France's identity, Mauriac treasures both the urban and the rural landscapes, including the natural habitat with its living organisms as well as human constructions. Here again, their unique, irreplaceable character appears as the cumulative imprint of many generations. While Mauriac focuses on famous poets, Parisian monuments, and "great moments" of history in the above-cited text, other "Bloc-notes" testify to the intimate connection of the physical habitat to the lives of unrecognized "everyday" people, and to a whole web of humanity left by the wayside in the wake of the implacable rural exodus underway in the France of the late 1950s and early 1960s.

Such is the case in March 1964, when Mauriac depicts his trip from Paris back to his traditional family dwelling in the Bordeaux region as a journey through time. Paris and Malagar represent rather opposite poles in Mauriac's temporal geography. The *Bloc-notes* often associates the bustling metropolis with the modern world's inhuman onslaught of highways and concrete, while linking Mauriac's provincial home to a rich network of accents, manners, and practices that have remained largely unchanged over the *longue durée* of the French rural world. He accordingly welcomes the prospect of traveling from the capital city back to his country dwelling as a voyage through the past, one that will bring him back into contact with the humanity still radiating from the hearth, the focal point of a vitality transcending differences of age and social class:

> Samedi 14 mars 1964
>
> Je suis au bord de ce plaisir que je vais connaître une fois encore: monter en voiture un matin, rouler sur une route familière, sachant que je ne m'arrêterai pas avant d'avoir atteint le seuil d'une certaine cuisine. . . . Je l'ai dans l'esprit, cette cuisine, telle qu'elle est depuis mon enfance, j'en respire l'odeur délicieuse; nous ne sommes jamais entrés dans la maison que par elle: c'est l'endroit le plus humain—moins peut-être à cause du feu sacré de l'âtre et des flambées de sarments qui, à l'heure de la grillade, l'embrasent qu'à cause de tant de pauvres femmes, qui depuis cent vingt ans, s'y sont affairées. Je me souviens d'un vers de Jammes: "Une servante morte au sourire docile. . . ." Il y en a toujours eu une que les enfants aimaient. (BN III, 451)
>
> [Saturday, 14 March 1964
>
> I am once more on the verge of experiencing the pleasure of getting into the car one morning and driving down a familiar highway, knowing that I will not stop before reaching the threshold of a certain kitchen. . . . I can see this kitchen in my mind just as it has been since my childhood, and I can breathe in its delightful smell. We never entered by any other door, and this is the most human place in the house, perhaps not so much because of the sacred fire in the hearth and the flames of the vine branches that make it flare up when meat is being grilled, but more because of the many poor women who have busied themselves over the fire throughout the last one hundred and twenty years. I remember a verse of Jammes's poetry: "A deceased servant with the docile smile. . . ." There was always one such woman whom the children loved.]

The fundamental opposition in Mauriac's portrayal of his contemporary world, however, is between, on the one hand, the steamroller of consumerism and technology, and, on the other hand, the web of relations tying humans to their habitat in both Paris and the provinces. Such a network has been accumulated over time and retained in the web of memory, as we see when the Auteuil train station connects Mauriac with the world of Verlaine:

> Qu'elle me paraît loin encore, cette cuisine alors que l'auto atteint à peine la gare d'Auteuil, celle où Verlaine, le dimanche, regardait Lucien Létinois descendre l'escalier "comme un ange le long de l'échelle céleste"! Je pense à eux, non pas chaque fois que je passe devant la gare, mais chaque fois que *la gare devient la première station d'un voyage à travers le temps révolu: le départ pour les vacances.* (BN III, 451)
>
> [How distant this kitchen seems to me as the car barely reaches the Auteuil train station, where, every Sunday, Verlaine would watch Lucien Létinois descend the steps "like an angel down the celestial ladder"! I think of them, not each time I go by the station, but each time that *the station becomes the first stop on a trip through times past: the departure for the vacation period.*]

Mauriac's nostalgic reverie neither provides him with an escape from the unsettling transformations of the contemporary world nor fosters any illusion as to the ultimate impact of the *exode rural:*

> Je roule à travers un passé qui fut tissé d'autant et de plus de malheurs que "le jour d'aujourd'hui." La trame de l'histoire et celle de mon histoire se confondent en moi, et en même temps un cri s'élève—ou plutôt une symphonie que je suis seul à pouvoir entendre; mais chacun écoute la sienne, si du moins il détient l'oreille qu'il faut pour capter cette musique du destin. . . .
>
> . . . Il m'arrive, contemplant cette campagne morte, de me réjouir sombrement de sa mort. Paris deviendra énorme. Les quelques métropoles de la province aspireront tout ce qui restera d'humanité autour d'elles. Mais enfin cette campagne deserte subsistera, cette solitude des champs où ceux qui sont capables de l'aimer trouveront toujours un refuge. . . .
>
> Non! c'est là une vue de l'esprit. En fait, une campagne désertée devient cadavre. Si l'obscur pays landais de mon enfance, très sauvage en apparence et très désert, demeure vivant dans mon souvenir, c'est qu'en réalité il était le lieu d'une histoire humaine: une famille vivait dans la

métairie la plus perdue, la plus éloignée de tout village. Si loin que nous nous enfoncions dans la grande lande, à travers des marais difficilement accessibles, toujours quelques clarines tintaient, nous entendions le cri guttural d'un berger, le piétinement du troupeau. La lande en ce temps-là fut un désert peuplé. Aujourd'hui les métairies qui n'ont pas brûlé sont pour la plupart abandonnées. Les champs n'existent plus, ni les troupeaux. Une campagne d'où les hommes se sont retirés est une morte. Les hommes disparus ont emporté avec eux un langage, ce patois que j'aimais, dont les dames de mon enfance usaient avec leurs servantes—et les moeurs qui réglaient toutes les circonstances de la vie et surtout les noces et les funerailles. (BN III, 451–53)

[I am traveling through a past woven from just as many and even more woes than those we have "right here and now." The fabric of history and the story of my own past join seamlessly together in me and at the same time a shout goes up—or rather a symphony only I can hear. But everyone listens to their own, at least if their ears are sensitive enough to tune in this music of destiny. . . .

. . . As I survey this dead rural area, I sometimes somberly rejoice at its death. Paris will someday be enormous. The few large cities in the provinces will suck in all that remains of the human population around them. In the end, however, this empty countryside will subsist, with these lonely fields where those capable of loving it will always find refuge. . . .

No! That is an intellectual view. In fact, a deserted rural area becomes a corpse. La Lande, the remote region native to me as a child, appears quite wild and uninhabited. Yet the reason it remains alive in my memory is because in reality it was the site of a human story in history: in the most obscure sharecropper's house the farthest from any village lived a family. As far as we might penetrate into the Lande region through highly inaccessible marshes, we could always hear the sheep bells ring, a shepherd's guttural cry, and the herd's trampling hoofs. In that time, La Lande was a populated wasteland. Now the sharecroppers' houses that have not burned down are for the most part abandoned. Neither the fields nor the herds are there anymore. A rural area deserted by humans is dead. Those who have disappeared have taken with them a language (this regional dialect that I loved as a child and that all the women used to speak with their servants), as well as the mores that used to order all occasions in life, especially weddings and funerals.]

In Mauriac's eyes, the gradual depopulation of the rural habitat thus signifies the disappearance of a rich network of life and culture. While his perspective is privileged in every sense and not totally free of an unwitting paternalism, it nevertheless testifies to the anxiety accompanying the radical cultural and social evolution brought on by the massive movement of rural inhabitants to urban centers in France, an anxiety that will ultimately be experienced not only by this bourgeois Catholic member of the Académie Française (as his critics and rivals would paint him), but by the entire spectrum of French citizens.

Obviously, Mauriac writes not as a sociologist or a demographer, but as one continuing to chronicle his daily encounter with history, as indicated in the preface to the *Bloc-notes*. We find the editorialist for the *Figaro littéraire* pointing out the threads tying him not only to the grandiose tapestry of momentous events but also to the homespun fabric woven by the loom of French history in everyday life. Seeing the customs, the language, and the physical habitat of the rural world disappear before his eyes is thus for Mauriac similar to experiencing the death of some intimate acquaintance. The conclusion of this "Bloc-notes" portrays the desertion of the French countryside as a symptom of a more general dehumanization of modern society and culture deeply unsettling to Mauriac the novelist:

> C'est parce que cette terre était vivante que j'aurai été un écrivain vivant, moi qui suis né d'elle et qui n'aurais rien été sans elle—et mes romans doivent tout à l'alios et à l'argile dans lesquels ils s'enracinent. . . .
>
> O Dieu! que je me sens loin de ce qui s'écrit aujourd'hui et de ce qui se traduit en images sur les écrans! Et que tout m'y paraît vidé de sève! . . . Cette sève, ce sang qui circulaient autrefois à travers tous les livres, à travers toutes les peintures: leur diversité infinie n'empêchait pas qu'ils ne fussent tous tributaires de cette circulation vivante et qui concernait les êtres et les arbres et la terre elle-même. Je souffrais d'une campagne d'où l'humain s'est retiré—mais il s'est retiré aussi de ce qui s'écrit, de ce qui se peint. . . . (BN III, 453)

> [It is because this land was alive that I, who was born from it and would have been nothing without it, have been a living writer. And my novels owe everything to the sandy loam and the clay in which they take root. . . .

God! How far I feel from all that is being written and translated into images on the screens nowadays! And how everything on these screens appears to me to be drained of its living substance! . . . This living substance, this lifeblood, used to circulate through all the books and through all the paintings. Their infinite diversity did not prevent them from all being tributaries of this living circulation that was connected with living beings and trees and the earth itself. I used to suffer from a rural area deserted by humanity, but now humanity has also deserted writing and painting. . . .]

We would do well to discount the ridiculous notion of literary production as somehow springing from the earth, a notion moreover flatly refuted by many other passages in the *Bloc-notes.* Mauriac clearly rejects the pathetic fallacy and sets his entire literary and journalistic work in direct opposition to the predatory violence (designated by "entre-dévorement" [mutual devouring]) that he sees as the primary law of nature. Any misgivings about the possibility of some romantic "return to nature" of any sort should be dispelled by the following two passages, in which Mauriac unequivocally repudiates such a notion:

> Une humanité condamnée à la puanteur des villes modernes a plus de raisons que l'homme du XVIIIe siècle et que les romantiques de vouloir revenir à la vie primitive:
>
> Mais la nature est là qui t'invite et qui t'aime;
> Plonge-toi dans son sein . . . [Lamartine, "Le vallon"]
>
> Eh, bien non; la nature ne nous invite pas et elle ne nous aime pas. Et il en a coûté gros à certains campeurs de se plonger dans son sein. . . . ("Malagar, mardi 7 septembre 1965," BN IV, 127)
>
> . . . mais sur le visage humain, fût-ce le plus ingrat, au fond du regard le plus morne, brille une lumière qui ne saurait venir de la matière aveugle et sourde, je sais bien que c'est impossible, ni de ce monde animal, dont la loi est de s'entre-dévorer. ("Mercredi 26 septembre 1962," BN III, 236)
>
> [A humanity that has been condemned to live in the stench of modern cities has more reasons than did eighteenth-century people and the romantics to want to return to a primitive life:

> But there is nature who invites you and loves you;
> Plunge into its bosom . . . [Lamartine, "The Valley"]

> Well, no, nature does not invite us and does not love us. And certain campers have paid a hefty price for plunging into its bosom. . . .

> . . . but on the human face, even the most unrewarding one, a light shines beneath the gloomiest gaze. This light could not possibly come from blind and deaf matter, I know that this is impossible. Nor could it come from this animal world, whose law is a mutual devouring.]

Throughout the *Bloc-notes* of the 1960s (and, more sporadically, of the 1950s), Mauriac deplores the loss of humanity occasioned by specific technological and artistic constructions (the nouveau roman, abstract painting, and the Roissy airport) built on the ruins of a more human world. In other words, he bemoans first and foremost what he perceives as a widespread dehumanization alienating him from contemporary culture.

This estrangement from the brave new world springing up around him receives more explicit expression in the following piece penned prior to another transition between Malagar and the writer's residence at Vémars just north of Paris. For Mauriac, the unbridled urbanization transforming the Paris region not only signifies a break with the past and the destruction of the rural habitat, but also marks the more general dehumanization. Hence the apprehension about returning to the Ile de France:

> . . . Ce n'est pas tant les hommes que je redoute (si redoutables qu'ils soient) que le monde tel qu'il devient sous nos yeux dans sa mutation accélérée: ce monde inhumain.
>
> Le monde inhumain, c'est cela qui frappe. C'était trop peu que de le dire absurde, car l'absurde peut encore être à la mesure de l'homme, comme l'est toute folie. Qu'y a-t-il de plus humain que les fous qui ont été nos maîtres: Baudelaire, Verlaine, Rimbaud? En revanche, la cité qui s'édifie sous nos yeux, cette termitière, est logique et raisonnable. Brasilia, que je considérais avec terreur sur le petit écran, est la conception d'un technicien équilibré, non le cauchemar d'un insensé comme le sont les châteaux de Bavière.
>
> La référence à l'homme, voilà le secret perdu non seulement pour l'architecture et pour ce qui concerne l'urbanisme. Les romans, les

poèmes, les galeries de peinture: l'absence de l'homme y est partout célébrée comme une victoire. Il n'y a plus de visage nulle part. Aucun coeur ne bat plus dans aucun livre. ("Malagar, vendredi 16 octobre 1964," BN III, 532)

[. . . I do not dread humans (as dreadful as they may be) as much as I dread the sort of world we see developing and mutating in fast motion: this world is inhuman.

What is striking is the inhuman character of the world. It was not enough to call it absurd, for what is absurd is still of human proportions, as are all forms of madness. What could be more human than the madmen who have been our masters: Baudelaire, Verlaine, Rimbaud? The city being built under our very eyes, this termite colony, on the other hand, is logical and reasonable. The Brasilia that I contemplated with terror on television is the conception of a mentally balanced technician, not the nightmare of some wildly unreasonable man, as are the chateaus in Bavaria.

The reference to humanity is the secret that has been lost not only from architecture but from all that is connected with urban development. The absence of humanity is being celebrated everywhere as a victory, in novels, poems, and art galleries. There is no longer any face anywhere. Not a single heart beats in any book.]

The methodically impersonal expanses of concrete emblematic of modern urban development in Brasilia and Paris illustrate for Mauriac the banishment of the human element from contemporary literature and art. Conversely, the animals, crops, and edifices of his rural dwellings at both Malagar and Vémars connect Mauriac with a vibrant network of human activity transmitting a tangible legacy of the past:

Mais même le monde est physiquement détruit. . . .

Je suis entré dans l'étable, où un boeuf demeure encore. Il y en avait quatre autrefois. Je voyais son grand oeil dans l'ombre; un rayon qui fusait par un trou de la porte touchait son pelage roux. J'écoutais ce bruit calme de la rumination, je respirais cette odeur puissante et douce qui avait baigné l'obscure existence de mes ancêtres oubliés. Et tout à coup . . . j'ai revu autour de ma maison de Seine-et-Oise ces prairies pour lesquelles il n'existe plus de faucheur. . . . Et puis je revoyais en esprit ces milliers de poissons crevés que roulaient l'Adour, il y a quelques semaines, et tant d'autres rivières. Enfin, je me suis souvenu de cette

> lourde glace de Venise qui vient de chez ma mère. Accrochée dans mon cabinet de Malagar, elle s'est détachée. . . . A tort ou à raison, cette chute [de la glace de Venise] fut attribuée à l'ébranlement causé par les avions qui passent le mur du son au-dessus de Malagar. Je le crois quant à moi, car il y a bien d'autres signes que ces murs séculaires et lézardés ne résisteront pas toujours à cette loi indéfiniment violée. (BN III, 532–33)
>
> [But even the material world is being destroyed. . . .
>
> I walked into the barn, where there is still a steer. There used to be four of them. I could see his large eye in the shadows; a ray of sunlight streaming in through a hole in the door touched his reddish brown hide. I listened to that calm sound of rumination as I breathed in the strong, sweet smell that had permeated the obscure lives of my forgotten ancestors. And all of a sudden . . . I saw again around my house in the Seine-et-Oise these prairies for which there are no longer any reapers. . . . And then I saw again in my mind the thousands of dead fish floating down the Adour river (and many other rivers) a few weeks ago. Finally, I remembered the heavy Venetian mirror from my mother's home. It fell off the wall of my study at Malagar. . . . Rightly or wrongly, this mishap was blamed on the shaking caused by planes breaking the sound barrier over Malagar. For my part, I believe it, for there are a good many other signs that these cracked, age-old walls will not hold up forever as this law is repeatedly violated.]

Hayfields abandoned by harvesters, streams choked with dead fish, heirlooms and walls damaged by sonic booms: all signal the violation and seemingly inexorable destruction of a venerable human habitat, breaking down the web of humanity connected with it. The disappearance of the agrarian society and physical environment not only creates an abrupt discontinuity and a sense of loss, but also constitutes an acute crisis of personal, social, and human identity for Mauriac.

The *Bloc-notes* moreover point to another source of estrangement, one that stems not from any inability to understand the contemporary world nor from the desire to return to the past (except by memory), but from the younger generation's indifference to the historical experience of their predecessors:

> Ils ne s'intéressent pas à cette histoire, la nôtre, qui est pourtant la leur. Ils croient qu'ils sont nés le jour de leur naissance, ces pauvres enfants.

> Nous autres, nous savions que notre destin s'était noué vingt ans avant notre venue au monde, quand Napoléon III, avec son énorme chapeau et son cigare, était entré dans la nasse tendue par Bismarck. ("Jeudi 14 avril, 1966," BN IV, 247)
>
> . . . les jeunes Français sont devenus indifférents à l'histoire que leurs pères ont vécue. Nous n'étions pas ainsi, nous autres, nous acceptions d'être des héritiers. Nous ne nous lassions pas d'apprendre ce qui était advenu à nos aînés, cette histoire d'avant notre naissance dont nous pressentions que notre génération allait faire les frais. ("Vendredi 24 septembre 1965," BN IV, 136)
>
> [They are not interested in this history, which is our history, but nevertheless theirs. These poor kids believe that they were born on the date of their birth. The rest of us know that our destiny had been fixed twenty years before we came into the world when Napoleon III, with his enormous hat and his cigar, fell into the trap set by Bismarck.
>
> . . . French young people have become indifferent to the history that their parents experienced. The rest of us were not like that: we accepted the fact that we were heirs. We never tired of learning what had happened to our predecessors. We had the presentiment that our generation would have to pay for the history that had taken place before our birth.]

Born in 1885, some fifteen years after the humiliating defeat that amputated the Alsace-Lorraine territory from France and set the stage for the terrible slaughters of World War I, Mauriac deplores the younger generation's willful, insouciant ignorance of their elders' experience of history.

The following passages testify to this disparity between his own strong sense of implication in the past and the younger generation's indifference. The first piece furthermore links his sense of alienation as a writer to the disruptions of the rural habitat, as he sharply contrasts the peaceful isolation of the countryside with the crowded hustle and bustle of highways and beaches:

> Vémars, 18 août 1964
>
> Passer de cette villa dans l'Esterel où j'étais hier soir à ce jardin du Valois où me revoilà ce matin, c'est prolonger la demi-conscience du voyage nocturne dans le train bleu. Je rêve encore: c'était hier le torride

été bruissant de cigales et, à peine franchies les limites enchantées de la forêt peuplée d'écureuils, un horrible grouillement humain et mécanique sur les plages et sur les routes. Et tout à coup l'automne s'annonce dans ce jardin aux arbres épais et trop serrés et que tourmente un vent pluvieux. Il n'y a plus personne ici dont me sépare ma vieillesse: ce ne sont plus mes petits-enfants, mais des hirondelles qui rasent la prairie. Je ne suis plus pour personne cette énigme dont le mot demeure aussi inconnu de ceux qui m'aiment que de ceux qui me haïssent. . . .

Ce mot de l'énigme je ne le cherche plus, et c'est sans doute pourquoi je n'écris plus de romans. (BN III, 512)

. . . l'écrivain [Mauriac lui-même] qui écrit sa page depuis cinquante-six ans . . . ressent une vague gêne et presque de la honte à parler encore, à écrire encore, alors que presque toutes les grandes voix se sont tues et qu'il reste si peu de témoins d'une histoire dont la génération d'aujourd'hui se détourne. . . . Mais c'est trop dire: car pour se détourner il faudrait qu'elle y ait un instant attachée sa pensée. En fait, rien de ce qui a précédé leur venue au monde n'a d'existence pour nos petits-enfants. ("Samedi 2 juillet 1966," BN IV, 287)

[Vémars, 18 August 1964

As I go from that villa where I was yesterday in the Esterel to this garden in the Valois where I find myself this morning, I prolong the semiconsciousness of a night trip on the blue train. I am still dreaming: yesterday it was a torrid summer rustling with locusts, and just after passing the enchanted edges of the forest populated with squirrels, one finds a horrible crowd of humans and machines on the beaches and the highways. Here I am no longer separated from anyone by my old age. Here it is not my grandchildren, but rather the swallows that skim over the prairie. I am no longer the enigma whose key remains just as unknown to those who love me as to those who hate me. . . .

I no longer search for the key to the enigma, and that's probably why I no longer write novels.

. . . the writer [Mauriac himself] who has been writing his editorials for fifty-six years . . . feels slightly embarrassed and almost ashamed to still be speaking and writing when almost all of the great voices have grown silent and when there remain so few witnesses to a history that today's generation is turning away from. . . . But that's somewhat of an exag-

> geration, for to turn away they would have had to focus their attention on it for an instant. The fact of the matter is that nothing that preceded their coming into the world has any existence for our grandchildren.]

As intimately as Mauriac ties his sense of loss and alienation to his own particular experience as a writer and a French citizen born shortly after the traumatic beginnings of the Third Republic, having come of age at the height of the Dreyfus affair, and having witnessed the successive traumas of World War I, the defeat and occupation of France by the Germans during World War II, and the Algerian war, these passages also testify to an interplay between history and memory that resulted from the very disruptions of "Les Trente Glorieuses" described lyrically in the *Bloc-notes.*

Masterfully documented in Pierre Nora's monumental *Les Lieux de mémoire*, France's rapid transformation from a largely traditional, agrarian, Catholic, nationalistic society to postindustrial consumerist society constituted a radical transition that left the world of "vieille France" by the wayside and ushered in a passion for memory often manifested in the preeminence of the historical over the literary. Nora moreover points to the constitution and celebration of "lieux de mémoire" as "le relais de la fiction défaillante" [taking up where fiction was leaving off]: "Histoire, profondeur d'une époque arrachée à sa profondeur, roman vrai d'une époque sans vrai roman. Mémoire, promue au centre de l'histoire: c'est le deuil éclatant de la littérature" (History, depth of an age torn away from its depth, the truthful novel of an age without any true novel. Memory thrust forward to the center of history: this is the overwhelmingly obvious grieving over the death of literature).[5]

Nora's observation applies perfectly to the *Bloc-notes*, which repeatedly and often explicitly aims to compensate for the human emptiness so often decried in the passages cited above (as well as in many others). Highly significant in this regard is Mauriac's commentary on a selection of Proust's correspondence, in which he associates the author of *A la Recherche du temps perdu* with his own concerns. Both indeed fear that times past may be doomed to oblivion. The disappearance of the rural habitat in the wake of the automobile, consumer society, and urban

5. Nora, "Entre mémoire et histoire," xlii.

sprawl only heighten such apprehensions for Mauriac. Once again, we find that the prospect of leaving one residence for another arouses disquietude over the fate of entire realms of memory inextricably linked to the rural landscape:

> Dieu sait que j'aimerais ne pas quitter Paris cet été. Mon plaisir s'accroîtrait à l'idée du torrent de moteurs sur les routes et de ces plages grouillantes. Mais je devrai me soumettre moi aussi au déplacement forcé. Je m'y résigne sans joie. Non que je ne sois attaché à ce jardin près de Paris où je vais aller d'abord. Trop près de Paris pour ne pas être condamné. Ces hêtres séculaires, je les sais aussi éphémères que moi: à peine me survivront-ils. Déjà la ville a jeté un tentacule d'autoroute dans notre direction et ne nous a manqués que de peu. Dans dix ou douze ans, tout sera consommé.
>
> . . . Il n'empêche que l'idée que ce jardin rejoindra bientôt dans le même néant celui de la rue La Fontaine, où jouait le petit Proust, m'en détacherait plutôt; quelle folie! puisque autant qu'il eût duré, ce jardin, ce n'eût été que l'espace d'une ou deux générations; l'intervalle de la mienne aura suffi pour que le feu détruise à Saint-Symphorien les secrètes forêts de mon enfance; le paysage bien-aimé a été partout effacé, comme un dessin d'écolier au tableau noir.
>
> Cette menace ne pèse pas sur Malagar, pourtant je n'y respire pas mieux qu'en Seine-et-Oise. C'est qu'une vieille maison, c'est qu'un vieux domaine finissent par ressembler à ces plaques sensibles sur lesquelles plusieurs photographies superposées ont été prises et où se confondent des visages brouillés. Je subis l'obsession de ces présences à demi effacés, et je participe moi-même de leur effacement. ("Dimanche 4 juillet 1965," BN IV, 104–5)
>
> [Lord knows I would love not to leave Paris this summer. That option becomes more and more attractive whenever I think of the flood of cars on the roads and the teeming crowds on the beaches. But I too will have to subject myself to a compulsory journey. I have reluctantly given in to the idea. It's not that I am insensitive to the charms of this garden near Paris where I am going first. It's too near Paris to escape condemnation [[by eminent domain or urban sprawl]]. I know that these age-old beech trees are as ephemeral as I am: they will barely outlive me. Already the city has thrust a tentacle of a freeway out in our direction and it just barely missed us. In ten or twelve years, the whole process will have been completed.]

Echoing Proust's desire to maintain or re-create the delicate but rich, if tiny, web of humanity that he sees gradually being undone, Mauriac finds in *The Remembrance of Things Past* a model for his own *Bloc-notes*, which so often reconnects us with the memorable past carried secretly by things present. The following commentary on George D. Painter's *Marcel Proust* clearly suggests that times past can be not only captured by Proust's inimitable weave of lyricism, imagery, and narration, but also be reflected and transmitted even in a more conventional account of another age, such as Painter's biography:

> Sur les points où mes souvenirs me permettent de faire des recoupements, sur des détails infimes, l'auteur anglais serre de si près la réalité qu'on s'étonne qu'il l'ait découverte à travers des correspondances et qu'il ne l'ait pas vécue lui-même. . . .
>
> J'écoute dans ce livre anglais comme la mer dans un coquillage l'immense et dérisoire rumeur de ce petit monde proustifiant auquel Proust ne doit rien et qui doit à Proust de n'être pas anéanti. ("Dimanche 27 février 1966," BN IV, 222–23)
>
> [On the points where my memories make it possible for me to cross-check, and on tiny details, this English author sticks so close to reality that one is surprised that he learned about it through letters and that he did not himself have any direct experience of it. . . .
>
> Just as one can hear the sound of the sea in a shell, I listen in this English book to the tremendous yet insignificant resonance of this little Proustifying world to which Proust owes nothing and which owes it to Proust not to have been swallowed up by oblivion.]

Mauriac's admiration for Painter's work clearly conveys his own interest in the remembrance of things past in his own *Bloc-notes:* if a biographer can duplicate the Proustian magic, how much more so a novelist and editorialist of Mauriac's talent?

Anticipating Nora's analysis of France's collective passion for history, Mauriac moreover attributes the drive for retrieving, retaining, and reinvesting a bygone world both to his own particular preoccupations and to the interest demonstrated by the general public, such as the visitors thronging the Vermeer exhibit at the Orangerie:

Pourquoi cette ruée quotidienne dans une exposition comme celle du musée de l'Orangerie? Ce n'est pas le snobisme des vernissages. Ces pauvres gens ne sont pas venus pour être vus, mais pour voir. Pour voir quoi? Infiniment plus que ce qui leur est montré. Ils savent que le sujet importe peu et qu'il ne faut pas attacher d'importance à ce que le tableau représente. Mais alors que cherchent-ils? *Comme Proust, qu'ils n'ont peut-être pas lu, ils sont à leur insu à la recherche du temps qu'il faut retrouver:* ce temps de Vermeer, ce temps de Chardin fixé par miracle sur un peu de toile et qui a résisté aux siècles: *un temps à la mesure de l'être humain, dont chacun de nous garde la nostalgie et que l'ère atomique a bousculé.* ("Vendredi 18 novembre 1966," BN IV, 350)

[Why this daily rush to see an exhibit such as the one in the museum in the Orangerie? This is not the snobbery of inaugural cocktail parties. These poor folks have not come to be seen, but to see. To see what? Infinitely more than what is displayed for them. They know that the subject matters little and that one must not attach any importance to what the picture represents. But then what are they seeking? *Like Proust, whom they have perhaps not read, they are unknowingly engaged in a search for the time that must be retrieved:* the time of Vermeer or of Chardin has been miraculously fixed onto a bit of canvas and has held up over centuries: *a time on a human scale, to which we all hark back, and which has been brushed aside by the atomic age.*]

Thus likening the crowds of commoners regularly packing the Orangerie's art exhibit to Marcel Proust's rather esoteric literary enterprise, Mauriac displays the full range of his talents as an essayist and commentator in the tradition of Montaigne and "les moralistes." The passage moreover testifies to his historical perspicacity. Linking the public's ostensibly aesthetic enchantment with the venerable paintings of Vermeer and Chardin to the unsettling context of the cold war, he gives powerful expression to the pathos of the 1950s and 1960s while at the same time pointing to a crisis of human identity.

Mauriac's repeated juxtaposition of the technocratic consumer society's amnesia with Proust's retrieval of the fragile little world of his childhood confirms Nora's observation on the interconnection between the demise of literature (moreover increasingly devoid of poetry and human drama) and the passion for history (accordingly invested with a rich palette of ideas and emotions). Though certainly not unrelated to Mauriac's advancing age nor, as we shall see in greater detail, to his increasingly Gaullist political convictions, this determination to obtain from historical memory the affective depth and intellectual adventure formerly situated in the novel is best understood as an emblem of a cultural phenomenon that concerned French society in general. As pointed out by François Furet, the enchantment with historical memory cut across the ideological categories that once so clearly distinguished right-wing Maurrassian nationalism from the internationalist idealism of the Left: the interest in roots, regional particularities, or "*terroir*" (the soil, the land of a particular region), and rural traditions that for so long were tied to the type of mythology of "la terre et les morts" (the land and the dead) exemplified by Barrès's *Roman de l'énergie nationale*, was from the late 1960s on widely embraced by the Left. Witness the phenomenal success of books on the "histoire des mentalités" (history of mentalities). This history, notes Furet, did not simply spring up spontaneously from documents and archival sources but rather was produced through an entire generation's response to the brusque separation from its own past that had been occasioned by the economic and social explosion of "Les Trente Glorieuses." And Furet goes on to specify that this explosion of historical memory represents not a reactionary attempt to return to the institutions and mores of "la vieille France," but rather from a desire to rediscover the particular ways in which the modern generation's ancestors had invested the world of their time with their own beliefs, emotions, and representations. The public and scholarly fascination for the "histoire des mentalités" thus evidenced the same connection between rapid change and nostalgia as Nora finds between history and memory. In both cases the disenchantment of literary culture corresponds to the frenzy for identifying and celebrating "lieux de mémoire": "Son secret [celui de l'histoire des mentalités] est d'abord un secret de sensibilité, par quoi elle investit le passé de l'inverse de notre présent, qui est encore notre présent" (Its secret [the secret of the history of mentalities] is first of all a secret of sensitivity, by which the past is invested in a way opposite to the present, which is still our present).[6]

6. Furet, *L'Atelier de l'histoire*, 24.

Although hardly a treatise on the "histoire des mentalités," the *Bloc-notes* does indeed provide a rich compendium of references to similarly enchanted places of memory, most often connected to Mauriac's family dwelling, Malagar, and to the surrounding region, as in the following lines. Once again, travel initiates a journey through time on the part of Mauriac's memory:

> Malagar, vendredi 29 mai 1959
>
> Hier, nous avons quitté Malagar au crépuscule. C'était un soir "doré et blond comme une pêche" tel que, dans une de ses Elégies, Francis Jammes décrit un soir de Bordeaux—de ce Bordeaux vers lequel nous roulions. Chaque village de la vallée garonnaise a un nom qui retentit en moi. J'ai donné celui de Virelade à la famille des *Mal Aimés.*
>
> Voici la ville où je suis né, des maisons où les miens ont vécu. . . . Voici le Grand Théâtre, ces marches que je gravis dans un songe éveillé. Même le *Concerto en si bémol* de Mozart joué par Clara Haskil, ne parvient pas à traverser l'épaisseur du temps révolu, dont cette salle ravissante me donne l'exacte mesure. Que de repères, ici, connus de moi seul! Mon oeil cherche un endroit du paradis. Nous y étions montés en cachette, un de mes frères et moi. C'était la première fois que je pénétrais dans un théâtre. Nous entendîmes le premier acte de *Mireille.* Qu'avais-je imaginé? Je me souviens de cette déception démesurée, et qui aura duré toute ma vie. . . .
>
> *Don Juan* mis à part (où "la voix sainte et terrible" retentit dans la musique) quel opéra échappe à la puérilité, à l'absurde, à la niaiserie?
>
> Voilà quelles étaient mes pensées dans l'auto qui nous ramenait à Malagar, à travers les villages endormis que la Garonne baigne, et dont les noms composent une des secrètes litanies de mes vacances d'enfant heureux: Villenave-d'Ornon, Beautiran, Virelade, Cérons, Barsac. . . . Musique d'au-delà de toute musique. (BN II, 264–65)
>
> [Malagar, Friday, 29 May 1959
>
> Yesterday we left Malagar at dusk. It was an evening "golden and blond like a peach" such as the one that, in his *Elegies,* Francis Jammes describes one evening in this city of Bordeaux where we are heading in our car. Each village in this Garonne valley river has a name that resounds within me. I gave the name Virelade to the family in *The Unloved.*
>
> Here is the town where I was born, and houses where my family lived. . . . Here is the Grand Théâtre and the steps that I climb up in my

daydream. Not even the *Concerto in B minor* can make it through the thick barrier of times past, whose exact dimensions are provided to me by this delightful hall. How many landmarks there are here known only to me! One of my brothers and I had secretly gone up into this hall one day. It was the first time I had been inside a theater. We heard the first act of *Mireille*. What had I imagined? I remember my overwhelming disappointment, and it has lasted all my life. . . .

Except for *Don Juan* (where the "holy and terrible voice" resounds in the music), what opera escapes the pitfalls of puerility, absurdity, and silliness?

Such were my thoughts in the car that was taking us back to Malagar, through the sleepy villages watered by the Garonne river: their names compose one of the secret litanies of the vacations I had in the happiness of my childhood: Villenave-d'Ornon, Beautiran, Virelade, Cérons, Barsac. . . . Music beyond all music.]

Mauriac thus finds the names of the villages surrounding his childhood home invested with the lyrical transports that he had for so long sought after and found lacking, or at least inadequate, in the aesthetic domain: while even Mozart's sublime music (to which Mauriac ascribes metaphysical status on several occasions in the *Bloc-notes*[7]) and opera cannot abolish the barrier of time, "l'épaisseur du temps révolu" (the thick barrier of times past), and recapture the magic of Mauriac's childhood world, the names and places of the "litanie" of villages recited here brings about just such transports.

As we might expect, Malagar itself, in spite—or perhaps because—of its temporal fragility constitutes an even more evocative "lieu de mémoire" whose every object carries its own story of how Mauriac's ancestors inhabited bygone eras:

Mercredi 3 avril 1963

Un printemps encore, et je le regarde naître avec attention comme s'il devait être le dernier. Je respire une fois encore l'odeur des sarments que j'allume. Aux murs et sur les consoles, toutes ces choses qui seront dispersées après moi me semblent aimantées par ce coeur dont j'écoute

7. See in particular "12 avril 1955," BN I, 263; "4 janvier 1957," BN I, 426; "5 mars 1966," BN IV, 227–28; "14 juillet 1967," BN IV, 483–84; and "27 avril 1969," BN V, 226. Mauriac often speaks of Mozart as a sublime consolation and as a testimony to the existence of something besides a drive for domination and power.

> les battements et par cette mémoire elle-même encombrée des souvenirs liés à chacun de ces objets. Si je leur prêtais une voix, si chacun d'eux racontait ce qu'il a vu, ce serait toute l'histoire d'une obscure famille d'autrefois, sans autres péripéties visibles que des morts, et que des héritages, et que des partages. (BN III, 333)
>
> [Wednesday, 3 April 1963
>
> Another spring is here, and I watch it come to life as attentively as if it were the last. Once again I breathe in the smell of vine cuttings that I ignite. On the walls and console tables, all these things that will be scattered after my death seem magnetically charged by this heart I hear beating and by this memory itself, laden with particular memories tied to each one of these objects. If I lent them a voice, if each one of them told the story of what it had seen, it would be the complete history of a little-known family of times past, without any other ups and downs than deaths, inheritances, and divisions of property.]

Countless other pages of the *Bloc-notes* connect the testimony of Mauriac's ancestral dwelling and its environs to a seemingly immemorial rural, provincial, "vieille France" past.

Yet as suggested in the allusion to the inevitable scattering of these objects treasured for all that his family's past has invested in them, Mauriac harbors no illusion as to the possibility of escaping history's movement nor even of living within a cocoon of souvenirs. The "Bloc-notes" immediately following the one cited above testifies to his lucidity on this score:

> Mardi 9 avril 1963
>
> Cette soudaine décoloration du monde tient sans doute à l'absence de soleil, mais aussi, j'imagine, à la bile au-dedans de moi. . . .
>
> Mais il existe une cause directe de mon désenchantement, le silence a été assassiné. Il n'y a plus de silence nulle part. Sur les vieilles propriétés où les oiseaux ne nichent plus autant qu'autrefois, de fous invisibles traversent le mur du son. Les murs qui ont résisté aux siècles frémissent jusque dans leurs fondements, les portes jouent, parfois les plafonds se fendent. Quand le vent souffle du sud, il apporte jusqu'à nous le fracas des moteurs, celui d'une perforatrice toute proche. Cette vallée de la Garonne qu'ourle la longue ligne sombre de la forêt landaise n'évoque plus pour moi, comme quand j'étais enfant, le vers que

j'aimais de "La maison du berger": "Les grands pays muets longuement s'étendront." C'est peu de dire que la plaine n'est plus muette. Et moi, je perds ce pouvoir que je détenais d'embellir ici les choses et les êtres. Je renonce à cet effort continu de réinvention pour maintenir le monde au niveau de mes songes.

Dès que je ne m'en mêle plus, il ne faut pas compter sur cet aigre printemps pour dissimuler la lèpre des murs décrépits, car la vigne vierge n'a pas encore de feuilles, et dans les tilleuls moribonds les boules du gui que je n'arrive pas à détruire sont des fibromes végétaux. Nous nous croyons préposés à l'orchestration de ce monde inhabitable, nous autres écrivains. Voilà que j'en ai assez, tout à coup. Le moteur règne sur la terre et dans le ciel. La chimie empoisonne les oiseaux, dont certaines espèces disparaissent. (BN III, 336–37)

[Tuesday, 9 April 1963

The world's sudden loss of color is doubtless due to the absence of sunlight, but also, I imagine, to my own bitter mood. . . .

However, there is a direct cause of my disenchantment: silence has been assassinated. There is no longer any silence anywhere. On the old estates where the birds no longer nest as much as they used to, invisible madmen are breaking the sound barrier. Walls that have withstood the centuries shake on their foundations, doors sway, and sometimes ceilings split. When the wind blows from the south, it even brings us the loud noise of motors and of a nearby drill. This Garonne river valley hemmed by the long, dark line of the Landes forest no longer conjures up for me, as it did when I was a child, the verse that I loved from "The Shepherd's House": "The great, silent regions will stretch out a long way." Needless to say, the plain is no longer silent. As for me, I am losing the capability I once had to make the objects and living things beautiful here. I have given up that continuous effort of reinventing the world in order to maintain it on the same level as my dreams.

Once I am no longer involved with it, one must not count on this sour spring to conceal the leprosy on these decrepit walls, for the virgin grapevine does not yet have any leaves and the beads of mistletoe in the dying linden trees that I cannot bring myself to destroy are vegetal fibroma. We writers believe that we have been designated to orchestrate this uninhabitable world. Now all of a sudden I have had enough. Motors reign on earth and in the sky. Chemicals are poisoning birds, and some species are becoming extinct.]

While striving to revive the past by reconstituting the web of humanity tied to places of national and personal memory, Mauriac nevertheless calls attention to the fragility of his own enterprise as a writer who ultimately cannot shelter himself from the march of time. Keenly aware of the historical evolution underway, he thus measures his own estrangement from the emerging postindustrial world by underscoring the gradual disappearance of the rural habitat that for so long had nurtured French society and French culture.

Mauriac not only acknowledges that he cannot live in the past: he refuses to present his *Bloc-notes* as a refuge from history. On one occasion, he even questions the powerful exercise of memory so evident in countless other pieces:

> A chaque retour [à Malagar], naguère encore, en franchissant le seuil, je ne savais jamais si je serais charmé ou déçu. Autrefois, le charme l'emportait presque toujours, et c'est maintenant le contraire. Jamais je n'ai tant souffert d'avoir glorifié avec si peu de vergogne cette pauvre terre, cette pauvre maison. Le vrai est que ce climat orageux, toujours mal supporté, d'aussi loin que je me souvienne, aujourd'hui m'accable. Qu'il est loin, le "paradis parfumé" dont rêvait Baudelaire quand il se souvenait de son enfance, qu'il est perdu le paradis où tout était "amour et joie." La source de cette joie était au-dedans de l'enfant qui créait son paradis: Malagar le sera à jamais pour Nathalie, pour Gérard, pour Pierre, qui dessinent en ce moment dans la cour un golf miniature.
>
> Mais moi, je redoute cet horizon et la vapeur qui en monte et qui m'oppresse. *Ce lieu commun du passé-refuge, et du souvenir qui serait une défense contre l'angoisse d'exister, quel mensonge!* C'est le contraire qui est vrai; c'est le présent, c'est le quotidien, et en particulier la politique, surtout la politique, qui m'aura protégé contre une émeute de souvenirs toujours grondante en moi. ("Malagar, jeudi 3 septembre 1964," BN III, 516–17)

> [Not so long ago, at each return [to Malagar], I never knew whether I would be charmed or disappointed upon stepping over the threshold. It used to be that the charm would almost always prevail, and now it's the opposite. Never have I suffered so much from having so shamelessly glorified this humble piece of land and this humble home. The truth is that this sultry climate that, for as long as I can remember, I always did

find hard to bear, is too much for me today. How far is that "fragrant paradise" that Baudelaire dreamed of when remembering his childhood. That paradise where all was "love and joy" is indeed lost. The source of that joy was within the child who created his paradise: Malagar will be such a place for Nathalie, for Gerard, and for Pierre, who are at this very moment etching out a miniature golf course in the yard.

For my part, however, I dread this horizon and the stifling haze that arises from it. *This commonplace of the past as a refuge and of memories that are supposedly a defense against the anxiety of existing, what a lie!* The very opposite is true. What has protected me from the onslaught of memories constantly seething within me is the present, everyday events, and above all, politics.]

Returning to Malagar as he often does in the *Bloc-notes*, Mauriac this time underscores not only the disjunction between his childhood world and his present preoccupations but also the artificiality of literary realms of memory. Without denying the significance of the past nor the validity of "lieux de mémoire," he refuses to use the past as a shield from pressing issues of the present, just as he refuses to use spirituality as a pretext for turning his back on history.

Mauriac seeks neither to collapse the distance separating contemporary French society from the "vieille France" of his youth, nor to abandon the present in favor of the past, but to understand the present in relation to the past and vice versa. Establishing this interconnection between current issues and bygone times is moreover entirely consonant with the constitution of places of memory as described by Nora. In no way restricted to nostalgia or narcissism, historical memory can prove to be a productive activity:

> Mémoire-miroir, dirait-on, si les miroirs ne reflétaient pas l'image du même, quand, au contraire, c'est la différence que nous cherchons à y découvrir; et dans le spectacle de cette différence, l'éclat soudain d'une introuvable identité. Non plus une genèse mais le déchiffrement de ce que nous sommes à la lumière de ce que nous ne sommes plus.
>
> C'est cette alchimie de l'essentiel qui, bizarrement, contribue à faire de l'exercice de l'histoire, dont la brutale poussée vers l'avenir devrait tendre à nous dispenser, le dépositaire des secrets du présent.[8]

8. Nora, "Entre mémoire et histoire," xxxiii.

[Mirror-memory, we would say, if mirrors did not reflect the identical image, when, on the contrary, what we are seeking to discover here is difference; and, in the spectacle of that difference, the sudden outburst of an identity so hard to find. It is no longer a genesis but the interpretation of what we are now in light of what we are no more.

Strangely, it is this alchemy of essences that contributes to making the exercise of history the depository of the present's secrets, even though the rush to the future should supposedly relieve us from having to do history.]

Such is precisely what we find in the *Bloc-notes:* Mauriac returns to the past as a means of better engaging the present while at the same time lending greater depth and substance to the issues at hand. The past thus takes on inherent value as an integral part of personal and national identity. However, Mauriac revisits it not to escape the challenge of current events but to reexamine, redefine, and yet reaffirm his identity as a writer, a Catholic, and a French citizen confronting the historical realities of media culture, dechristianization, and decolonization. Once again, Nora's characterization describes perfectly Mauriac's use of historical memory:

> Le passage de la mémoire à l'histoire a fait à chaque groupe l'obligation de redéfinir son identité par la revitalisation de sa propre histoire. Le devoir de mémoire fait de chacun l'historien de soi. (Nora, xxix)

> [The transition from memory to history compelled each group to redefine its identity by reviving its own history. The duty to remember makes each group and every person become historians of their own past.]

Nora thus connects France's relatively rapid transition from "mémoire" (i.e., the traditional society of "la vieille France" that transmitted its customs and rituals through "memory") to "histoire" (the society of contemporary France that has grounded its institutions on "history," a conscious analysis and reconstruction of the past), with the frenzy of commemorations and historical investigation characteristic of postindustrial France.

The long editorial penned only two days after the Paris police's brutal repression of a demonstration against the OAS, in which a number of protesters were crushed in a stairway at the Métro Charonne,[9] provides a vivid example of how Mauriac engages pressing issues while at the same time shuttling between momentous figures and events from France's past and the drama of the present. Mauriac first situates his journalism with respect to the monumental literary work undertaken by Montaigne amid the horrors of the religious wars:

> Samedi 10 février 1962
>
> Montaigne commença à écrire ses *Essais* en 1572, l'année de la Saint-Barthélemy. Les *Oeuvres Morales* de Plutarque, traduites par Amyot, parurent cette année-là et devinrent son bréviaire. Je ne crois pas à un hasard: Montaigne cherchait un refuge dans l'écriture. Il s'agissait pour lui d'échapper à l'horreur de vivre dans un royaume éternellement divisé contre lui-même. Nous ne sommes pas sortis, depuis quatre siècles, des guerres de religion: les prétextes changent, non la haine ni les attentats. De petits crimes au nom de grands principes, c'est presque toute l'histoire de France.
>
> Et nous aussi, dont l'écriture est le métier, nous rêvons comme Montaigne d'échapper à l'évènement par l'essai et d'en faire notre miel. La tentation se double, si nous sommes chrétiens, et si nous avons reçu la grâce d'un coeur sensible à Dieu, du pouvoir qui nous est donné de la fuite par en haut. Oui, une tentation—et il n'y faut pas céder. Les saints qui fuient le monde dans les cloîtres y souffrent et y meurent pour le monde. Notre vocation à nous, les laïcs, qui ne sommes pas des saints, ce n'est pas de fuir les hommes en Dieu, mais au contraire de trouver Dieu dans les hommes, fût-ce au plus épais d'une misérable politique.
>
> Il nous faut donc reprendre le commentaire de cette monotone et basse histoire quotidienne sans nous flatter d'en faire, à notre humble niveau, une oeuvre durable comme sont les *Essais*, car il n'est rien de plus éphémère que la politique intérieure française. . . . (BN III, 130–31)

9. This incident as well as those of October 1961 have recently (and in particular at the outset of the Papon trial in October 1997) become the focal point for renewed scrutiny of violations of human rights by French armed forces and police during the Algerian war. See Paul Thibaud, "Retour sur une tragédie," *L'Express*, 10 November 2001 (or online at <http:www.lexpress.fr/Express/Info/France/Dossier/octobre61.dossier.asp?n>).

[Saturday, 10 February 1962

Montaigne began writing his *Essays* in 1572, the year of the Saint Bartholomew's Day Massacre. Plutarque's *Moralia* [[or *Philosophy Commonly Called the Morals*]], translated by Amyot, were published the same year and became his breviary. I don't believe this was a coincidence: Montaigne was seeking refuge in writing. For him, it was a matter of escaping the horror of living in a kingdom perennially divided against itself. Four centuries after the religious wars, we have not gotten out of this state of affairs: pretexts change, but not the hatred nor the criminal attacks. Little crimes committed in the name of grand principles: that pretty much sums up all of French history.

We too, whose profession it is to write, dream like Montaigne of escaping events and of making our honey from them with our essays. And for us Christians who by God's grace have a sensitive heart, there is another temptation: the one that stems from our capacity for fleeing on high. Yes, a temptation—and we must not yield to it. The saints who flee the world for the cloisters suffer and die there for the world. As for us laypersons who are not saints, our vocation is not to flee human beings in search of God, but on the contrary to find God in human beings, be it in the thick of a miserable political situation.

We must therefore resume our commentary on the sordid, monotonous, daily story of history without presuming, on our own humble level, to make from it a work as durable as the *Essays*, for nothing is more ephemeral than France's domestic politics. . . .]

As is so often the case in the *Bloc-notes*, these lines depict the violent conflicts of the Algerian war as simply the latest episode in a long string of criminal conflicts characteristic of France, that "royaume éternellement divisé contre lui-même" (kingdom perennially divided against itself). And though Mauriac insists that he is no Montaigne and his *Bloc-notes* no *Essais*, an undeniable parallel remains: claiming to plunge into the political fray that Montaigne supposedly sought to flee, his extended commentary on the "basse histoire quotidienne" (sordid daily story of history)—monotonous only in its unceasing horror—recalls the Renaissance essayist's painstaking self-scrutiny and studious reflection on the "humaine condition," this time explored through the editorialist's encounter with history past and present.

History unfailingly filters the perception of the present in the *Bloc-*

notes and provides the inescapable frame of reference for understanding current events. Paradoxically, Mauriac identifies precisely this tendency to view the present in the light of the past as another source of estrangement from the contemporary world. Shuttling back and forth between the two, he accentuates the difference alluded to by Nora:

> Samedi 2 octobre 1965
>
> Cette distance que le grand âge met entre nous et l'événement, c'est ce qui fait croire qu'un vieil homme est devenu insensible et qu'il ne réagit plus à rien. Le vrai est que, si engagé qu'il soit en apparence, tout lui apparaît déjà comme de l'autre rive à chaque instant plus proche. On dirait que son oeil s'accommode à la vision qui sera bientôt éternellement la sienne.
>
> La vie fait tableau sous mon regard. . . .
>
> . . . quelle joie de découvrir une réédition du *Jules César* de Jérôme Carcopino! Je vais revivre la guerre des Gaules, persuadé d'y retrouver à deux mille ans de distance ces traits de notre nature qui vont à la mort dès qu'il y a à nos portes, pour en profiter, César ou Hitler. (BN IV, 139–41)
>
> [Saturday, 2 October 1965
>
> This distance that old age puts between me and events is what leads people to believe that I have become an insensitive old man who no longer reacts to anything. The fact of the matter is that, as politically committed as I may seem to be, everything already appears as if I were already viewing it from the other shore [[of death]] that is drawing nearer every instant. It is as if my eye were adjusting to the vision that will soon be mine for eternity.
>
> Life stretches out under my eyes as if composed for a painter's canvas. . . .
>
> . . . what a joy to discover a new edition of Jérôme Carcopino's *Jules César!* I am going to relive the Gallic wars, convinced that two thousand years later I will rediscover these traits of our [[French]] character that invariably appear as soon as some Caesar or Hitler shows up at our gates to take advantage of them.]

If the history of the Gallic wars holds up a distant mirror reflecting deep-seated traits of the French people, Mauriac nevertheless remains acutely aware of the distance separating the present from the past. His invariably historical perception (situating the present against the backdrop of time) thus clashes with the younger generation's blissful (and willful) ignorance of history:

> Samedi 11 décembre 1965
>
> Je ne puis parler de rien d'autre. A l'âge que j'ai, ne me détacherai-je pas de cette histoire qui est au moment de se poursuivre sans moi, et quelle chance subsiste que je pénètre très avant dans le prochain chapitre? Cette histoire, nous les fils de la IIIe République, nous l'avons vécue de trop près, au jour le jour, depuis notre adolescence, mais aussi siècle après siècle, nous qui fûmes peu ou prou historiens—et il n'en est aucun que nous n'avons eu le pouvoir d'habiter en esprit: *on peut dire que l'histoire de France tout entière se transcrit dans l'instant actuel*, que les mêmes passions y créent les mêmes complicités que durant les trois derniers siècles avec une puissance étrangère (qui n'est jamais la même: il y a beau temps que ce n'est plus l'Espagne!). Une continuité et une permanence: c'est cela notre destin, et qu'il nous faut aimer, oui, aimer désespérément pour ne pas céder au mépris. . . . (BN IV, 179–80)
>
> [Saturday, 11 December 1965
>
> I can speak of nothing else. At my age, shall I not be detached from this story of history that is about to go on without me, and what chance remains for me to get very far into the next chapter? We children of the Third Republic have experienced this story of history too closely from day to day since we were adolescents; and those of us who were in the slightest way inclined to be historians have lived this story of history century by century. And every single one of us has been able to inhabit this history in our minds: *one can say that the entire story of France's history is transcribed into the present moment*, that the same passions create here and now the same complicities with a foreign power (which is never the same: it has not been Spain for a long time) that can be observed over the last three centuries. A continuity and a permanence: that is our destiny, a destiny that we must love, yes, desperately love so as not to give in to contempt. . . .]

One would be hard-pressed to charge the past with more significance than does Mauriac in these lines, which once again present France's history as the depository of a common experience, and therefore constitutive of national identity. Yet Mauriac occupies a decidedly uncomfortable position here: steeped in history to the point of living current crises as new chapters in a long drama, he ironically finds himself estranged from those insensitive to the legacy of the past.

Thus understood from the perspective of history, the present is not isolated, not autonomous, not disconnected, but rather appears as another episode in a larger drama that has been unfolding for generations. Just as for Georges Lefebvre the French Revolution formed one coherent block, so for Mauriac French history—however violent may be its inner turmoils or catastrophic its relations with other countries—constitutes one integral story, an overarching, continuous set of events that have to be understood in relation to each other and to the entire saga. Even in the most divisive, somber, tragic moments, history offers Mauriac the possibility of maintaining a cohesive national identity and affirming continuity with the past.

The *Bloc-notes*'s continual references to the ordeals of France's past as both the setting and source of its contemporary conflicts enact the dynamic process described by Nora: memory holds up the past as a sort of mirror to the present, but it is precisely by interpreting the "spectacle de cette différence" (the spectacle of that difference) separating past from present that we come to (re)define and (re)form our contemporary identity.[10] The references to the St. Bartholomew's Day Massacre in Mauriac's "Bloc-notes" of "10 février 1962" are a case in point. Considering the event as emblematic of the endemic violence and civil warfare marking so many chapters of French history, he does not in the final analysis assimilate one to the other nor attribute both to some impersonal, immutable process unfolding outside of human responsibility and impervious to human intervention. In other words, he does not incorporate specific events into a grandiose logical chain of causes and effects or into some Hegelian dialectic that in the end trivializes (if not dissolves) violence and oppression by making them inevitable or even necessary to the overall scheme of things.

In the editorial inspired by the Métro Charonne massacre, Mauriac is not content merely to invoke the criminal conflicts of Montaigne's time: he goes on to denounce Minister of the Interior Roger Frey's ac-

10. See Nora, "Entre mémoire et histoire," xxxiii.

count of the incident and to accuse Michel Debré of complicity with the OAS (see BN III, 131–32, and Touzot's notes). Mauriac's reaction to the terrorist bombings carried out by the OAS against the most vulnerable segments of the Muslim population of Algeria is even more telling, not only of the tension between his invocation of the past (once again the St. Bartholomew Day Massacre) and his analysis of the present, but also of his own contradictions as one of the "gaullistes de gauche" (Gaullists on the left) who remain supportive of the general even while decrying the politics of his prime minister (see BN III, 132–33).

Contrary to the previously cited editorial referring to Montaigne and the religious wars, the following piece progresses from Mauriac's immediate surroundings, to Camus's lyrical depiction of Algeria, and on to the OAS's campaign of terror. Mauriac then connects this wave of violence with other political crimes in France's past before spelling out the implications for the current political situation. In order to appreciate the dynamic tension between Mauriac's political analysis of the present and his reference to the past, one must perceive the interrelation between these different parts of this "Bloc-notes." The passage therefore bears quoting at length:

> Mercredi 9 mai 1962
>
> Ces pâques tardives dont j'avais attendu des merveilles ne m'auront servi de rien puisque le printemps n'est pas venu à son heure et qu'avril aura été un mars frissonnant. Je comptais bien, cette année, voir les roses; la seule que j'aie cueillie, ce fut le matin du départ, avant de monter en voiture. La veille, au crépuscule, quelques roulades interrompues m'avaient rassuré: les rossignols étaient là, mais ils n'ont pas chanté dans la nuit trop froide. Ainsi les choses nous trahissent, il ne faut pas s'y appuyer plus que sur les êtres. L'attachement à des arbres et à des pierres est trompé comme tous les amours.
>
> Mais rien ne peut faire que l'histoire ne continue. "Solidaire, solidaire de ce monde où les fleurs et le vent ne feront jamais pardonner tout le reste . . ." (*Carnets* d'Albert Camus). Je pense tout à coup à une lettre que j'ai reçue: attaché comme je le suis à une maison, à une terre, où pourtant je n'habite que trois mois de l'année, je devrais être plus sensible que je ne le montre à l'arrachement imposé aux déracinés de l'Algérie. La lecture des *Carnets* de Camus me fait sentir ce qu'est cette terre algérienne, son pouvoir d'ensorcellement. D'où vient mon appar-

ente insensibilité? Car il ne s'agit que d'une apparence. Dès que j'arrête ma pensée sur un cas particulier, j'entre aisément dans cette angoisse. (BN III, 180–82)

[Wednesday, 9 May 1962

I had expected this late Easter to be wonderful, but since spring has not come on time, my hopes were for naught: April has turned out to be a chilly month of March. I was really counting on seeing the roses this year, but the only one I picked was on the morning I left, just before getting into the car. The previous day at dusk, I had been reassured by a few birds I heard warbling off and on: the nightingales were there, but did not sing during such a cold night. Thus it is that things betray us: we must not count on them any more than on living beings. Affection for trees and stones is betrayed as are all loves.

Yet nothing can change the fact that history goes on. "I am in deep, deep solidarity with this world where flowers and wind will never bring us to excuse all the rest . . ." (Albert Camus, *Journal*). I suddenly think of a letter that I received: as fond as I am of a house and a piece of land, even though I only spend three months out of the year there, I should be more sympathetic than I let on to the wrenching separation imposed on those who had to leave behind their homes in Algeria. Reading Camus's *Journal* gave me a sense of that Algerian land and its power of enchantment. What does my apparent insensitivity stem from? For it is only an appearance. Whenever I fix my mind on a particular case, I can easily share a similar anxiety.]

Particularly notable here is the critical distance Mauriac once again takes with respect both to his own favorite place of memory and to the importance accorded to "lieux de mémoire" in general. Rather than allowing his own passion for the realms of memory of his childhood home lead him to sympathize with the partisans of an "Algérie française," he denounces the crimes perpetrated by the OAS, who built their whole ideology on the attachment and loyalty to their own version of Barrès's "la terre et les morts":

Ce qui m'en sépare [de l'angoisse des déracinés européens de l'Algérie], c'est ce grand tas de morts qui épaissit et qui monte jour après jour, ces cadavres de pauvres, d'enfants, de femmes de ménage, qui recouvrent chaque soir les cadavres de la veille, ces victimes désignées par le hasard mais appartenant toutes au même peuple, le plus démuni, le plus humilié, le plus offensé depuis cent trente ans; les chrétiens qui l'ont humilié et offensé n'ont pas tous part à l'abomination d'aujourd'hui, je le sais bien, et beaucoup la blâment. Il n'empêche que les récits des témoins concordent: ces crimes s'accomplissent dans une sécurité absolue, non pas presque toujours, mais toujours. La complicité de l'homme de la rue est patente. Et que la peur y entre pour une grande part, je le crois; mais enfin toute épreuve pâlit en comparaison de celle qui est infligée à ce peuple; toute injustice paraît légère confrontée à ce crime innombrable, ininterrompu, en quelque sorte mécanique.

Les tueurs appartiennent à une espèce connue, à une faune qui s'est manifestée à divers moments de l'histoire; mais il s'agissait d'un massacre, comme la Saint-Barthélemy, avec un commencement, un milieu et une fin; ou de journées révolutionnaires. Je doute si à aucune époque et dans aucun temps il se soit rien passé de tel que ce qui s'exécute froidement en plein jour, et selon un plan préconçu, sur les trottoirs des villes algériennes, depuis des semaines et des mois.

Cette boucherie répond à un calcul. Elle a été conçue par une réflexion lucide; et s'il ne se trouve pas beaucoup de Français, même de droite, pour l'approuver, il s'en trouve beaucoup en revanche pour absoudre les assassins et pour charger de leurs crimes celui qui, selon eux les a rendus possibles par une politique qu'ils détestent. (BN III, 181–82)

[What distances me [[from the anxiety of those Europeans who had to leave their homes in Algeria]] is this big heap of dead bodies that is growing larger and taller every day: these are corpses of the poor, of children, of maids, and every evening their bodies cover those who were killed the day before. Although chosen at random, these victims all belong to the same group of people: those who have been the poorest, most humiliated, and the most insulted for a hundred years. I know quite well that not all the Christians who have humiliated and insulted them have taken part in today's abominations. Many condemn these acts. Nevertheless, eyewitness accounts are all in agreement: these crimes are carried out with absolute impunity, not almost always, but always. I am willing to believe that fear might have a lot to do with it. Still, all other ordeals pale in comparison with the one inflicted on this group of people; all other injustices seem minor in comparison with this uninterrupted, clockwork series of crimes on such a huge scale.

The killers belong to a known type of people that has shown up at various times in history. In the past, however, the phenomenon occurred at events such as the Saint Bartholomew's Day Massacre, with a beginning, a middle, and an end, or else during one of the insurrectional days of a revolution. I doubt that in any other era or at any other time there has been anything similar to the events that have been going on for weeks and months in the cities of Algeria and that are still happening today: actions are being carried out in broad daylight and according to a preconceived plan.

This butchery is the product of cold calculation. It has been carefully and consciously thought out. And even if there are not many French people, not even on the right, who approve of it, there are, however, a good many willing to absolve the killers and blame their crimes on the man who, according to them, has made these actions possible by a policy that they hate.]

If Mauriac refers here to that (in)famous place of historical memory, the Saint Bartholomew's Day Massacre, it is not to present the bombings as some sort of inevitable event only to be expected given the circumstances—although it would have been easy to use such an argument—but on the contrary in order to better gauge the gravity and ponder the implications of the OAS's violence. In Mauriac's view, its campaign of terror was all the more unsettling in that it corresponded not to some momentary rash of political rage or fanaticism but rather to a political strategy coldly carried out over an extended period of time with the massive complicity of the local population.

The entire editorial is a marked exercise of historical realism emphatically opposed to any idyllic depiction: here as elsewhere, Mauriac rightly sees France's past as divisive and bloody, and there can be no question of returning to another time or any previous order either in Algeria or in mainland France. Yet it is precisely this historical lucidity that leads him to proclaim an unswerving loyalty to de Gaulle and to embrace the general's admittedly idealistic vision of French history. The "Bloc-notes" written for 30 October 1960 reveals why, in Mauriac's view, the vision of the past inherent in de Gaulle's "certaine idée de la France" makes the general the ideal person to lead France through the Algerian crisis. Before citing Mauriac's comments on de Gaulle's epic view of French history, we should note that they come after several paragraphs relating a series of anxieties over the present situation, all of which implicitly incline the aged editorialist toward de Gaulle. Once again, a transition between the provincial world of his ancestral home at Malagar and the Parisian metropolis prompts highly negative remarks about the modern urban world:

> Aujourd'hui, c'est de nouveau Paris et ses banlieues: cinq ou six millions d'âmes, eût-on dit autrefois. Il faut dire aujourd'hui: des millions de moteurs. Au-dessus du plus grand garage de l'Europe, le mazout entretient jour et nuit sa calotte de poisons. (BN II, 492)
>
> [Today, it's Paris and Parisian suburbs again: five or six million souls, one would have said in other times. Today, one has to say: millions of motors. Day and night, fuel oil maintains it cap of poisons over the biggest garage in Europe.]

This observation of a sort of mortality in the capital city leads Mauriac to contemplate his own mortality, to posit a permanence and continuity not contingent upon any historical event, and then to reaffirm his irrevocable "engagement" or implication in the *res publica:*

> Ce qui demeure, nous le tenons au-dedans de nous. Nous le possédons à jamais. Non que nous nous détournions du monde: nous lui appartenons jusqu'à la fin; il ne dépend pas de nous d'en sortir avant l'heure. L'engagement n'est pas un acte délibéré: nous sommes engagés, que nous le voulions ou non. (BN II, 492)
>
> [We hold within us that which abides. We possess it forever. Not that we turn away from the world: we belong to it until the end, and it is not up to us to leave before it is time. Commitment is not a deliberate act: we have committed ourselves whether we like it or not.]

Mauriac next proceeds to clarify the specific nature of this political commitment: strongly condemning "le fanatisme nationaliste" (nationalist fanaticism, both that of the FLN and of the OAS, but the latter in particularly strong terms) responsible for the most serious violations of human rights in Algeria, he finally presents his support for de Gaulle as an attempted synthesis of various contrasting views:

> Tel est ce noeud de contradictions que je ne démêle ni ne romps. "Mon amitié pour certains hommes" dont parlait Mounier? Elle tient à ceci qu'un homme au pouvoir, si je l'estime, l'incarne, cette contradic-

tion qui est en moi. Mendès France hier, de Gaulle aujourd'hui, s'efforcent de rejoindre cette vérité qui n'a pas de camp, cette justice due à la fois au peuple algérien et aux Français d'Algérie—due aussi à cette France historique qui existe dans la pensée d'un de Gaulle avec un autre visage que dans la pensée d'un militant de gauche: celui-ci voit un peuple souffrant et peinant, et tendant à se libérer, de génération en génération, et de Gaulle voit des soldats, des rois, des ambassadeurs, des Assemblées, qui donnent à notre destin sa figure éternelle. N'importe: c'est bien de la même France qu'il s'agit et à laquelle la justice est due comme à tout autre peuple. (BN II, 493)

[Such is the knot of contradictions that I neither untangle nor break. As for "my friendship with certain men" that Mounier used to claim, it comes down to this: if I esteem a man who holds political power, it's because he embodies this contradiction that is in me. Yesterday Mendès France and today de Gaulle have sought to reach that truth that has no political camp and that acknowledges that justice must be rendered both to the Algerian people and to the French in Algeria. Justice must also be rendered to this France of history that exists in the thought of de Gaulle and that has a different face from the one we find in the thought of a leftist activist: the latter sees a people suffering and struggling from generation to generation to free itself, while de Gaulle sees soldiers, kings, ambassadors, and assemblies that give our destiny its perennial face. No matter: we are talking about the same France, to which justice is due, just as for any other nation.]

As idealistic—and therefore decidely unrealistic, since it is inattentive to the political crimes that Mauriac sees so prominently in French history—as de Gaulle's "certaine idée de la France" may be, Mauriac finds in it a unity, continuity, and connection to the past that compensate for civil strife, political instability, and historical amnesia so characteristic of the disheartening present. Such lines—not at all uncommon in the *Bloc-notes*—should suffice to dispel the notion that Mauriac's allegeance to de Gaulle stemmed from blind ideological loyalism. We find on the contrary a complex, carefully articulated, and reasoned political stance.

Mauriac did of course distinguish—or in the eyes of his detractors, discredit—himself in an unflagging defense of de Gaulle's sovereign command of France in numerous editorials, particularly those of the

1960s. But he was neither unaware of nor indifferent to the significant tensions between his own views and those of the general. In the "Bloc-notes" penned for "Jeudi 28 mars 1963," Mauriac reflects on the passion for history that irresistibly draws him to de Gaulle in spite of his own misgivings over certain chapters of French history that the general seems to ignore. Mauriac begins by measuring the disparity between de Gaulle's epic vision and the current citizenry of France, stating that he (Mauriac) admires first and foremost in de Gaulle, a "chef qui . . . demeure fidèle à cette idée de la France à laquelle les Français vivants ressemblent si peu et qui pourtant correspond pour lui à une idée irrécusable" (BN III, 331; leader who . . . remains faithful to this idea of France that resembles so little present-day French people, yet which for him represents an irrefutable notion). He then proceeds, by means of carefully nuanced reasoning, to explain the gap between de Gaulle's grandiose view of history and his own analysis of the "brouillamini d'erreurs et de violence" marking France's past:

> De Gaulle croit, lui, que la France demeure la grande nation dans tous les ordres. C'est par là qu'il date, répliquent ses adversaires, et que sa politique relève d'un nationalisme révolu. Mais lui se moque bien de passer pour un nationaliste. Il garde sa foi, ou plutôt il fonde sa certitude sur des données qui ne relèvent pas seulement de l'histoire. Convenons-en: il est plus facile à M. Spaak[11] qu'à de Gaulle d'être un bon Européen. (BN III, 331)
>
> [For his part, de Gaulle believes that France is still a great nation on all levels. His adversaries retort that this notion is dated, and that his policies hark back to an antiquated nationalism. But he could care less about being seen as a nationalist. He keeps his faith, or rather he founds his certitude on facts that are based on other things than history. Let's admit it: it is easier for M. Spaak to be a good European than for de Gaulle.]

Mauriac clearly perceives the measure of braggadocio in de Gaulle's claims to French grandeur, and makes a point of setting his own outlook apart from that of the general and, notably, of Maurras:

11. Touzot (BN III, 331, n1) explains that the Belgian foreign minister Paul Henri Spaak sharply opposed de Gaulle's European policies.

Non que je partage tout à fait sa foi. Je vois, par un effort de volonté, cette France que voit de Gaulle, celle que voyait Péguy, dans ma jeunesse, que voyait Barrès, que ne voyait pas Maurras, qui, lui, éliminait ce qu'il haïssait et menait sa guerre civile personnelle à travers l'histoire. De Gaulle, il me semble, ne choisit pas: Robespierre et Saint-Just entrent dans la composition du tableau au même titre que Saint Louis et que Jeanne d'Arc. Oui, je la vois, cette France, mais sans lui donner tout mon coeur. Notre histoire me fascine et m'horrifie. Si je ne craignais pas de faire rire, j'avouerais qu'une part de moi-même ne s'est jamais consolée de la croisade albigeoise, jamais consolée de la Saint-Barthélemy, ni des dragonnades, ni de la destruction de Port-Royal, ni de la Terreur, ni du procès de la Reine, ni du martyre de Louis XVII, ni de tout le reste, jusqu'à la dernière torture, en Algérie, du dernier torturé.

De tout cela, l'idée de la France que se fait de Gaulle se nourrit. Il ne renie rien de cette grandeur, cimentée par le sang des héros, mais aussi par celui des victimes, et façonnée par une pensée politique constante de Philippe le Bel à Richelieu et de Richelieu à de Gaulle. Incapable de ressentir ce qu'il ressent (ce que j'imagine qu'il ressent), j'incline à croire comme à une possibilité que l'histoire lui donnera raison contre ceux qui ont décidé que la France était devenue à jamais une nation de second ordre. J'entre dans son parti pris de ne pas mesurer la patrie à ses concitoyens vivants. Je parie pour la grande nation, sans renier pour autant l'Europe. (BN III, 331–32)

[Not that I completely share his faith. Putting my mind to it, I can see this France that de Gaulle sees, the one that Péguy saw, the same one that, when I was a youth, Barrès saw and Maurras did not see. Maurras eliminated what he hated and carried out his personal civil war through history. De Gaulle, it seems to me, does not pick and choose: Robespierre and Saint-Just enter into the composition of his painting as rightfully as Saint Louis and Joan of Arc. Yes, I can see this France, but without giving it all my heart. Our history fascinates and horrifies me. If I were not fearful of making people laugh at me, I would admit that a part of me has never been consoled over the crusade against the Albigenses, nor Louis XIV's use of soldiers to stamp out Protestantism, nor the destruction of Port-Royal, nor the Reign of Terror, nor the queen's trial, nor the abuse suffered by Louis XVI's young son, nor all the rest, right down to the last act of torture and the most recent victim of torture in Algeria.

All of that enters into the idea of France formed by de Gaulle. He re-

> pudiates none of that grandeur cemented by heroes'—but also by victims'—blood, and fashioned by political thinking that has been a constant from Philippe the Fair to Richelieu and from Richelieu to de Gaulle. Although incapable of feeling what he feels (what I imagine he feels), I am inclined to believe in the possibility that history will prove him right over those who decided that France had definitively turned into a second-rank nation. I take his side in choosing not to measure our country by the citizens now living. I wager for the great nation, without repudiating Europe in the process.]

These lines exhibit neither blind adherence nor total submission to de Gaulle's politics of grandeur. It takes a willful effort for the editorialist to perceive France's past as de Gaulle sees it, and even then Mauriac has to admit that, far from inspiring transports of national pride, some chapters leave him queasy: "Notre histoire me fascine et m'horrifie" (Our history fascinates and horrifies me).

But Mauriac's adhesion to de Gaulle's grandiose idea of French history is all the more fascinating precisely because he underscores the tensions—if not contradictions—of de Gaulle's logic. He clearly perceives the Gaullist narrative of French history as an artful construction that does not account for political crimes committed against various groups. As fanciful as it may be as an account of the past, however, de Gaulle's certain idea of France wins Mauriac's enthusiastic endorsement as a political strategy for integrating the disparate elements of the nation's past into a coherent project for the present.

Mauriac had after all said as much in reaffirming his support of de Gaulle while at the same time castigating Prime Minister Michel Debré and Debré's government after the brutal suppression of anti-OAS demonstrators at the Métro Charonne. After explicitly admitting the contradiction that finds him torn between "fidélité à de Gaulle" (fidelity to de Gaulle) and "fidélité à ce peuple dont le flot sombre recommence à rouler, comme en d'autres journées d'histoire, entre la République et la Nation" (BN III, 133; fidelity to the people who, as on other historic days, once again are flowing somberly down the avenue between the Place de la République and the Place de la Nation), Mauriac voices his confidence in de Gaulle:

> Il incarne la France de l'histoire; il donne une réalité charnelle à ce qui n'était qu'une idée. . . .
>
> De Gaulle est le cerveau et le coeur d'une grande nation rassemblée, d'une grande nation une et indivisible qui n'existe pas. ("Samedi 10 février 1962," BN III, 133, 134)
>
> [He embodies the France of history; he gives a flesh-and-blood reality to what was only an idea. . . .
>
> De Gaulle is the heart and mind of a great nation gathered together, a great nation one and indivisible that does not exist.]

To Mauriac's mind, de Gaulle's attraction stems from this capacity to translate an idealistic (hence fanciful, even artificial) historical vision into concrete political reality, or in other words to lead France back to its international grandeur by the seductive power of an epic narrative.

As courageous and uncompromising as he was in denouncing the fascistic nationalism so conducive to torture and oppression in Algeria and in identifying the affinities between nazism and the nationalist accusers of Dreyfus, Mauriac ends up embracing de Gaulle's generous, forward-looking nationalism for reasons that closely resemble the novelist's continued admiration for Barrès. While warning that one can no longer read Barrès's exposition of nationalism without keeping in mind "la sinistre histoire nazie" (BN IV, 134; the sinister history of nazism), Mauriac's preface to Barrès's complete works stresses Barrès's importance for the dramatic history of the Third Republic and even modern literature. In all his ambivalence, Barrès remains a "lieu de mémoire" for Mauriac on a personal and a national level.

It is furthermore no mere coincidence that Mauriac characterizes Barrès's political ambition in virtually the same terms as de Gaulle's: "ce qui lui importe d'abord . . . c'est d'inspirer et de diriger la politique française à partir de l'idée de France qu'il porte au-dedans de lui et qu'il découvre à la racine de son moi" ("Vendredi 24 septembre 1965," BN IV, 138; what is first and foremost important to him is to inspire and conduct French policy based on the idea of France that he carries within him and that he finds at the root of his personal identity). Indeed, Mauriac explains the enthusiasm for de Gaulle that suffuses the *Bloc-notes* of the mid- and late 1960s in terms of the general's ability to impose an epic vision of France's past on a rather reticent, motley electorate, "ce peuple de grippe-sous, occupé de tiercé, de nourriture et de télévision" ("Vendredi 25 juin 1965," BN IV, 101; this tight-fisted people focused on horse races, food, and television). Even though Mauriac acknowledges that de Gaulle's narrative stems from a very personal vision of "une France qui n'existe pas" (a France that doesn't exist), the editorialist nevertheless embraces and celebrates it as a remedy not only to address the factionalism that threatens to tear asunder or disgrace the French nation but also to confront everything in postindustrial France that chagrins or alienates him.

Whereas religious, social, and ideological divisions generate recurrent civil warfare (as so vividly recalled by Mauriac's many allusions to the Saint Bartholomew Day Massacre and the Dreyfus affair, among others), de Gaulle's ideal of "la France eternelle" reconciles the warring factions by incorporating them all into one continuous narrative of national permanence and grandeur. Just after referring to the Gallic wars as emblems of the internecine strife so characteristic of France's long history, Mauriac presents de Gaulle as the cure to this age-old "mal français" (French complaint):

> Peut-être est-ce de cela [la tendance française de s'entre-déchirer] que notre peuple a pris conscience, grâce à de Gaulle. Nous en aurons bientôt le coeur net. Le problème à résoudre pour lui ou pour son successeur est de faire vivre ensemble des Français qui ne s'aiment pas, chacun ayant ses raisons particulières, enracinées dans l'histoire, la plus lointaine et la plus proche, de détester tous les autres. ("Samedi 2 octobre 1965," BN IV, 141)
>
> [Perhaps our nation has become aware of this fact [[France's propensity for internecine strife]] thanks to de Gaulle. We shall soon know one way or another. The problem that he or his successor will have to resolve is that of getting French people to live peacefully together even though they don't like each other: each group has its particular reasons, rooted in the most recent or most distant history, for hating all the others.]

De Gaulle's politics of idealized *memory* thus compensate for the tragic reality of French *history*. Mauriac accordingly sums up Gaullism's merit as the power of de Gaulle's "certaine idée de la France" to galvanize the French into a cohesively functioning nation. What ultimately justifies de Gaulle, contends Mauriac, is "cette permanence de la vieille nation, c'est l'idée que s'en fait de Gaulle et qui ne serait rien si elle ne répondait pas à la réalité" ("Vendredi 25 juin," BN IV, 102; this permanence of the old nation, the idea that de Gaulle has formed of this nation, and which would be nothing if it did not respond to reality). Similarly, Gaullism's strength, Mauriac argues in the same piece, "tient à cette découverte que les Français ont faite d'un pouvoir de la France demeuré intact à travers une histoire horrible" (BN IV, 103; stems from the French people's discovery that a certain French capability has remained intact through a horrible series of historical events). As fanciful as it may be in the light of historical truth, de Gaulle's ideal construct neverthless links the various factions of the French people to each other by anchoring them all to a venerable, albeit traumatic, past transcending the limitations of the present.

Conversely, we find that just prior to the December 1965 presidential elections the younger generation's insensitivity to de Gaulle's notion of "la France éternelle" troubles Mauriac. Not having seen France totter on the brink of irreparable disaster during World War I and World War II, they do not appreciate the "résurrections" that Mauriac attributes to the general:

> . . . ils [les jeunes] ne sont remontés d'aucun de nos abîmes, ils n'ont pas même à les oublier puisqu'ils ne les ont pas connus. Alors que nous, qui avons eu vingt ans avant 14, à quoi n'avons-nous pas survécu? De Gaulle incarne ces résurrections successives, mais pour un garçon de vingt ans. . . . ("Dimanche 12 décembre 1965," BN IV, 181)
>
> [. . . they [[the young]] have not climbed back out of any of the depths we had fallen into, they don't even have any need to forget them since they never experienced them. We who turned twenty before 1914, on the other hand, have lived through all sorts of calamities. De Gaulle embodies these successive resurrections, but for a young man aged twenty today. . . .]

After de Gaulle's reelection, Mauriac returns to the same idea, reiterating his conviction that "De Gaulle disparaîtra, mais ce qui a déferlé à travers lui vient du fond de l'histoire et continuera après lui" ("Dimanche 26 décembre 1965," BN IV, 187; de Gaulle will pass away, but the tide that rolled in with him comes from the depths of history and will continue on after he is gone).

The quasi-religious aura that Mauriac's use of terms such as "résurrection" attribute to the general are by no means an anomaly in the *Bloc-notes* of the mid- to late 1960s. Our editorialist not only has frequent recourse to a personification of France, he often goes so far as to situate this human incarnation of the French nation in the person of Charles de Gaulle. While such near-monarchist sentiments may constitute a rather shocking inconsistency on the part of one who had so courageously defended the dignity of the human person against the reason of the state in his outspoken denunciation of torture and oppression in Algeria, it is important to note here that Mauriac's habit of idolizing de Gaulle has everything to do with his passion for history and memory, and nothing at all to do with any "mystical" inclinations.[12]

Seeing de Gaulle as the embodiment of a paradoxically timeless French identity fashioned from the successive ordeals that the nation has endured over centuries offers two tremendous benefits to the octogenarian author of the *Bloc-notes:* on the one hand, it allows him to rescue the rich patrimony of the past from oblivion, and, on the other hand, it provides an antidote to the dissolution of French identity that Mauriac sees in the general dehumanization of a world of rampant technology and Americanization. Two pieces in particular articulate the twofold remedy that Gaullist memory administers to Mauriac's historical angst. In the first, we find Mauriac once again irritated with the younger generation's insensitivity, if not total indifference, to the treas-

12. In his *Mauriac et de Gaulle*, Malcolm Scott attributes Mauriac's fervent Gaullism to mystical intimations (71) and even contends that the editorialist assimilates the general to Christ (197–98). In addition to truncating a citation and thus making it say the opposite of what Mauriac meant, Scott seems to ignore or forget that (a) Mauriac sees Christ as the archetype of all who experience oppression or suffering, and that (b) accordingly, a number of people, including Pierre Mendes France and Alfred Dreyfus, appear as Christ figures in the *Bloc-notes.* Moreover, the very notion of "mysticism," implying direct communication or even unity with the divine, is utterly foreign to Mauriac, who both in his novels and in the *Bloc-notes* repeatedly decries the absence of God. Scott seems to use "mystical" as synonymous with "spiritual."

ures of intelligence and courage that, in Mauriac's eyes, France has acquired through the vicissitudes of its long past:

> Jeudi 16 juin 1966
>
> Quelques jeunes Français, cette semaine, répondent à l'enquête d'un hebdomadaire: "La patrie? Un petit coin de terre. Ça ne représente pas grand-chose." Ou encore: "A partir du moment où on conquiert l'espace, le mot patrie ne veut plus rien dire." Le mot patrie ne leur dit plus rien. Que leur diraient, à ces subtils garçons, le mot Montaigne, le mot Descartes, le mot Port-Royal—ou le mot Résistance, le mot Mont-Valérien, le mot Vercors? Quel écho éveillerait en eux cette litanie de héros, d'inspirés et de saints dont nous pouvons nous bercer nous-mêmes, sans sortir de notre histoire? Qu'est-ce que l'espace auprès d'une seule de ces pensées? Mais de quoi vais-je leur parler?
>
> Le vieil homme [Charles de Gaulle] que la Russie acclamera au moment où paraîtra ce bloc-notes incarne la jeunesse éternelle d'un peuple. . . . Mais il suffit qu'un peuple prenne conscience de lui-même dans quelques-uns—et peut-être, à certaines heures, dans un seul. (BN IV, 280–81)
>
> [Thursday, 16 June 1966
>
> This week, a few French youth have responded to a survey in a weekly news magazine. "Our country? A little corner of earth. It does not represent much." And then: "Once the conquest of space has begun, the word 'country' no longer means anything." What would the word Montaigne, the word Descartes, the word Port-Royal, or the word Resistance, the word Mont-Valérien, the word Vercors mean to these clever young men? We can take comfort in this litany of heroes, inspired figures, and saints without looking outside our own history, but what would they stir up inside these youth? What is space in comparison with a single one of these thoughts? But what am I going to talk to them about?
>
> The old man [[Charles de Gaulle]] that Russia will be acclaiming when this "Bloc-notes" will come out embodies the perennial youth of a nation. . . . But it is enough for a country to become aware of itself in a few people, and perhaps, at certain times, in one single person.]

Just as de Gaulle's embodiment of a certain idea of French history bridges the abyss of amnesia separating the generation of the 1960s from the ranks of their illustrious predecessors, so his affirmation of

France's proud autonomy in the face of American hegemony preserves the specific identity that France has acquired as a prominent, long-standing European power. To those decrying de Gaulle's habit of identifying the French nation with his own person, Mauriac therefore protests that, far from succumbing to megalomania, the general has rendered a singular service to his compatriots:

> Et voici que de Gaulle vous démontre, et dans un temps où d'énormes empires croyaient nous avoir relégués au niveau des petits peuples, que cette France de 1965 garde intact son pouvoir sur les coeurs et sur les esprits; et elle le garde en dépit de l'entreprise d'avilissement et de l'attentat permanent contre l'homme dont les techniques modernes (cinéma, radio, télévision) sont les agents. . . .
>
> Le général de Gaulle ne se prend pas pour la France, mais peut-être (peut-être . . .) a-t-il rendu beaucoup de Français conscients de ce qu'il n'appartient à personne, individus ou nations, de renier: ce qui constitue pour chacun son être même, ce qui le rend différent de tous les autres—non certes supérieur aux autres ni meilleur—mais ce qui le rend irremplaçable. C'est à partir de cette connaissance que l'Europe pourra naître enfin. ("Vendredi 25 juin," BN IV, 102–3)
>
> [And now, in a time when huge empires thought they had relegated us to the level of a little country, de Gaulle is demonstrating to you that the France of 1965 has kept intact its power over hearts and minds; and France has kept it in spite of the debasing onslaught of modern technology (cinema, radio, television) against humanity. . . .
>
> General de Gaulle does not presume to be France, but maybe (just maybe . . .) he has made many French people aware of something that no one, no individual or nation, has the right to repudiate: this is what constitutes the very being of each one of them, what makes each different—granted, not superior or better—from all the others, that which makes it irreplaceable. On the basis of this knowledge, Europe will finally be able to see the light of day.]

What more eloquent or at least more pertinent definition could one give of the "exception française" that, from de Gaulle to Mitterrand to Chirac, France's leaders have so insistently asserted vis-à-vis American presumptions throughout the last forty years. Most noteworthy for our present discussion, however, is the quite visible link between de Gaulle's uncompromising affirmation of French sovereignty and Mauriac's preoccupation with defending the delicate tapestry of humanity against the encroachments of the modern world.

The very personal realms of memory visible in Mauriac's many descriptions of the vibrant past—which as we have seen are connected not only to his family dwelling at Malagar but also to the surrounding rural provincial world—ultimately find themselves parallel to the "lieux de mémoire" so vital to France's national identity. On both the personal and the collective levels, we observe the same passion for preserving the stores of memory that, for Mauriac, as for so many of his compatriots, constitute the substance of self and country.

It is this ardor for France's historical heritage that leads Mauriac to embrace some rather embarrassing Barrésian notions of national identity and to utter certain regrettable and at times flagrant excesses. Take for example the lines he penned in the wake of the Ben Barka affair.[13] Although deeply troubled by the murky circumstances of the incident,[14] Mauriac adamantly refused to make an analogy with the Dreyfus affair that might tarnish de Gaulle. Without entering into the details of this controversy, we can observe with no little amazement that Mauriac's ultimate disculpatory argument in defending de Gaulle is the criminal nature of history itself:

> Il n'empêche que ce qui s'est toujours passé ne devrait plus se passer sous de Gaulle. Cela, le peuple l'a senti. Les adversaires eux-mêmes, en s'étonnant et en se scandalisant, ont rendu un hommage involontaire à l'homme exécré. Mais moi, je sais que l'histoire est criminelle et qu'il ne dépend de personne, et pas plus de De Gaulle que, dans les siècles des siècles, de Titus, de Marc Aurèle ou de Saint-Louis, de la rendre innocent. . . .
>
> L'histoire est criminelle et elle pose des énigmes redoutables à ses élus. . . . il n'a pas dépendu de lui [de Gaulle] d'éviter les flaques de boue et les flaques de sang, pas plus que cela n'a dépendu, au cours de

13. Mehdi Ben Barka, the leader of the Moroccan opposition, was kidnapped and killed in autumn 1965 by two French police officers who later implicated their superiors; see Touzot, BN IV, 201 n2.

14. An ex-convict having set up the ambush/trap for Ben Bella was, at the moment of his arrest, found to have "committed suicide" in a highly suspect manner; see Touzot, BN IV, 201 n2.

l'histoire, de la volonté d'aucun prince, si saint ou si sage qu'il ait été: "On ne gouverne pas innocemment." Mais c'est peut-être le seul domaine, la politique, où il arrive que le renoncement à l'innocence devienne mérite et devienne vertu. ("Samedi 19 février 1966," BN IV, 217–18)

[The fact remains that what has always occurred should not have occurred under de Gaulle. The French people have sensed that. In their surprise and indignation, de Gaulle's adversaries themselves paid unwitting tribute to the man they execrate. But, as for me, I know that history is criminal and it is up to no one, not de Gaulle anymore than it was up to Titus, Marcus Aurelius, or Saint Louis, to make it innocent throughout all these centuries. . . .

History is criminal and it presents dreadful dilemmas to its elect. . . . [[I]]t was not up to him [[de Gaulle]] to avoid the mud puddles and the pools of blood, no more than it ever was up to any prince over the course of history, however saintly or wise he may have been: "One does not govern innocently." But politics is perhaps the only domain in which it sometimes becomes a merit and a virtue to turn one's back on innocence.]

What a stunning about-face for the author of the *Cahier noir*, justly admired as a Resistance piece for its unequivocal denunciation of Machiavellian politics, and what an apparent lapse of conscience for the editorialist of *L'Express* who, in denouncing the torture and oppression perpetrated for reasons of state during the Algerian war, constantly reminded his readers that history has a human face and courageously insisted that neither France's elected officials nor the citizens who elected them could escape responsibility for crimes committed on behalf of the government. Rather than appearing as the result of human, all-too-human, enterprises, however, the "history" invoked here seems to unfold implacably outside the realm of human will.

The concluding words to this effort to insulate de Gaulle from the Ben Barka affair illustrate a notable lapse into the idolization of de Gaulle alluded to above:

De Gaulle incarne tout ce qu'ils [ses détracteurs] ne peuvent souffrir: une certaine idee de l'indépendance de la nation à l'égard de toutes les autres et surtout de la plus puissante, la religion d'un honneur français à sauvegarder et à défendre, de cette "fortune de la France" que les rois et les républiques se sont passée de siècle en siècle jusqu'à de Gaulle et que lui, le dernier, il élève au-dessus de vos têtes furieuses. (BN IV, 219)

[De Gaulle embodies everything that they [[his detractors]] cannot bear: a certain idea of the independence of our nation with respect to all others, and above all to the most powerful nation; the religion of a French honor to be preserved and defended, of the "French destiny" that our kings and republics have passed on from century to century right down to de Gaulle, and that he, the latest in this long tradition, raises above your furious heads.]

Not only does Mauriac liken the founder of the Fifth Republic to a consul, a sovereign, and a monarch, he even depicts him here as a sort of high priest of a "religion d'un honneur français" (religion of a French honor) raising the glorious body of the immortal French nation for all to worship.

In a February 1967 editorial, he readily approves de Gaulle's personal exercise of power and then recalls what is perhaps the most famous episode of Barrès's nationalist trilogy *Le Roman de l'énergie nationale* in order to illustrate what he considers to be the general's prime virtue:

> . . . à aucun moment de l'histoire, en France, l'Etat n'aura été quelqu'un au degré où il l'est aujourd'hui.
>
> Ce qui irrite ou exaspère, ou consterne tant de mes contemporains (du moins ceux dont l'esprit s'est formé sous les deux précédentes républiques), je conviens que je m'en accommode moi-même le mieux du monde, sans aucune vergogne: on ne saurait être moins gêné que je ne suis par le pouvoir personnel, ayant souffert durant toute ma vie d'une absence de pouvoir que d'ailleurs autour de moi chacun déplorait: "Il n'y a plus d'Etat!," gémissait-on. C'était évident, et ce qu'il en a coûté à la nation, nous le savons. ("Dimanche 12 février 1967," 398)
>
> [. . . never at any other time in history in France has the state been embodied in someone to the degree that it is today.
>
> That is what irritates, exasperates, or worries so many of my contemporaries (at least those whose minds were trained under the two preceding republics). I admit that I am on the contrary shamelessly comfortable with this state of affairs. One could not be less upset than I am by the personal exercise of power, since I have throughout my life

suffered from an absence of power that everyone around me moreover used to deplore: "There is no longer any governmental authority!" people would moan. The fact was obvious, and we know what price our nation paid because of that state of affairs.]

Having thus stated his satisfaction at seeing a prestigious, willful individual embody the state, Mauriac proceeds to salute de Gaulle for embodying the essence of French identity in his policies:

Relisant ces jours-ci *Les Déracinés* de Maurice Barrès, dans la belle édition du Club de l'Honnête Homme, je me demandais si ce livre avait compté pour le jeune de Gaulle comme pour mes amis et pour moi-même. Ce qui est sûr, c'est que l'humble vérité politique, celle qui ne tient pas à une construction de l'esprit mais aux données du destin français, de Gaulle a pu en prendre là de la graine, et il l'a semée plus tard, en d'autres temps, et sous quelle tempête de grêle, et dans quelle boue, hélas!

Monsieur Taine, au chapitre VII des *Déracinés*, nous le voyons qui donne comme but à sa promenade un platane du square des Invalides. Monsieur Taine admire que cette masse puissante de verdure "obéisse à une raison secrète, à la plus sublime philosophie qui est l'acceptation des nécessités de la vie. Sans se renier, sans s'abandonner, il a tiré des conditions fournies par la réalité le meilleur parti, le plus utile." (BN IV, 398)

[As I was rereading Maurice Barrès's *Les Déracinés* [*The Uprooted*] in the fine edition published by Le Club de l'Honnête Homme, I wondered if this book had meant as much to the young de Gaulle as it had to my friends and to me. One thing is sure: de Gaulle could take from this book the seed of the humble political truth that does not stem from any construction of the mind but from the basic facts of France's experience. Later, in another era, he sowed this seed in considerable muck and during a terrific hailstorm!

In Chapter 7 of *Les Déracinés*, we find Monsieur Taine, who has designated a plane tree on the Square des Invalides as the end point of his walk. Monsieur Taine marvels at the fact that this powerful mass of greenery "should obey a secret logic, the most sublime philosophy, which is the acceptance of life's necessities. Without repudiating itself or letting itself go, it has taken the best and most useful advantage of the conditions provided by reality."]

The image of the plane tree drawing every parcel of its vitality and even the subtle beauty of its fluttering leaves from the soil and seed from which it grew dramatically figures an organic conception of national identity: individuals are rooted in the land and the people from which they originate. Hence the Barresian cult of "la terre et les morts." In opposition to the "abstract ideas" of cosmopolitan intellectuals and international socialists, Barrès formulated an organic, quasi-biological conception of French identity in which the past was paramount. National history was seen as almost genetically ingrained in individuals. Rather than a conscious knowledge of events, the past embodied in "la terre et les morts" provided a set of reactions, instincts, sensibilities, practices, and traditions—in other words, a memory understood as an organic substance transmitted through bloodlines, and not constituted as a result of a conscious will to recall, select, and conserve.[15]

Numerous "Bloc-notes" lucidly question both personal and national memory; Mauriac clearly treasures his nation's past, but many of his editorials scrutinize the most unsettling pages of French history. Such is the case even with Barrès, whom Mauriac could no longer dissociate from the sinister legacy of both the Dreyfus affair and nazism. His strong adherence to de Gaulle's politics of grandeur should therefore not be interpreted as a return to the integral nationalism championed by Barrès at the turn of the century. At the same time, however, the invocation of the famous episode from *Les Déracinés* is indicative of a significant resurgence of nationalist sentiment unmistakably tinted with the Barrésian doctrine of "la terre et les morts" that continued to fascinate Mauriac.

To better define Mauriac's attitude here, we can contrast it with that of his literary (though not always political) nemesis, Sartre. One of the most famous episodes of *La Nausée* places Sartre's highly autobiographical protagonist Roquentin precisely before an imposing plane tree whose large, gnarled roots create an intense physical and metaphysical nausea. In its massive accumulation of material substance, the tree has received its essence from the seed and earth out of which it was gradually formed. It thus figures the "en-soi" (being in itself), or everything that

15. Cf. Winock, *Le siècle des intellectuels*, 13, 16–17.

Roquentin/Sartre vehemently feels he must negate in order to "exist" autonomously and take his existence into his own hands. In other words, Roquentin/Sartre's attitude toward the past is exactly opposite from that of Mauriac, who finds it inconceivable that a person or a nation could exist autonomously without maintaining the specific identity constituted first and foremost by the rich patrimony of experience painstakingly acquired over a lifetime and inherited from previous generations.

Since de Gaulle's politics of national grandeur offered the possibility of integrating the vast—although, as evident from the many passages of the *Bloc-notes* cited in this chapter, always ambivalent and fragile from Mauriac's perspective—heritage of France's past into a dynamic, coherent story of history, it is not surprising that Mauriac came to overtly embrace the general's exercise of personal power. More regrettable is the fact that on several occasions he even condoned actions that he knew to be deceitful, unjust, and difficult to reconcile with the ethical imperative entailed by his own conviction, often reiterated in the *Bloc-notes*, that "*Deus caritas est*" (God is love). As we have already seen in several passages, it is as if Mauriac saw in the very person of Charles de Gaulle the remedy to the oblivion, amnesia, and dehumanization decried so often in the *Bloc-notes* of the 1960s. Hence the recurrent use of the verb "incarner" (to embody):

> . . . Il [de Gaulle] *incarne* la France de l'histoire; il donne une réalité charnelle à ce qui n'était qu'une idée. ("Samedi 10 février 1962," BN III, 133)
>
> De Gaulle *incarne* ces résurrections successives. . . . ("Dimanche 12 décembre 1965," BN IV, 181)
>
> De Gaulle *incarne* tout ce qu'ils ne peuvent souffrir: une certaine idée de l'indépendance. . . . ("Samedi 19 février 1966," BN IV, 219)
>
> Le vieil homme [de Gaulle] que la Russie acclamera au moment où paraîtra ce bloc-notes *incarne* la jeunesse éternelle d'un peuple. . . . ("Jeudi 16 juin 1966," BN IV, 280)
>
> . . . à aucun moment de l'histoire en France, l'Etat n'aura été quelqu'un au degré où il l'est aujourd'hui. ("Dimanche 12 février 1967," BN IV, 398)

> [. . . He *embodies* the France of history; he gives flesh and blood reality to what was only an idea.
>
> De Gaulle *embodies* these successive resurrections. . . .
>
> De Gaulle *embodies* everything they cannot stand: a certain idea of independence. . . .
>
> The old man that Russia will acclaim when this "Bloc-notes" comes out *embodies* the perennial youth of a nation. . . .
>
> . . . at no time in the history of France has the state been a person to the extent that it is today.]

Mauriac's passionate attachment to the rich experience that has formed French history through a long series of trials and tribulations thus leads him not only to embrace de Gaulle's "certaine idée de la France" but even to literally idolize the general on more than one occasion.

The most telling example of the intimate link between Mauriac's adulation of de Gaulle and his ardent desire to see the unity, permanence, and specific identity of the French nation achieved through a reaffirmation of the legacy of the past is found in the "Bloc-notes" relating the rich succession of memories evoked by a visit to Strasbourg. The embodiment of history that Mauriac finds in the Alsatian city's cathedral is all the more striking since it follows on the heels of three paragraphs decrying the devastation of the rural habitat brought about by the construction of the Roissy airport. The first lines accordingly present the venerable gothic edifice as a powerful antidote to the dehumanized urban landscapes dominated by machinery and concrete:

> Strasbourg, vendredi 24 juin 1966
>
> Ici, pour la première fois, la mécanique est vaincue, nous ne la voyons plus, nous ne l'entendons plus. Ici ce sont les pierres qui crient, leur clameur couvre tout, et l'histoire l'emporte. On me dira que tout se passe au-dedans de moi, dans mon imagination de vieil homme élevé par les vaincus de 70 et par Barrès. Eh bien, non: les hommes et les femmes qui erraient dans la demi-ténèbre de la cathédrale n'étaient plus ces touristes qu'ils redeviendraient à la sortie. Tous étaient comme frappés, dégagés du temps, ou plutôt incorporés dans l'histoire. Les grandes orgues retentirent tout à coup. La dernière fois que je les avais entendues, c'était pour entonner le *Te Deum* de la Libération. Le

général de Gaulle se dressait debout à droite dans le choeur. Le canon proche grondait moins fort que les cloches. Aujourd'hui, après vingt-deux ans, j'entre dans la chapelle où est gardé le pain de vie. Je ne sais pas par coeur le *Te Deum*, alors c'est le *Magnificat* qui monte de mon coeur à mes lèvres, et ce coeur déborde d'une certitude qui éclaire en profondeur la politique de de Gaulle: C'est qu'une nation est quelqu'un réellement, et qui a une vocation, et qui a un destin particulier, et qui a des intercesseurs. Comment ne reconnaissez-vous pas, vous qui avez vécu ce dernier quart de siècle, que nous avons été protégés et sauvés? (BN IV, 286–87)

[Strasbourg, Friday, 24 June 1966

Here, for the first time, the machines have been overcome: we no longer see or hear them. Here, it is the stones that cry out: their clamor drowns out all the rest, and history prevails. People will say that all this is going on within me, in the imagination of an old man raised by the losers of 1870 and by Barrès. In fact, no: the men and women wandering about in the dimly lit cathedral were no longer the tourists that they would once again become upon going out.

It was as if all had been stunned and lifted out of time, or rather incorporated into the story of history. The great organ suddenly resounded. The last time that I had heard it was when people joined in to sing the *Te Deum* at the Liberation. General de Gaulle was standing to the right in the chancel. The bells were louder than the rumbling of a nearby canon. Today, twenty-two years later, I enter the chapel where the bread of life is kept. I do not know the *Te Deum* by heart, so it is the *Magnificat* that rises up to my lips from my heart, and my heart overflows with a certitude that fully elucidates de Gaulle's political strategy: a nation is really a person who has a vocation, a particular destiny, and intercessors. How can you who have experienced the last twenty-five years not acknowledge that we have been protected and saved?]

All the various anxieties about historical amnesia and the dissolution of France's historical identity are summed up and dispelled in the transports expressed for the parallel figures of de Gaulle and the Strasbourg cathedral, both transformed into "lieux de mémoire" in this passage. Even the dehumanizing effects of technology alluded to in the first line are overcome by the majestic music emanating from both the architecture and the organ. Mauriac likens the construction of the cathedral to the historical magnum opus realized by de Gaulle's "certaine idée de la

France": just as the rough-hewn stones have been incorporated into a grandiose human "oeuvre" that preserves their particular qualities while at the same time giving them a transcendent permanence, so de Gaulle allies the democratic idealism of the Third Republic with Barrès's nationalist fervor, thus maintaining France's identity while reaffirming its "vocation" in a world dominated by the United States and the Soviet Union. This realization of national unity in such a dynamic synthesis is conveyed by Mauriac's lyrical description of what momentarily bonds him, the "veil homme élevé par les vaincus de '70 et par Barrès" [old man raised by the losers of 1870 and by Barrès] to "ces touristes" wandering about in the cathedral: "Tous étaient comme frappés, dégagés du temps, ou plutôt incorporés dans l'histoire" (BN IV, 286; It was as if all had been stunned and lifted out of time, or rather incorporated into the story of history).

The numerous editorials that Mauriac penned in defense of de Gaulle throughout the mid- to late 1960s often present the regal-mannered French president as a living monument of (highly idealized) French history, to which Mauriac vows an unfailing loyalty, even in cases when he knows that de Gaulle is wrong. When reacting to Israel's overwhelming victory in the Six Days War of 1967, for example, De Gaulle cavalierly spoke of the Israelis as "un peuple d'élite, sûr de lui et dominateur" (an elite people, sure of itself and overbearing). (See Winock, *Le Siècle des intellectuels*, 555–63.) Mauriac rejects the distorted image of Israel as the aggressor, but condones the general's attitude for reasons of state:

> Je l'ai dit et le redis: je ne ferai pas semblant d'admettre que dans cette guerre de six jours Israël fut l'agresseur; mais je comprends que de Gaulle s'interdise un seul mot qui puisse porter atteinte à cette constante de la politique française depuis Charlemagne, depuis François Ier, ou, sans remonter au déluge, depuis Evian,[16] et qui est l'entente de la fille aînée de l'Eglise avec le grand Turc. ("Vendredi 1er décembre 1967," BN IV, 548)
>
> [I have said and resaid it: I shall not pretend to admit that Israel was the aggressor in this six-day war. However, I understand why de Gaulle might refuse to utter a single word that could undermine the good rela-

16. It was in Evian that the accords ending the Algerian war were signed in March 1962.

tions between the "eldest daughter of the Church" with the grand Turk. This has been a constant in French policy ever since Charlemagne, François I, or, without going all the back to the flood, ever since Evian.]

Mauriac goes on to admit that he yields to the reason of state as long as there is no crime involved, as had been the case in the Dreyfus affair and the war in Algeria. He therefore accepts de Gaulle's posture with respect to Israel in spite of its injustice, not only in the name of the historical continuity invoked in the preceding passage, but also on the basis of what, like de Gaulle, Mauriac claims to be France's rightful place in world affairs, particularly in the face of American hegemony. The justification offered for this claim is none other than the prestige accruing to France from her rich and proud historical heritage:

> Quand il s'agit de nations comme celles de la vieille Europe, qui ont une histoire de mille ans, une histoire politique et militaire mais aussi celle des savants, des philosophes, des artistes et des saints, qui pourrait admettre de bonne foi, à moins d'être un imbécile qu'une seule d'entre elles consentira jamais à remettre une part de ses pouvoirs à une autorité supra nationale? (BN IV, 549)
>
> [In dealing with nations such as those of the old Europe that have a thousand-year history, a political and military history, but also one of scientists, philosphers, artists, and saints, who but an idiot could in good faith admit that any single one of them would ever consent to giving a part of its powers to some supranational authority?]

Thus grounded in an illustrious past, the national sentiment inspiring de Gaulle's foreign policy wins Mauriac's adhesion, even when it means constructing a nuclear strike force. In this sense, the *Bloc-notes* of the late 1960s returns to some of the ethnocentric presumptions that characterized Mauriac's attitude prior to his decision to protest the violence and oppression of France's policies in North Africa in 1952. Such lapses and contradictions, however, should not overshadow the larger contours of Mauriac's approach to history in the *Bloc-notes.* One would be wrong to think that he ultimately came full circle. The following chapter adumbrates the enduring originality of his perspective on the ongoing story of France's history.

6 THE *BLOC-NOTES* IN HISTORY

Si je me "défoule" dans ce bloc-notes, c'est que depuis tant d'années que le mystère du mal me tourmente, j'ai tout de même le remède à ma portée: non une réponse qui puisse satisfaire ma raison, mais, comme un homme dont les vêtements seraient en feu et qui se jetterait à la mer, *je me jette dans cet océan de bonté que demeure tout de même l'histoire humaine; elle est criminelle, et pourtant elle est sainte.* ("Vendredi 15 décembre 1967," BN IV, 556)

[If I am "letting off steam" in this "Bloc-notes," it's because throughout all these years that the mystery of evil has tormented me, I have after all had the remedy at hand. Not an answer that could satisfy my mind, but as a man with his clothes on fire would throw himself into the sea, *I throw myself into this ocean of goodness that the story of human history nevertheless remains: the story is criminal, yet sacred.*]

One would be hard-pressed to find a writer who took history more seriously than does François Mauriac in the *Bloc-notes;* as one of the first to identify the particular significance of new developments (as attested by his precocious commentaries on subjects as diverse as the literary début of Françoise Sagan, the beginning of hostilities in Algeria, the sudden eclipse of a rural provincial world, or the advent of television in the political arena), he invariably places the here-and-now sub specie aeternitatis,[1] seeing each event as the latest turn in a drama un-

1. Cf. Henri Peyre's assessment, as cited by Cocula, *Mauriac, le Bloc-notes,* 114: "Il pos-

folding since time immemorial, charging the present with the burden—but at the same time the legacy—of an enduring past.

As amply demonstrated by the passage cited above, history mattered, and mattered infinitely for Mauriac, in ways that liken him to his contemporaries yet set him apart. Both the specificity and the enduring value of his approach to the past in the *Bloc-notes* can best be appreciated in contrast with Sartre and de Gaulle, whose highly antagonistic perspectives on history largely dominated France's ideological landscape in the 1950s and 1960s. Indeed, if François Mauriac's stature as a major intellectual figure in postwar France has heretofore been largely neglected (if not entirely overlooked) in the United States, it is to no small degree due, on the one hand, to his unblinking Gaullism, and, on the other hand, to Sartre's preeminence as the quintessential leftist intellectual and master thinker who had skewered—and summarily dismissed—Mauriac as a bourgeois Catholic author of psychological novels. Add to that the fact that the *Bloc-notes*, which has now established Mauriac's reputation as France's premier polemicist of the postwar era, if not of the entire twentieth century,[2] remained largely unknown and inaccessible until Jean Touzot's 1993 Points-Seuil edition, and it is not surprising that Sartre's caricature of the author of *Thérèse Desqueyroux* has often obscured the journalist who, three years before Henri Alleg's book published under the same title, penned *La Question*.

Contrary to what Sartre (and even certain critics) would have us believe, the author of the *Bloc-notes* can hardly be dismissed as some

---

sédait le don de capter l'événement, pour le transposer de l'éphémère évanescent, qui est son milieu propre, dans l'éternel et situer le relatif dans le sillage de l'absolu" (He had the gift of capturing events, taking them out of the evanescence of topical commentary, which is their natural setting, and transposing them into timelessness, thus situating the relative in the realm of the absolute). In all its eloquence, however, this formulation is too lyrical to take on value as a critical analysis. In particular the "absolu" and "éternel" can be better delineated in terms of the notions of history that Mauriac shared with generations of his compatriots while at the same time adapting them to his own particular perspective.

2. According to Jean Daniel, "Mauriac fut peut-être le plus grand polémiste du XXième siècle" (Mauriac was perhaps the greatest polemical writer of the twentieth century); see "Extrait de 'François Mauriac,'" in *Mauriac et la polémique*, ed. André Séailles (Paris: L'Harmattan, 2001), 101. Georges Suffert and André Séailles articulate similar assessments in their contributions to the "Dossier François Mauriac" published by *Magazine littéraire*, no. 215, February 1985, pp. 43–48.

starry-eyed writer lost in the musings of his peculiar novelistic imagination. The editorials that we have examined squarely confront the question of history, probe Mauriac's own irrevocable implication in France's politics, and, with courageous condemnations of torture and oppression in North Africa, testify to a concrete political commitment that makes him just as much an "écrivain engagé" (committed writer) as Sartre. Even more important for us today, however, is what sharply distinguishes Mauriac's views on history from those championed by Sartre, espoused by the dominant figures of the Parisian intelligentsia throughout the "Trente Glorieuses," and perpetuated even today, notes Finkielkraut, by certain "militants de la memoire" (memory activists).[3]

It took nothing less than a second world war and a Nazi Occupation of France for Sartre to finally "reach [his] rendez-vous with history" and realize that all he enjoyed as a brilliant young philosophy professor and author whose conspicuously bohemian lifestyle deliciously scandalized the bourgeois was contingent upon political conditions forged by collective human action in the specific events of history. Jolted out of an insouciant skepticism that refused the limitations inevitably attendant to political commitment, thrown into the confrontation of humanity with its negation, Sartre concluded that existence was fundamentally historical.

Since oppression, suffering, and death were in every case attributable to social or political situations that were to be combated, history was in Sartre's eyes inherently conflictual and violent. There could be no middle ground, nor any realm of human activity sheltered from politics. For the novelist who in *La Nausée* had conveyed such an acute sense of radical contingency, the implacable conflict of the war era nevertheless offered meaning.[4] If an omnipresent history constantly forces a choice between submission and resistance, then each act, every deed, takes on special significance, as Sartre dramatically asserts in one of his accounts of the Dark Years:

3. Alain Finkielkraut, *Une voix vient de l'autre rive* (Paris: Gallimard, 2000), 124, 126–27.

4. Alain Finkielkraut, "La persistante solitude de Char et de Camus," in *Une voix vient de l'autre rive* (Paris: Gallimard, 2000), 120–24.

> Puisque le venin nazi se glissait jusque dans notre pensée, chaque pensée était une conquête; puisqu'une police toute-puissante cherchait à nous contraindre au silence, chaque parole devenait précieuse comme une déclaration de principe; puisque nous étions traqués, chacun de nos gestes avait le poids d'un engagement. Les circonstances souvent atroces de notre combat nous mettaient enfin à même de vivre, sans fard et sans voile, cette situation déchirée, insoutenable qu'on appelle la condition humaine. L'exil, la captivité, la mort surtout que l'on masque habilement dans les époques heureuses, nous en faisions les objets perpétuels de nos soucis, nous apprenions que ce ne sont pas des accidents évitables, ni même des menaces constantes mais extérieures: il fallait y voir notre lot, notre destin, la source profonde de notre réalité d'homme; à chaque seconde nous vivions dans sa plénitude les sens de cette petite phrase banale: "Tous les hommes sont mortels."[5]
>
> [Since the Nazi venom was even seeping into our thinking, each thought was a conquest; since an all-powerful police sought to force us to be silent, each spoken word became valuable as a declaration of principle; since we were being hunted down, each one of our acts carried the weight of our political commitment. The often horrific circumstances of our fight finally put us in a position to experience this wrenching, unbearable situation called the human condition without any exterior artifices. We made exile, captivity, and above all death, which remains skilfully masked during happy eras, the constant focus of our concern. We learned that they are not avoidable accidents, nor even constant but exterior threats. We had to see them as our lot, our destiny, and the ultimate source of our human reality; with each second we kept on experiencing the full meaning of this little commonplace sentence: "All humans are mortal."]

And yet, even for the writer who had staged a powerful drama of existential despair in *Huis clos* [*No Exit*], there was hope in the very midst of this stark mortality. For if all oppression and injustice were historical, that is, caused by humans, these scourges could be combated and ultimately eradicated.[6]

Few would contest that Sartre's bold claim to the human freedom

5. Jean-Paul Sartre, "La république du silence," in *Situations III* (Paris: Gallimard, 1947), 11–12.

6. Finkielkraut, "La persistante solitude de Char et de Camus," 123–24.

and dignity acquired in the face of Nazi repression and terror constituted a brilliant characterization of resistance on all levels. Sartre's persistent interpolation of the fierce struggles and irreducible oppositions of the war into the general domain of history throughout the 1950s and 1960s, however, is much more problematical.[7] Indeed, for some three decades after World War II had ended, Sartre and many others continued to advocate revolutionary violence as a necessary means of ridding humankind of the shackles impeding history's march toward a utopian future. If so many French intellectuals pursued the revolutionary fantasy for so long, points out Finkielkraut, it was in no small part because the values and institutions inherited from the past were viewed as mere "constructions" of history to be dismantled and cleared away in preparation for a new order.[8]

As an active member of the intellectual resistance who attended the meetings of the Comité National d'Ecrivains along with the mercurial young philosophy professor who had so unceremoniously ridiculed his novels, Mauriac would have doubtless subscribed to Sartre's depiction of the human condition during the German Occupation of France. To legitimate and even celebrate violence as the midwife of history, as does Sartre from his graphic description of the murder of Clytemnestre and Egisthe in *Les Mouches* [*The Flies*] to his enthusiasm for the slaying of Europeans by third world nationalists in his preface to Frantz Fanon's *Les Damnés de la terre*, however, would be unthinkable: the *Bloc-notes* invariably deplores violence as either tragic or criminal.

It is just such a refusal to formulate any justification for the destruction of human life that moved Mauriac to explain why he viewed the murder of a seven-year-old boy by a fifteen-year-old boy as the latest illustration of all that was criminal in humanity and history:

> Ce qui nous serre la gorge dans un crime si étrange, c'est qu'en vérité il n'est pas étrange, qu'il n'est que le plus horrible des faits divers, mais un fait divers dans cet interminable massacre d'innocents qui, depuis le meurtre d'Abel, s'est perpétué tout au long de l'histoire appelée sainte, à chaque sac de ville ("ils n'épargnèrent ni les femmes ni les petits en-

7. Finkielkraut, "La persistante solitude de Char et de Camus," 120–22.
8. Finkielkraut, *L'humanité perdue*, 57–64.

> fants . . .") comme au long de l'histoire tout court et en particulier durant les croisades et les guerres de religion, les plus féroces de toutes et où chacun des deux partis avait mobilisé l'Etre infini. (BN IV, 556)
>
> [What grips our throat in such a strange crime is that in fact it is not strange. It is just the most horrible tragedy in the news. It is another tragedy in this interminable massacre of innocents that, ever since the murder of Abel, has been perpetuated throughout so-called sacred history, every time a city was plundered ("they spared neither the women nor the small children . . ."), just as it has been perpetuated throughout history in general, particularly during the crusades and religious wars, the most ferocious of all, in which both sides had mobilized the Eternal Being.]

In this same piece, Mauriac depicts predatory violence as a "law": "la loi qui régit les rapports entre les êtres vivants, du végétal à l'animal le plus évolué" (the law that governs relations between living things, from plant life to the most highly evolved animal). He even formulates the neologism "l'entre-dévorement" (mutual devouring) to designate the phenomenon (BN IV, 555)

Refusing to view violence as a norm or a principle to be emulated, Mauriac decries murder as "la négation absolue en apparence de cet Amour en qui nous avons foi" (BN IV, 555; the obviously absolute negation of the Love in whom we have faith]. Conversely, he unequivocally rejects all attempts to invoke a metaphysical absolute, namely, the Deity, in support of a group or nation at war. While Sartre and other fellow travelers were willing to make ethical choices and political action subservient to the progress of history,[9] Mauriac knew that evil could never be completely eradicated from humanity or society. He accordingly takes exception to the notion of progress: "Il faut renoncer à cette prétention que le progrès s'est manifesté aussi dans le crime" (BN IV, 555; We must give up this claim that progress has also manifested itself in crime).

Mauriac's refusal of the Marxist-Hegelian ideology not only sets him apart from Sartre and the Parisian intelligentsia of the 1950s and 1960s,

9. See Tony Judt, *The Burden of Responsibility* (Chicago: University of Chicago Press, 1997), 12–20.

but also parallels Tzvetan Todorov's critique of the totalitarian approach to history. Both fascism and communism, observes Todorov, are based on rather Darwinist notions of history as a struggle for survival and dominance; since violence is perceived as the fundamental mode of life and survival, it therefore becomes encoded as the principle of politics. Thus claiming to follow the laws of biology or history, communism and nazism both set out to hasten the processes supposedly at work in nature or human events. And both the adherents of communism and those of nazism, notes Todorov, were willing to exterminate their enemies and destroy the heritage of the past in order to construct their brave new worlds.[10]

That the bourgeois Catholic member of the Académie Française to whom we owe the *Bloc-notes* was not swayed by the considerable seductive powers of postwar Marxism will hardly astonish students of French intellectual history, even if his 4 January 1957 analysis of the cracks already appearing in the Stalinist regimes has been largely confirmed by the collapse and breakup of the Soviet bloc. But Mauriac's refusal to see history as all-encompassing and normative cannot simply be attributed to the a priori's of class and religion in France, a priori's that he moreover conspicuously flouted on a number of levels throughout his career. Nor did he simply invert Sartrian politics, replacing the philosopher's negations with affirmations and vice versa.

Contrary to what one might expect, for example, Mauriac rejects the notion that the will of God is immanent in historical events and adamantly refuses any teleology that wittingly or unwittingly tends to justify the murder of a child and the "massacre d'innocents": ". . . je demeure imperméable aux arguments des théologiens qui ont réponse à tout" (BN IV, 555: . . . I remain impervious to the arguments of theologians who have an answer for everything). The violence so evident in humanity and history, as we see in the lines cited at the beginning of this chapter, remains a "mystère" that torments Mauriac. Not even the celebration of Christmas offers any logical explanation for what Mauriac terms "ce monde incompréhensible" (BN IV, 557; this incomprehensible world).

10. Todorov, *Mémoire du mal*, 42–43, 49.

In history Mauriac finds no overarching principle, no underlying force, and no ultimate end bestowing meaning on each event or leading the entire drama to resolution. Whereas for Sartre history endowed the world with an abundance of signification, events in Mauriac's view are never totally transparent, but rather opaque and polyvalent. The drama of history proves moreover to be tragic in that suffering and injustice remain largely irremediable: many passages of the *Bloc-notes* decry historical crimes—and in particular the atrocities committed by Mauriac's compatriots and correligionaries—with no attempt to find justification or reparation in some subsequent event.

Ultimate redemption is situated outside of human time, beyond his grasp. The remedy at hand ("le remède à ma portée") is specifically designated not to be an intellectual key to a rational explanation of history ("non une réponse qui puisse satisfaire ma raison" [BN IV, 556: not an answer that could satisfy my mind]), but a pragmatic comportment: "comme un homme dont les vêtements seraient en feu et se jetterait à la mer, je me jette dans cet océan de bonté que demeure tout de même l'histoire humaine" [BN IV, 556: like a man whose clothes were on fire would throw himself into the sea, I throw myself into this ocean of goodness that the story of human history nevertheless remains]). The veritable leap of faith so dramatically figured by imagery here most decidedly does not constitute any sort of oneness with history, be it mystical or ideological. These lines offer on the contrary yet another illustration of the radical disjunction between self and history that we have so often encountered in passages of the *Bloc-notes* dealing with particularly violent events. Mauriac's initial instinctive reaction is one of repugnance and recoil: the unending brutality of the human saga instills a sense of irreparable brokenness and separation. It takes a willful effort of "engagement" such as the one symbolized by the burning man's plunge into the sea for Mauriac to accept his part in the "brouillamini d'erreurs et de violence" that is history.

At the same time, nothing could be more foreign to Mauriac than the notion of reinventing humanity (cf. Sartre: "L'homme est à faire" [Humanity remains to be invented]) by making a clean slate of the past and liquidating its onerous heritage. Contrary to Sartre's famous dictum, Mauriac sees humans as intricately fashioned by the innumerable vicissitudes of historical experience constituting their collective identity. Keen on preserving and passing on the rich (if ambivalent) legacy so painfully acquired over millenia, Mauriac ultimately exemplifies what Finkielkraut has termed "gratitude" toward the past: a deep sense of attachment, indebtedness, and respect for the humanity of preceding generations.[11] Such is eminently the case when, after articulating one of his most poignant indictments of the violence that has never ceased to characterize the human story, Mauriac nevertheless represents history as an ocean of goodness into which he plunges. The leap of faith in no way removes the crime or repairs the damage: it rather reaffirms Mauriac's full implication in the human drama and a commonality of human experience that transcends the boundaries of time and the divisions of society. The plunge into the sea of human history does not figure the achievement of any ultimate end, but the desire for full participation and the affirmation of human solidarity spanning temporal and political divides.

As we have seen, it was a similar desire to embrace a national identity that affirmed the unity of the French people throughout its long history and beyond its often fierce ideological divisions that best accounts for Mauriac's enthusiastic support of de Gaulle and his politics of "grandeur." A quick analysis of de Gaulle's epic discourse reveals why Mauriac held it in such admiration. As was the case for Sartre, it was in response to the ordeal of defeat and occupation and the saga of resistance and liberation that de Gaulle articulated a powerful sense of history infusing past and present with compelling signification. His triumphant march down the Champs-Elysées on 26 August 1944 thus marked not only the dramatic end of the Nazis' humiliating occupation of the French capital but also the apotheosis of the upstart leader of La France Combattante as the personal embodiment of the nation's reborn identity. Such is at least the view expressed in de Gaulle's own description of this truly monumental (in Nora's sense of "lieu de mémoire") event, which the general's talented pen transforms into a veritable epiphany of national identity as forged out of French history and revealed in his very person:

11. Finkielkraut, *L'humanité perdue*, 159.

> Il s'agit, aujourd'hui, de rendre à lui-même, par le spectacle de sa joie et l'évidence de sa liberté, un peuple qui fut, hier, écrasé par la défaite et dispersé par la servitude. Puisque chacun de ceux qui sont là a, dans son coeur, choisi Charles de Gaulle comme recours de sa peine et symbole de son espérance, il s'agit qu'il le voie, familier et fraternel, et qu'à cette vue resplendisse l'unité nationale.[12]
>
> [Today, by flaunting its joy and displaying its freedom, it is important to restore to its rightful status a nation that only yesterday had been crushed by defeat and scattered by servitude. Since all of those who are here have in their hearts chosen Charles de Gaulle as a recourse for their suffering and a symbol of their hope, it is important that they see him, familiar and fraternal, and that, upon seeing him, national unity should once again shine for all to see.]

The national unity celebrated here is constituted along two axes. The diachronic axis establishes continuity between past and present by linking the euphoria of the Liberation to a long, illustrious record: "A chaque pas que je fais sur l'axe le plus illustre du monde, il me semble que les gloires du passé s'associent à celle d'aujourd'hui" (With each step I take down the most illustrious thoroughfare in the world, its to me as if the glories of the past are associated with the glory of today).[13] De Gaulle's grandiose narrative proceeds with an epic catalogue of these national glories from Saint-Louis to Foch and Clemenceau, then concludes by observing: "L'Histoire, ramassée dans ces pierres et dans ces places, on dirait qu'elle nous sourit" (It is as if history, gathered up in these stones and in these city squares, were smiling at us).[14] Even more striking is the unity among the myriad of French individuals, various social groups, and different generations achieved across the synchronic axis:

> Il se passe, en ce moment, un de ces miracles de la conscience nationale, un de ces gestes de la France, qui parfois, au long des siècles, viennent illuminer notre Histoire. Dans cette communauté, qui n'est qu'une seule pensée, un seul élan, un seul cri, les différences s'effacent, les indi-

12. De Gaulle's account is reproduced in Christine Levisse-Touzé, *Paris libéré, Paris retrouvé* (Paris: Gallimard-Paris Musées, 1994), 92.

13. Levisse-Touzé, *Paris libéré*, 93.

14. Levisse-Touzé, *Paris libéré*, 94.

> vidus disparaissent. Innombrables Français dont je m'approche tour à tour, à l'Etoile, au Rond-Point, à la Concorde, devant l'Hôtel de Ville, sur le parvis de la cathédrale, si vous saviez comme vous êtes pareils![15]
>
> [What occurs now is one of these miracles of our national consciousness, one of these sagas of France that at various times over the centuries come to illuminate our history. In this community, which is of one mind, one single élan, one sole cry, differences are erased, individuals disappear. You countless people of France to whom I draw near first at the Place de l'Etoile, then at the Rond-Point, again at the Place de la Concorde, and finally in front of the Paris city hall and outside of the Notre Dame cathedral, if only you knew how similar you are!]

The intensity of such unanimism can only be appreciated in relation with the highly fractious character of French society and the precarious tenure of the many regimes and constitutions having controled France's political institutions since 1789 (moreover recalled by de Gaulle in a paragraph subsequent to the lines cited above): for the wildly cheering multitude assembled along the Champs Elysées on that 26 August 1944, the traumatic split between Vichy and de Gaulle's France Combattante, which had pitted the *Milice* against the Resistance and brought the country to the brink of civil war, provided the most recent example.

The volatile, contingent character of French politics—illustrated again by the turbulent episodes of the war in Algeria, from Guy Mollet's ignominious capitulation to a tomato-throwing mob in Algiers to the botched attempts to stage a military coup and assassinate de Gaulle—was, as we have stressed, certainly foremost in Mauriac's unswerving support of de Gaulle. And the author of the *Bloc-notes* could hardly remain insensitive to "cette émotion profonde et sacrée" (this deep and sacred emotion) inspired by the resuscitation of French pride and honor and experienced during "des minutes qui dépassent chacune de [leurs] pauvres vies" (minutes that transcend each one of [their] poor lives) by the Parisian throngs upon the liberation of *la ville-lumière.*[16]

And yet, in spite of momentary, if notable, lapses into a virtual idol-

15. Levisse-Touzé, *Paris libéré,* 92.

16. These words are from de Gaulle's famous speech at the Paris city hall on 25 August 1944; the speech is quoted in Levisse-Touzé, *Paris libéré,* 95.

ization of de Gaulle in his waning years, Mauriac consistently approaches history in general and France's past in particular from a standpoint quite distinct from that of the first president of the Fifth Republic. As we noted in Chapter 3, Mauriac admired de Gaulle's "certaine idée de la France" not as a faithful record of the past—since the darker chapters of French history had been glossed over or simply omitted—but rather as a dynamic political platform and a rallying point for restoring national unity and international stature. De Gaulle's heroic narrative of France's past was perfect for furthering the general's political agenda, and since Mauriac subscribed to his politics he gave the Gaullist epic his pragmatic support. In the end, however, he never departed from his own perspective on history, which remained fundamentally tragic.

When all is said and done, history represented for Mauriac a moral drama in which humanity plays out its ideals and passions, a story of occasional triumph and redemption (as with de Gaulle) but with seemingly unending crime and retribution. Hence the many allusions to the story of Cain and Abel, to which Mauriac frequently returns when characterizing human history in general, as in the above-cited lines decrying "cet interminable massacre d'innocents qui, depuis le meurtre d'Abel, s'est perpétué tout au long de l'histoire appelée sainte" (BN IV, 556; this interminable massacre of innocents that, ever since the murder of Abel, has been perpetuated throughout so-called sacred history). There and throughout the *Bloc-notes*, Mauriac's overriding preoccupation is not some triumphant tale of a particular nation but rather the criminal violence manifested in every epoch and perpetrated by groups of all ideological, national, and religious persuasions, beginning with those most intimately linked to his own identity: the European Christians. We find the clearest expression of this perception in the lines written in response to unspeakable historical crimes depicted by Erwin Leiser's film *Mein Kampf*. The parallels that Mauriac draws between Nazi crimes and various chapters of French history are as uncompromising as they are ahead of their times (since it was only in the 1970s that a general reflection on the Holocaust as a cataclysm called into question European history and culture in general). And his conclusion proves unsettling to any and all conceptions of history, including Mauriac's own:

Que la génération qui aura été témoin de ces choses ne soit pas tombée à genoux en se frappant la poitrine et qu'au contraire. . . . A quoi bon rien ajouter? Je me tiens au noeud d'une contradiction qui, je le sais, ne sera pas résolue ici et maintenant. Il n'y a pas à essayer d'accorder ce monde de *Mein Kampf* (qui fut aussi dans la douce France, celui de la guerre des Albigeois, de Caboche, de la Saint-Barthélemy, des tueries révolutionnaires, des journées de juin, de la Commune et de Versailles) avec le *Deus caritas est.* Je ne supporte plus d'entendre, à ce sujet, un théologien me donner ses raisons. La conformité me suffit de la Croix avec la souffrance des hommes. Quelqu'un m'a dit un jour, et je ne l'ai jamais oublié: "C'est l'amour que nous avons crucifié, et que nous continuerons de crucifier jusqu'à la fin du monde." *C'est cela l'histoire, et il n'y a pas d'autre histoire.* ("Lundi 28 novembre 1960," BN II, 508)

[The fact that the generation that has witnessed these things has not fallen to their knees while beating their breasts and that, on the contrary. . . . But why go on? I am standing at the heart of a contradiction that I know will not be resolved here and now. There is no use in trying to make this world of *Mein Kampf* (which in our sweet France was also that of the war against the Albigenses and Caboche, that of the Saint Bartholomew Day's Massacre, of the revolutionary slaughters, the insurrectional days of June, the [[uprising of the]] Commune and [[the repression by troops from]] Versailles) with the [[New Testament dictum]] *Deus caritas est* [["God is love"]]. I can no longer bear to hear some theologian give me his reasons on the subject. The conformity of the Cross with human suffering is enough for me. I have never forgotten what someone said to me one day: "What we have crucified is love, and we will keep on crucifying love until the end of the world." *That is the story of history, and there is no other.*]

Even when writing at the apogee of his Gaullist fervor some seven years later, Mauriac still presents the question of history as coextensive with the problem of evil (cf. "le mystère du mal" in the December 1967 passage cited at the outset) and as indicative of the criminal capacity of humanity that must be openly confronted. Such is the case in his "Bloc-notes" for "Jeudi saint 7 avril 1966" (Maundy Thursday, 7 April 1966). Rather than taking sides in the controversy over the censorship of the film production of *La Religieuse* (which had just been banned), Mauriac turns to what he sees as the real scandal confronting Catholics:

. . . je voudrais rappeler une vérité que nous n'aimons pas à regarder en face, nous autres catholiques, et que l'Eglise elle-même ne regarde vraiment en face, semble-t-il, que depuis Vatican II.

Cette vérité, comment la formulerai-je? L'homme est de tous les animaux le plus féroce: il se manifeste comme tel à tous les moments de l'histoire. D'un siècle à l'autre, c'est le style de la férocité qui change, non sa virulence. Simon de Montfort[17] est couvert de moins de sang, je ne dis pas que Hitler et que Staline, mais que le grand Churchill exigeant la destruction de Dresde ou Truman celle d'Hiroshima et de Nagasaki. Dans ce musée historique de l'horreur, ce qui assigne une place à part aux chrétiens, ce n'est pas qu'ils aient été pires que les autres, c'est que les bûchers allumés, les villes détruites l'aient été au nom du Christ. Ce que les Espagnols ont fait du Nouveau Monde, ils l'ont fait la croix à la main. Le seul nom de croisade, dont l'histoire était contée à notre enfance comme une sainte épopée, résume l'effroyable équivoque qui dure depuis Constantin et dont la guerre civile espagnole a constitué le dernier épisode. (BN IV, 243)

[. . . I would like to recall a reality the we Catholics don't like to confront, and that the Church itself has only really confronted since Vatican II.

How shall I formulate this reality? Human beings are the most ferocious of all animals: they have displayed their ferocity in every period of history. From one century to another, only the style of this ferocity has changed, not its virulence. Simon de Montfort is covered with less blood than, I won't say Hitler and Stalin, but the great Churchill demanding the destruction of Dresden or Truman that of Hiroshima and Nagasaki. What assigns a special place for Christians in this museum of historical horrors is not that they were worse than the others but the fact that the burnings at the stake and the destruction of cities were done in the name of Christ. In the New World, the Spanish perpetrated their deeds with the cross in their hands. The very word crusade, whose story was told like a sacred epic when we were children, sums up the frightful misconception that has prevailed ever since Constantine: the Spanish civil war constituted the final episode of this legacy.]

17. Simon de Montfort was the military leader of the campaign against the Albigenses, marked by repeated scenes of torture, mutilation, and civilian massacre. See Zoé Oldenbourg, *Le bûcher de Montségur* (Paris: Gallimard, 1959), 158–74, 189–251.

We thus see even the dyed-in-the-wool Gaullist Mauriac of the late 1960s lashing out not only against the atrocities committed in the name of Christianity but also against any pretension of recounting a holy history. These lines testify to a certain idea not of France, but of human history, the history so prominent in the editorials of the Algerian war period (as pointed out in Chapter 4) and that we find intact in the late 1960s. Poring over the legacy of Christendom and the Church—precisely the domains that one might expect to inspire hagiography and epic discourse—Mauriac finds not triumphant grandeur, but a tragic coexistence of sainthood and criminality:

> Après deux mille ans de guerres fratricides, mais aussi de sainteté, nous devons, nous les contemporains de Vatican II, tout assumer du passé, et même du pire, mais sans le séparer du meilleur. . . .
>
> Aujourd'hui, les jeux sont faits, il n'y a rien à dissimuler d'une histoire dont certains chapitres font horreur. Il faut tout prendre sur soi de cet héritage de l'Eglise et en tirer la leçon. . . .
>
> Et puis nous devons consentir au jugement du monde sur l'histoire révolue dans la mesure où ce jugement est juste. (BN IV, 245)
>
> [After two thousand years of fratricidal wars, but also of sainthood, we the contemporaries of Vatican II must assume responsibility for everything, even the worst, in our past, but without separating it from the best. . . .
>
> Today, the stakes are up, and there is nothing to gain from concealing a history in which certain chapters make one shudder. We have to take responsibility for this entire legacy of the Church and draw the lessons. . . .
>
> And then too we must consent to the world's judgment on the history of these bygone years, to the extent that this judgment is right.]

As devoted to the Catholic Church as he certainly is, Mauriac refuses to mitigate historical crimes by assimilating them into some divine plan or providential dialectic (as would a Claudel, for instance). Though politically charmed—and arguably seduced—by de Gaulle's narrative of grandeur on a political level, the *Bloc-notes*, to borrow a term from Finkielkraut, continually "disenchants history" to the extent that Mauriac never identifies the unfolding of events with reason, divine will, or any scheme of things that justified unspeakable acts of violence.[18]

The divergence from de Gaulle's approach to the past is unmistakable. Whereas, in order to galvanize national sentiment and forge a dynamic political strategy, de Gaulle writes off the dark chapters of France's past (thus considering Vichy, for example, "nul et non avenu" [null and void]),[19] the *Bloc-notes* frequently dwells on the most disturbing crimes not only of human history in general but also of the French nation and, as in the passage just cited, Christendom. Mauriac invites his readers to ponder the darkest chapters of French and ecclesiastical history, and even to submit themselves to the judgment of others ("le jugement du monde") outside their own national and religious group, injunctions unthinkable for de Gaulle.

Instead of enrolling history into the service of some predetermined political agenda, Mauriac probes the past for a source of collective and individual identity, guided by a sense of ethics: the question of history is ultimately not so much the question of national or ideological destiny or even temporality, that is, the nature and origins of society's evolution.[20] It is the question of humanity in its moral dimensions. And it is on that score that Mauriac's preoccupations most clearly diverge from de Gaulle's discourse of grandeur as well as from the Parisian intelligentsia's commitment to progressive dialectics. For as Mauriac affirms in his 15 January 1957 "Bloc-notes," history does not tell the whole story of humanity.

> Cette histoire totale, je doute qu'elle soit la seule vraie. Au-delà de "l'histoire dite par un idiot, pleine de fracas et de furie et qui ne signifie rien. . . ." . . . Je crois qu'il existe une autre histoire que l'Histoire: la mienne, la vôtre—autant d'histoires que d'êtres humains. C'est le secret des romanciers; et chacune d'elles contient les éléments d'un chef d'oeuvre irremplaçable. (BN I, 433)

18. Cf. Finkielkraut, "Y a-t-il un devoir de mémoire?," in *Une voix vient de l'autre rive*, 21.

19. See Nathan Bracher, "The Trial of Papon and the Tribulations of Gaullism," in *The Papon Affair: Memory and Justice on Trial*, ed. Richard J. Golsan (New York: Routledge, 2000), 115–30.

20. Cf. Furet, *L'atelier de l'histoire*, 17.

[I doubt that this total story of history is the only one that is true. Beyond the "tale told by an idiot, full of sound and fury, signifying nothing. . . ." . . . I believe that there exists a story other than the story of history: my story, yours—as many stories as there are human beings. That is the novelists' secret; and each one of these stories contains the makings of an irreplaceable masterpiece.]

Irrevocably implicated in the violence and tragedy of history, each human being nevertheless remains autonomous, irreducible to the socioeconomic and political vectors governing the course of events. It is precisely the preoccupation with these other eminently human and personal "histoires" (stories of history) that on the one hand compels Mauriac to refuse "[c]ette histoire totale" (this total story of history)—the Marxist-Hegelian logic that Sartre and *Les Temps modernes* saw as trumping personal ethics—while on the other hand preventing him from melding these myriad individual destinies into "une seule pensée, un seul élan, un cri" (one single mind, one single élan, one cry), even if he is unquestionably inspired by de Gaulle's saga of national glory.

Mauriac's rejection of unanimism is attested by many passages of the *Bloc-notes*, not only during the most intense period of the Algerian war (such as in the 15 January 1957 piece cited above), but also at the height of de Gaulle's power and prestige. Witness the following lines from "Mardi 27 septembre 1966":

> Chacun des êtres qui ne sont plus que poussière et que cendre a eu une histoire, et qui continue, un destin singulier qui ne peut être confondu avec aucun autre, pas plus que son visage, unique lui aussi, différent de tous les visages qui ont existé avant lui et existeront après lui. Tel qu'il fut, il a été aimé, il est aimé, non des autres qui ne sont plus, mais de Celui qui est de tout temps à jamais. Ce n'est pas moi qui l'invente, si c'est moi qui le crois. Je crois à cette promesse de l'éternel amour. (BN IV, 322)

> [Each of these persons [[literally "beings"]] who are now but dust and ashes had a story, and it continues: it is a singular itinerary that cannot be confused with any other, no more than their faces, which are also unique, and different from all the faces that existed before them and that will exist after them. Just as they were, they were loved, they are loved, not by others who are no longer, but by Him who is from ever-

> lasting to everlasting. It was not I who invented this, though I do believe it. I believe in this promise of eternal love.]

Not only does history always have a human (if often barbaric) face in Mauriac's eyes, this human face tells a story of history. If often full of sound and fury, but it is a tale that never signifies nothing, and that moreover remains irreducible to any Hegelian prose of the world and inassimilable to any saga of national grandeur. Embroiled in the "brouillamini d'erreurs et de violences qu'est l'Histoire" (imbroglio of errors and violence that is history), answerable for the plight of others as was Cain for Abel, each human being remains distinct and autonomous. And Mauriac grounds this inalienable status in the divine.

This Christian perspective is absolutely crucial for Mauriac's approach to history in the *Bloc-notes.* On the one hand, he adamantly refuses to interpret either the specific outcome of events or their inherent logic in terms of the "will of God." On the other hand, his explicitly Christian understanding of humans as beings created in the image of the divine prevents him from seeing history as humanity's unique or ultimate frame of reference. This same Christian humanism compels him to posit a special status for humanity, one that, both in the lines just cited and in those used as an epigraph to this chapter, the *Bloc-notes* repeatedly defines as each person's irrevocable title to dignity, respect, and justice. In his "Bloc-notes" for "Samedi 18 février 1967" (Saturday, 18 February 1967), Mauriac articulates his ongoing *engagement* with history as well as with this other human story that runs distinct, yet parallel to it:

> Je m'agite encore, je m'inquiète encore, je me soucie de cette histoire humaine, de cette histoire de France qui n'est pas finie, et puis, dans un ordre infiniment plus élevé, il y a cette autre histoire, celle de la grâce dans le monde, si ce que j'ai cru est vrai, ou enfin si les formules, si les rites auxquels j'ai adhéré recouvrent de quelque manière que ce soit ce "je suis!" que saint Jean met dans la bouche du Christ: "Avant qu'Abraham fût, je suis."[21] (BN IV, 401–2)

21. Mauriac's citation of the book of the New Testament is taken from John 8.58, and not from chapter 9, as Touzot, BN IV, 402 n1, erroneously indicates.

> [I still get worked up, I still worry, I am still concerned with this story of human history, with this story of France's history that is not over. And then, on an infinitely higher level, there is this other story, the story of grace in the world, if what I believe is true, or at least if the formal expressions and the rituals that I have adhered to correspond in some way or another with the "I am" that Saint John places in Christ's mouth: "Before Abraham was, I am."]

To be sure, these lines exhibit the contemplative attitude increasingly dominant in Mauriac's final years. But the basic contours of the two realms (the secular and the sacred) and the relation of one to the other remain those of the historical perspective found throughout the *Bloc-notes.*

As keen as he was on ensuring the continuity and permanence of the French nation in the face of consumerism, media culture, and a bipolar geopolitical hegemony, Mauriac was first and foremost engaged by history on the level of his Christian humanism. And it was clearly his position as an impenitent exponent of Christianity that most sharply distinguishes him from his Gaullist and Sartrian counterparts on the French intellectual scene. From one end of the *Bloc-notes* to the other, he cites Scripture in denouncing torture and oppression, and professes his Christianity to a public that he knows to be no longer even hostile to faith but bemused by it.

When invoking the Gospel, however, Mauriac rejects the representations that depict events as the historical embodiment of divine will. His approach to history thus remains diametrically opposed to that of kings and emperors such as Constantine, who, as Henry de Montherlant ironically recalled in "Le Solstice de juin,"[22] laid claim to divine endorsement for his reign by conspicuously inscribing the cross on his banners with the words *In hoc signo vinces* (In this sign you shall be victorious).[23] Notwithstanding his steadfast Gaullism, Mauriac consistently sees the likeness of Christ not in conquering heroes nor in triumphant regimes —and when de Gaulle is on occasion presented as a Christ figure, it is invariably when Mauriac depicts him as an isolated man enduring

22. Henry de Montherlant, *Essais* (Paris: Gallimard, 1963), 954, 959–60.

23. "Locutions latines et étrangères," *Le Petit Larousse illustrée* (Paris: Librairie Larousse, 1975).

taunts and insults—but rather in the faces of people past and present who have suffered torture and oppression at the hands of some powerful regime, most often French, European, or culturally Christian (as in the case of the United States).

Citing *Deus caritas est* as the basis of his ethics, Mauriac makes no claim to any authoritative knowledge of the process or end of history: events remain opaque, indeterminate, and approachable primarily in terms of specific people and situations. Here again the contrast with Sartre and the majority of French intellectuals of the 1950s and 1960s is distinctive. Insisting that the working class must not be abandoned or left hopeless (cf. "Il ne faut pas désespérer Billancourt" [We must not lead Billancourt into despair]),[24] professing their eagerness to share in the plight of the proletariat, they nevertheless invoked a privileged insight into the march of history largely inaccessible if not incomprehensible to the common people. Indeed, even Camus was found incapable by the editors of *Les Temps modernes*, who ridiculed his heretical denunciation of deified history in *L'Homme révolté* as a sort of fuzzy-headed sentimentalism stemming largely from Camus's supposed incapacity to master the dialectics of progress.

Openly declaring himself impervious to esoteric discourse, and despite attempts to qualify his views as "mystical," Mauriac never grounds his affirmations on any pretension of having received some sort of psychic telegram from the Deity. The one claim he does make (particularly during the 1960s) to a privileged perspective on current events is grounded in his long experience as an observer of France's tumultuous twentieth-century history from the Dreyfus affair to the presidency of Charles de Gaulle. In other words, he sharpens his perception with references to his *memory*. And throughout the succession of political crises and cultural upheavals marking the postwar decades, it was precisely his intimate familiarity with the past that made him so sensitive to what was original—but also commonplace—in the present.

Pointing out the frequent disparity between contemporaneously for-

24. Cf. Todorov, *Mémoire du mal*, 218. In other words, Sartre, along with others, maintained that one must not demoralize the working class by pointing out the criminal abuses of Stalinist regimes.

mulated observations and our subsequent perception of events, Tony Judt contends that most French intellectuals of the twentieth century were not good guides to what was really unfolding in their time.[25] The opposite is true for Mauriac. It is paradoxically because he found himself out of step with the *Nouvelle Vague* of the 1950s and the counterculture of the 1960s that, for all their idiosyncrasies, his commentaries on the gradual disappearance of the rural habitat and the advent of media culture and hedonistic consumerism give us "inside" access to what we now recognize as the profound evolutions of "les Trente Glorieuses."

This capacity for astute observation and sound judgment served Mauriac equally well in his political assessments. If the *Bloc-notes* is now widely recognized as a masterpiece and its author saluted as France's premier polemicist of the 1950s and 1960s (if not for the entire twentieth century), it is to a large degree thanks not only to Mauriac's early, outspoken, and eloquent condemnations of torture, but also to his unforgettable portrayals of the historical personalities and events both past and in the making under his keen eyes. One only has to read his description of the young François Mitterrand as an indomitable Rastignac,[26] or his remark concerning the Giscard d'Estaing of the late 1960s cloaking his equally unbounded ambitions in the phony casualness of a turtleneck sweater,[27] or his warning about the French army's use of torture that he issued at the outbreak of the war in Algeria[28] to conclude that Mauriac's political acumen and human judgment were rarely led astray.

Contrary to the stances taken by Sartre and the Parisian intelligentsia on a whole range of issues, Mauriac's positions on the cold war, Stalinism, decolonization, the decline of the Fourth Republic, de Gaulle's return to power, the constitution of the Fifth Republic, and the basic contours of French foreign policy in the 1960s have not only withstood the test of time, they have even been confirmed by a veritable chorus of praise for de Gaulle in the 1990s, moreover echoed in the books of such

25. Judt, *The Burden of Responsibility*, 11.
26. See Appendix, Section C.
27. See Appendix, Section D.
28. See Appendix, Section E.

prominent intellectuals of diverse backgrounds as Régis Debray, André Glucksmann, and Max Gallo.[29]

Conversely, the historical assessments and political stances advanced by the dominant figures on the French intellectual scene during the 1950s and 1960s have for the most part been thoroughly discredited by subsequent developments. Indeed, the disparity between doctrinal pronouncements on history and the actual workings of events transforming the postwar world leads Tony Judt to conclude that Sartre and most other members of the Parisian intelligentsia, given over to axiomatic reasoning and ideological dogma, prove to be out of touch with history.[30] No such accusation could be leveled at François Mauriac. While testifying to the political crises and dramatic cultural changes marking the postwar era in France, the *Bloc-notes* nevertheless expresses an overriding concern for history and *engagement* that Mauriac shared with an entire generation.

Here again, however, the very elements that put Mauriac out of step with the dominant intellectual trends of his day promise him a lasting place in history. Thoroughly "engaged" by France's colonial wars and the death throes of the Fourth Republic, he shunned utopianism in favor of de Gaulle, whom he pragmatically considered France's best hope for securing a democratic regime against the threat of a fascist putsch and for maintaining a place of honor in the context of a bipolar hegemony. Undaunted by de Gaulle's quasi-monarchical exercise of presidential power that claimed to embody the French nation, enchanted by the "certaine idée de la France" that de Gaulle successfully propagated

29. Régis Debray, who acquired considerable renown as a leftist militant by participating in Che Guevara's revolutionary combat in Latin America and later served as a political advisor to François Mitterrand in the early 1980s, penned *A demain de Gaulle* (Paris: Gallimard, 1990). André Glucksmann, who rose to prominence as a *nouveau philosophe* by abandoning revolutionary Marxism and taking up the cause of universal human rights in the 1970s, wrote *De Gaulle, où es-tu?* (Paris: Jean-Claude Lattès, 1995). Max Gallo, a Socialist elected to the National Assembly in 1981, served as spokesman for François Mitterrand in the early years of his presidency, and later published a monumental four-volume biography of Mitterrand's nemesis: *De Gaulle, Vol. 1: L'appel du destin* (Paris: Robert Laffont, 1998), *De Gaulle, Vol. 2: La solitude du combattant* (Paris: Robert Laffont, 1998), *De Gaulle, Vol. 3: Le premier des Français* (Paris: Robert Laffont, 1998), and *De Gaulle, Vol. 4: La statue du commandeur* (Paris: Robert Laffont, 1999).

30. Judt, *The Burden of Responsibility*, 12–17.

through his inimitable words and deeds, Mauriac—particularly during the Algerian war but even in the late 1960s—displayed stubborn resistance to any doctrinaire, ideological history: witness the *Bloc-notes*'s repeated reflections on the most unsettling episodes in the annals of his own (bourgeois) society, (Catholic) religion, (French) nation, and (European) civilization. Engaging and narrating history in terms of specific people and events, Mauriac remained immune to the stridently Marxist approach to history prevalent among French intellectual circles of the 1950s and 1960s, and in all likelihood impervious to esoteric philosophical reasoning in general. But neither was he a "problem solver" sporting expertise in political science or economics: his distinctive talent resides rather in his ability to articulate the ultimate stakes of historical events in terms of ethics and human identity. Understanding humanity through the drama of history (and vice versa), recognizing the irrecusable character of *engagement*, Mauriac refuses to collapse the distance between moral dilemmas and historical dialectics, and insists that each human being constitutes a personal story. The *Bloc-notes* can be best appreciated for leading us to read the story of its author and the history of his times through the past darkly.

APPENDIX

Section A

Without the slightest word of regret or remorse, Aussaresses relates in great detail acts of torture, executions, and "disappearances" used in the fight against the rebels' wave of terrorist bombings in Algiers. See "Algérie: Le général Aussaresses se confesse," *Le Figaro*, 2 May 2001. See also the dossier "France, guerre d'Algérie et torture" published by *Le Monde* on the Internet: <http://www.lemonde.fr/dossier/0,5987,3208-3515—,00.html>. As related in "Une amende de 7.5000 euros pour Aussaresses," *Le Figaro*, 25 January 2002, Aussaresses was tried and convicted for explicitly condoning war crimes. The Aussaresses affair was in fact just the latest and most spectacular of a long series of developments focusing public attention on the war in Algeria. In October 1997, toward the beginning of his long crimes-against-humanity trial, the question of Maurice Papon's responsibility in the brutal killings of unarmed Algerian demonstrators in October 1961 created no little stir. See "Les 'ratonnades' du 17 oct. 1961," *L'Express*, 11 October 2001. Other dossiers, including "Torture in Algérie. Comment clore le dossier," *L'Express*, 11 January 2001, and the Institut National de l'Audiovisuel's "La guerre d'Algérie à la télévision française," published on the Internet at <http://www.ina.fr/voir_revoir/algerie/>, offer further evidence of the renewed interest in the war in Algeria. The latter dossier incidentally contains an article, "Mauriac était un visionnaire" (Mauriac was a visionary), on François Mauriac's vigorous denunciations of torture. There are of course many other repercussions of these and other related issues, too numerous to cite here.

Section B

Fidélité d'une maison et de quelques arbres! Le lieu commun pour article littéraire, le cliché devient ici objet d'expérience. Sensation que j'éprouve aussi nette que celle du froid et du chaud, d'être ici sorti du temps—non certes de la vie: mais je respire dans un monde intermédiaire où le train de l'univers ne me concerne plus. *J'échappe à l'histoire des hommes*—comme si je me trouvais dans une sorte de pas perdu. ("Lundi 12 mars 1956, sur la route," BN I, 331)

Mais il me suffit du courrier pour que l'enchantement se dissipe. Les journaux, les lettres replongent le solitaire dans l'horreur quotidienne de l'histoire. ("Mardi 13 mars 1956," BN I, 331)

[What fidelity in a house and a few trees! The commonplace for a literary piece becomes here an object of experience. I experience the feeling of have stepped out of time just as clearly as the sensation of hot and cold. Of course I have not escaped life, but I am breathing in an intermediary world in which the course of the universe no longer concerns me. *I have escaped the story of human history*, as if I were in a sort of waiting room.

But the mail is all it takes to dissipate this enchantment. The letters and newspapers plunge the loner back into the daily horror of history.]

Section C

While defending Mitterrand in "l'Affaire des fuites" (the affair of the leaks), Mauriac gave the following bemused portrait of the ambitious young ministre de l'intérieur:

Vendredi 8 octobre 1954

Pour comprendre la réaction violente de François Mitterrand, il faut se rappeler ce qu'il coûte à un homme politique d'être calomnié, même lorsque la calomnie est dénoncée et reconnue par tous. . . .

Ce Mitterrand, je l'aime bien et depuis des années, si je ne le rencontre guère. C'est un garçon romanesque, je veux dire, un personnage de roman. Il sort, à quelques lieues de chez moi, du terroir charentais, comme Rastignac. . . .

Mais avant de subir ces attaques sordides et policières, Mitterrand en a connu d'autres: il a mérité que son premier ministère ait été celui des Anciens Combattants. L'ambition politique chez un jeune homme est une passion noble dans la mesure où elle se confond avec l'ambition pour la grandeur de la patrie. Ainsi, chez François Mitterrand qui avance d'un pas tranquille—du pas de ceux qui se rappellent l'avertissement de Saint-Just: "L'empire appartient aux flegmatiques." (BN I, 207–9)

[Friday, 8 October 1954]

In order to understand François Mitterrand's sharp reaction, one must remember how much a politician suffers from being calumnied, even when the calumny is acknowledged and condemned by everyone. . . .

I have liked this Mitterrand for years, although I rarely meet up with him. He is a novel young man, I mean a character out of a novel. Like Rastignac, he comes from the Charente area, a few dozen miles from where I live. . . .

But Mitterrand had seen a good many things before suffering these sordid police attacks: he earned the distinction of heading the Ministry of War Veterans as his first government appointment. Political ambition in a young man is a noble passion inasmuch as it is part and parcel of an ambition for his country's grandeur. Such is the case with François Mitterrand, who strides confidently forward with the gait of those who remember Saint-Just's warning: "The empire belongs to the cool-headed."]

Section D

Valéry Giscard d'Estaing's appearances on television in 1967 and 1968 prompted Mauriac to make the following commentaries, unforgettable for their perspicacity and acid wit:

> Valéry Giscard d'Estaing, lui, est un autre monsieur. Si étudié soit son numéro, il atteint sans effort apparent au naturel. Le plus jeune ministre des Finances de tous les temps est obligé de ralentir, de faire du surplace pour ne pas arriver trop tôt, pour ne pas être obligé de s'asseoir sur les marches du perron de l'Elysée. Que c'est beau à voir, l'héritier d'une grande dynastie bourgeoise! ("Dimanche 26 février 1967," BN IV, 405)

Mardi 2 mai 1967

"Le giscardisme est une ambition et non une pensée." C'est Philippe de Saint-Robert qui le dit avec son insolence de page,—mais l'insolence ici ne porte que parce qu'elle fait mouche. Souscrire à ce jugement, ce n'est pas d'ailleurs s'en indigner; l'ambition est la chose du monde la mieux partagée: vivre, c'est désirer. Un jeune être comblé dès le départ de tous les dons, ceux de la naissance, de l'intelligence, de l'argent, au degré ou fut ce Giscard, n'en est plus même à se demander: "Jusqu'où ne monterai-je pas?" Car il sait très bien où il va, où il ne doute pas de parvenir, et qu'il n'y a qu'une place à sa mesure en France, et qui est la première. (BN IV, 441)

Que celui-ci paraisse au petit écran moulé dans un pull-over, ou qu'il renonce au pull-over, ou qu'il s'adresse au peuple, comme l'autre jour, assis familièrement sur un coin de table, nous le voyons avec plaisir, sous notre nez, retoucher jour après jour le personnage du plus jeune ministre des Finances qu'il a été et du plus jeune président de la République qu'il sera, s'il plaît à Dieu et s'il n'y a pas d'accident de parcours. ("Mardi 16 juillet 1968," BN V, 104)

[Mr. Valéry Giscard d'Estaing is for his part quite another leading character. As well-rehearsed as his performance may be, he manages to come off looking effortlessy natural. The youngest minister of finance of all time is obliged to slow down and run in place so as not to get to the finish line too soon and then have to sit on the front steps of the Elysee [[the presidential residence]]. What a fine sight it is to see the inheritor of a great bourgeois dynasty!

Tuesday, 2 May 1967

As Philippe de Saint-Robert insolently says, Giscardism is an ambition and not a system of thought. The accusation stands out because it hits the nail on the head. One can agree with this assessment without indignation. Ambition is the most commonly found commodity in the world: to live is to desire. Any young man gifted with everything from the outset, including a distinguished ancestry, intelligence, and money to such a degree as was Giscard, can no longer wonder: "Just how high will I climb?" He knows good and well where he is going without any doubts as to his success. And there is but one place in France that is fit for him: the very first.

> Whenever he appears on TV, be it with or without a tight-fitting sweater, or be it informally seated at the table with common folks, as we saw him the other day, we enjoy seeing him perfecting right under our eyes his act as the youngest minister of finance that he has been and the youngest president of the Republic that he will be, if it pleases God and if no unexpected misfortune befalls him.]

The query that Mauriac places in Giscard's mind, "Jusqu'où ne monterai-je pas?" (Just how high will I climb?), is an allusion to Nicolas Fouquet, another ambitious young minister of finance who invited the young king Louis XIV to extravagant festivities at his sumptuous Château de Vaux, which prominently displayed the ambitious minister of finance's Latin motto: "Quod non ascendam?" (Just how high will I climb?). Shortly thereafter, Louis XIV had Fouquet arrested, convicted for embezzlement, and emprisoned for life. See Colette Dubois Brichant, *La France au cour des âges: Grands jours et vie quotidienne* (New York: McGraw-Hill, 1973), 249.

Section E

Mauriac immediately grasped the gravity of the situation:

> L'horreur de ce qui va se déchaîner doit être tout de suite adoucie par une offensive concertée contre les bas salaires, le chômage, l'ignorance, la misère et par les réformes de structure qu'appelle le peuple algérien. Et, coûte que coûte, il faut empêcher la police de torturer. ("Mardi 2 novembre 1954," BN I, 214)
>
> [The horror that is about to be unleashed must immediately be mitigated by a concerted offensive against low wages, unemployment, ignorance, and dire poverty, and by the structural reforms that the Algerian people are calling for. And, at all costs, we must prevent the police from torturing.]

BIBLIOGRAPHY

François Mauriac (Selected Postwar Writings)

Bloc-notes 1952–1970. 5 vols. Edited and annotated by Jean Touzot. Paris: Éditions du Seuil (Points-Essais), 1993.

L'imitation des bourreaux de Jésus-Christ. Paris: Desclée de Brower, 1984.

Mémoires politiques. Paris: Grasset, 1967.

"Le métier d'écrivain" (Interview). *L'Express*, 5 April 1957, pp. 17–20.

Twentieth-Century France and Intellectual History

"Algérie: Le général Aussaresses se confesse." *Le Figaro*, 2 May 2001.

"Une amende de 7.5000 euros pour Aussaresses." *Le Figaro*, 25 January 2002.

Appollonia, Ariane Chebel d'. *Histoire politique des intellectuels en France 1944–1954.* 2 vols. Brussels: Éditions Complexe, 1991.

Aron, Raymond. *Leçon inaugurale au Collège de France, 1er décembre 1970.* Paris: Collège de France, 1972.

Aussaresses, Paul. *Services spéciaux, Algérie 1955–1957.* Paris: Perrin, 2001.

Biondi, Jean-Pierre. *Les anticolonialistes.* Paris: Robert Laffont, 1992.

Birnbaum, Pierre. *L'affaire Dreyfus: La République en péril.* Paris: Gallimard Découvertes-Histoire, 1994.

Bracher, Nathan. "The Dreyfus Affair in François Mauriac's *Bloc-notes.*" *Contemporary French Civilization* 26, no. 1 (Winter–Spring 2002): 12–29.

———. "Facing History: Mauriac and Lévinas on Nazism." *Journal of European Studies* 23 (1993): 159–77.

———. "Mauriac and Decolonization: Civilization, History, and National Identity." *Contemporary French Civilization* 18, no. 2 (Summer–Fall 1994): 167–87.

———. "Memory Null and Void?: The Broken Record of Vichy Polemics in the Papon Case." *Contemporary French Civilization* 23, no. 1 (Winter–Spring 1999): 65–80.

———. "La mémoire vive et convulsive: The Papon Trial and France's Passion for History." *French Review* 73, no. 2 (December 1999): 314–24.

———. "Timely Predications: The Use and Abuse of History in Contemporary France." *Soundings* 81, no. 1–2 (Spring–Summer 1998): 235–56.

———. "The Trial of Papon and the Tribulations of Gaullism." In *The Papon Affair: Memory and Justice on Trial*, edited by Richard J. Golsan, 115–30. New York: Routledge, 2000.

Browning, Christopher R. *Ordinary Men: Reserve Police Battalion 101 and the Final Solution in Poland.* New York: HarperCollins, 1992.

Cocula, Bernard. "Le *Bloc-notes*, lieu de mémoire." In *François Mauriac 5: De mémoire en Mémoires*, edited by Jacques Monférier, 61–74. Paris: Minard-Lettres Modernes, 1995.

———. *Mauriac, le Bloc-notes.* Bordeaux: L'Esprit du temps, 1995.

Cohen-Solal, Annie. *Sartre.* Paris: Gallimard, 1985.

Conan, Eric, and Henry Rousso. *Vichy: An Ever-Present Past.* Translated and annotated by Nathan Bracher, with a foreword by Robert O. Paxton. Hanover, N.H., and London: University Press of New England, 1998.

Debray, Régis. *A demain de Gaulle.* Paris: Gallimard, 1990.

De Gaulle, Charles. *Mémoires de Guerre, Vol. 1: L'appel.* Paris: Plon, 1954.

Delcroix, Olivier. "Astérix, le dernier mythe français." *France-Amérique*, 5–11 February 2000, p. 32.

"Dossier François Mauriac." *Magazine Littéraire*, no. 215, February 1985, pp. 16–52.

Dubois Brichant, Colette. *La France au cour des âges: Grands jours et vie quotidienne.* New York: McGraw-Hill, 1973.

Duhamel, Alain. *Le complexe d'Astérix.* Paris: Gallimard, 1985.

Duhamel, Olivier. "Eux et nous." *L'Express*, 21 April 1997, p. 21.

Duranton-Crabol, Anne-Marie. "Du combat pour l'Algérie française au combat pour la culture européenne. Les origines du Groupement de Recherche et d'Etudes pour la Civilisation Européenne (GRECE)." In *La guerre d'Algérie et les intellectuels français*, pp. 59–78.

Evans, Richard J. *In Defense of History.* New York and London: W. W. Norton, 1999.

Finkielkraut, Alain. *L'humanité perdue.* Paris: Seuil, 1996.

———. *Une voix vient de l'autre rive.* Paris: Gallimard, 2000.

Fouilloux, Etienne. "Intellectuels catholiques et guerre d'Algérie." In *La guerre d'Algérie et les intellectuels français*, 79–114.

"France, guerre d'Algérie et torture." *Le Monde*, online at <*http://www.lemonde.fr/dossier/0,5987,3208-3515—,00.html*>.

Furet, François. *L'atelier de l'histoire.* Paris: Flammarion, 1982.

Gallo, Max. *De Gaulle, Vol. 1: L'appel du destin.* Paris: Robert Laffont, 1998.

———. *De Gaulle, Vol. 2: La solitude du combattant.* Paris: Robert Laffont, 1998.

———. *De Gaulle, Vol. 3: Le premier des Français.* Paris: Robert Laffont, 1998.

———. *De Gaulle, Vol. 4: La statue du commandeur.* Paris: Robert Laffont, 1999.

Girardet, Raoul. *L'idée coloniale en France.* Paris: La Table Ronde, 1972.

———. *Le nationalisme français.* Paris: Seuil, 1983.

Glucksmann, André. *De Gaulle, où es-tu?* Paris: Jean-Claude Lattès, 1995.

Golsan, Richard J., ed. *The Papon Affair: Memory and Justice on Trial.* New York: Routledge, 2000.

———. *Vichy's Afterlife: History and Counterhistory in Postwar France.* Lincoln: University of Nebraska Press, 2000.

Goodman, Ellen. "May All Wars Be Fought in the Movies." Syndicated column, June 4, 2001.

Goudineau, Christian. *César et la Gaule.* Paris: Errance, 1990.

———. "Nos ancêtres les Romains." *L'Express,* 9 September 1999, pp. 10–13.

Holy Bible (New International Version). Grand Rapids, Mich.: Zondervan, 1984.

Jackson, Julian. *France: The Dark Years, 1940–1944.* New York: Oxford University Press, 2001.

Judt, Tony. *The Burden of Responsibility.* Chicago: University of Chicago Press, 1998.

———. *Past Imperfect: French Intellectuals, 1944–1956.* Berkeley, Los Angeles, and Oxford: University of California Press, 1992.

Lacouture, Jean. *François Mauriac.* Paris: Seuil, 1980.

"La guerre d'Algérie à la télévision française." L'Institut National de l'Audiovisuel. Online at *<http://www.ina.fr/voir_revoir/algerie/>.*

Le Goff, Jacques. "L'histoire nouvelle." In *La nouvelle histoire,* pp. 34–75.

———, ed. *La nouvelle histoire.* Paris: Editions Complexe, 1988.

Levisse-Touzé, Christine. *Paris libéré, Paris retrouvé.* Paris: Gallimard-Paris Musées, 1994.

Monférier, Jacques, ed. *François Mauriac 5: De mémoire en Mémoires.* Paris: Minard-Lettres Modernes, 1995.

Montherlant, Henry de. "Le solstice de juin." In *Essais,* 953–63. Paris: Gallimard, 1963.

Nora, Pierre. *Les lieux de mémoire, Vol. 1: La République.* Paris: Gallimard, 1984.

Oldenbourg, Zoé. *Le bûcher de Montségur.* Paris: Gallimard, 1959.

Ory, Pascal, and Jean-François Sirinelli. *Les intellectuels en France.* Paris: Armand Colin, 1992.

Petit Larousse Illustré. Paris: Larousse, 1975.

Petit Larousse Illustré 1994. Paris: Larousse, 1993.

Prost, Antoine. *Douze leçons sur l'histoire.* Paris: Seuil, 1996.

"Les 'ratonnades' du 17 oct. 1961." *L'Express,* 11 October 2001.

Rioux, Jean-Pierre. "La guerre d'Algérie dans l'histoire des intellectuels français." In Rioux and Sirinelli, *La guerre d'Algérie et les intellectuels français,* 33–55.

Rioux, Jean-Pierre, and Sirinelli, Jean-François, eds. *La guerre d'Algérie et les intellectuels français.* Paris: Editions Complexes, 1991.

Rouart, Jean-Marie. "Héros de la France franchouillarde." *France-Amérique,* 5–11 February 2000, p. 32.

Rousso, Henry. *La hantise du passé*. Paris: Les Editions Textuel, 1998.

———. *The Vichy Syndrome*. Translated by Arthur Goldhammer. Cambridge, Mass., and London: Harvard University Press, 1991.

Sartre, Jean-Paul. "La République du silence." In *Situations III*, 11–14. Paris: Gallimard, 1949.

———. "M. François Mauriac et la liberté." In *Situations I*, 33–52. Paris: Gallimard, 1947.

———. "Qu'est-ce que la litérature?" In *Situations II*, 55–330. Paris: Gallimard, 1948.

———. "Villes d'Amérique." In *Situations III*, 93–111. Paris: Gallimard, 1949.

Scott, Malcolm. *Mauriac et de Gaulle*. Bordeaux: L'Esprit du Temps, 1999.

———. *Mauriac: The Politics of a Novelist*. Edinburgh: Scottish Academic Press, 1980.

Séailles, André, ed. *François Mauriac entre la Gauche et la Droite*. Paris: Klincksieck, 1995.

———. *Mauriac et la polémique*. Paris: L'Harmattan, 2001.

Sirinelli, Jean-François. *Deux intellectuels dans le siècle: Sartre et Aron*. Paris: Fayard, 1995.

———. "Les intellectuels français en guerre d'Algérie." In *La guerre d'Algérie et les intellectuels français*, 11–32.

———. "Mauriac, un intellectuel engagé." In *François Mauriac entre la Gauche et la Droite*, edited by André Séailles, 145–58. Paris: Klincksieck, 1995.

Thibaud, Paul. "Retour sur une tragédie." *L'Express*, 10 November 2001 (or online at <*http:www.lexpress.fr/Express/Info/France/Dossier/octobre61.dossier.asp?n*>).

Todorov, Tzvetan. *Face à l'extrême*. Paris: Seuil, 1994.

———. *Mémoire du mal, tentation du bien*. Paris: Robert Laffont, 2000.

———. "Ten Years without Primo Levi." *Salmagundi* 116–17 (Fall–Winter 1997): 3–18.

"Torture in Algérie. Comment clore le dossier." *L'Express*, 11 January 2001.

Vovelle, Michel. "L'histoire et la longue durée." In *La nouvelle histoire*, 77–108.

Winock, Michel. *Nationalisme, antisémitisme et fascisme en France*. Paris: Seuil, 1990.

———. *La République se meurt*. Paris: Gallimard Folio-Histoire, 1985.

———. *Le siècle des intellectuels*. Paris: Seuil, 1997.

Wylie, Laurence, and Jean-François Brière. *Les Français*. 3rd ed. Upper Saddle River, N.J.: Prentice-Hall, 2001.

INDEX

Through the Past Darkly: History and Memory in François Mauriac's 'Bloc-notes'
was designed and composed in Adobe Minion by Kachergis Book Design,
Pittsboro, North Carolina; and printed on 60-pound Glatfelter
Natural and bound by Edwards Brothers, Inc.,
Lillington, North Carolina.